D0705938

Teaching Dance Skills
A Motor Learning and Development Approach

Marliese Kimmerle, PhD
University of Windsor
Windsor, Ontario, Canada

and

Paulette Côté-Laurence, PhD
Brock University
St. Catharines, Ontario, Canada

J. Michael Ryan Publishing, Inc.

Teaching Dance Skills: A Motor Learning and Development Approach
Marliese Kimmerle and Paulette Côté-Laurence

Library of Congress Control Number: 2002096417

ISBN 1-887064-08-7

J. Michael Ryan Publishing, Inc.
24 Crescent Drive North
Andover, New Jersey 07821
www.jmichaelryan.com

Printed in the United States of America

10 9 8 7 6 5 4 3 2 1

Copyright © 2003 J. Michael Ryan Publishing, Inc. All rights reserved. No part of this book may be reproduced or transmitted in any form or by any means, electronic or mechanical, including photocopying, recording, or any information storage and retrieval system, without permission in writing from the copyright holder.

*In memory of my mother and father, and to my
favorite dance partner Val.*
— Marliese Kimmerle

*To Mike, Jean-Christophe, Gabrielle, and
Benjamin, who make it all worthwhile. I thank
them for their continued love and support.*
— Paulette Côté-Laurence

Acknowledgments

Teaching Dance Skills was conceived following a presentation given to dance educators at the Canadian-American Research Forum at the Canadian Association for Health, Physical Education and Recreation Conference in 1991. Thus began a process of translating doctoral studies in motor skill acquisition to the practical problems of dance teaching. Paulette's acceptance to collaborate on this venture allowed us to combine backgrounds in motor development and motor learning with our experience teaching a variety of dance forms at all educational levels. Our mutual efforts to make movement science theories accessible to current and future teachers served as a major driving force to produce this book.

The theoretical content of the book comes from our respective academic roles at the University of Windsor and at Brock University. Here, the concepts and models have been developed in undergraduate courses. We are grateful to our students for their assistance as we refined and validated the usefulness of the dance analysis and skill acquisition models.

A special note of appreciation is given to the dance teachers who allowed us access to their classes and to their students: Barbara Robinson, Academy Ste. Cecile, Windsor; and Louise Paquette, School of Dramatic Art, University of Windsor; Eva Romanowski-Annett and Rachel Spencer of Ballet Etc... Studio for the Arts, St. Catharines; and Paulette Côté-Laurence, Department of Physical Education and Kinesiology, Brock University. We thank the photographers Josie Hazen, Panagiota Klentrou, and Gabrielle Laurence, who caught the class action, and Tory James and Divino Mucciante, who contributed the photographs of the authors that appear on the back cover.

Marliese Kimmerle and Paulette Côté-Laurence
December 2002

Contents

Preface ix

Introduction xiii

Part One
Foundations of Effective Dance Teaching

Chapter 1
Effective Dance Teaching 3
  Obstacles to Teaching Dance Skills
    Inappropriate Dance Material
    Ineffective Teaching Methods
    Isolation Between Dance Teachers and the Movement Sciences
    Isolation Between Teachers in Various Dance Forms
  Solutions – Need for a Knowledge Base
    The Dance Material
    The Learning Process
    The Learners' Capabilities
  Goals for Teaching
  The Role of the Effective Dance Teacher

Chapter 2
How to Analyze the Dance Material 11
  The Communication Problem in Dance
  The Function of Dance Skill Analysis
  Terminology
    Movement
    Motor Skill
    Dance Skill
    Dance Techniques
  Levels of Dance Analysis
    Level I: Body Action
    Level II: Components
    Level III: Context
  The Complexity of the Dance Material
    Simple to Complex Dance Skills
    Simple to Complex Context

Chapter 3
Organizing the Dance Material **33**
   Making Choices in Different Dance Forms
   Making Choices in Body Actions
   Making Choices in Components
   Making Choices in Context
      Skill Sequences
      Pathway in Space
      Other Dancers
      Accompaniment

Chapter 4
How a Student Learns Dance Skills **51**
   A Learning Model
   A Learning Model for Dance Skills
      Stage One – Attempt Stage
      Stage Two – Correct Stage
      Stage Three – Perfect Stage
   Progressing Through the Stages of Learning
      Combination One - Jazz Inside Turn (8 Counts)
      Combination Two - Jazz Phrase (32 Counts)
      Combination Three - Jazz Dance (80 Counts)

Chapter 5
The Novice Adult Learner **67**
   Physical Capabilities
   Repertoire of Dance Skills
   Learning Abilities – Information Processing Abilities
      Perceptual Abilities
      Attention Capacity
      Memory Capacity
      Error Detection and Correction Capacity

Chapter 6
The Child Learner **87**
   Comparing Child and Adult Beginners
   The Young and the Older Child
   Physical Limitations Due to Growth
      Growth Spurt
      Proportion
      Bones, Joints and Muscles
   Competency of Fundamental Skills
   Experience in Dance Skills
   Learning Abilities
      Information Processing
      Learning Strategies
      Perceptual Skills

Motor Planning and Control
Cognitive Skills

Chapter 7
The Experienced Dancer 115
What is an Experienced Dancer?
The Role of Practice
Physical Abilities
Repertoire of Dance Skills
Learning Abilities – Information Processing Abilities
What is an Expert Dancer?
Knowledge Base
Body Structure
Information Processing Abilities
Practice

Part Two
Applying the Foundations to Dance Teaching

Chapter 8
Effective Dance Teaching 137
The Dance Teacher's Role
Preparing for the Dance Lesson: Evaluation and Selection
Observing During the Dance Lesson: Adaptation
Approaches to Observation
Learning Outcomes

Chapter 9
Selecting Dance Skills for the Learner 149
Evaluating the Dance Material
Evaluating a Dance Skill
Evaluating a Combination/Dance
Evaluating a Lesson/Unit
Evaluating the Needs of the Learner
Physical Abilities
Repertoire of Fundamental Motor Skills
Repertoire of Dance Skills
Learning Abilities
Characteristics of the Learner
Selecting Appropriate Material
Selecting Material for the Novice Versus the Experienced Dancer
Selecting Material for the Child Dancer

Chapter 10
How to Select Instructional Methods 169
Verbal Instructions
Clarity of Instructions

Use of Imagery
Quantity of Instructions
Repetition of Instructions
Demonstration
Role of Demonstration in the Dance Class
What Elements Can be Demonstrated
Frequency of Demonstration
The Model: Teacher or Student?
Location of Model
Learning Strategies
Assessing the Effectiveness of Instructional Methods

Chapter 11
How to Provide Feedback **189**
The Role of Feedback in the Dance Class
Types of Feedback Appropriate for the Dance Class
Extrinsic Feedback
Intrinsic Feedback
Timing of Feedback
Frequency of Feedback
The Role of Observation in the Dance Class
What Should the Teacher Observe?
When is Observation Important?
Evaluating Instructional Practices

Chapter 12
Looking Into the Future **209**
Where We Are Now – The Movement Sciences and Dance
Revisiting the Knowledge Base in Dance
Where Do We Go From Here – Looking Into the Future
Research on the Learning Process Across Dance Forms
Research on Children's Capabilities as Learners of Dance
Research on Effective Teaching in Dance
Recommendations

Glossary **217**

Index **221**

Teaching dance can be challenging, and so can trying to learn and perfect dance skills. A typical dance class includes students of a particular age group who display a wide range of skill levels and experiences. In order to accommodate all students, a dance teacher is expected to be familiar with developmental characteristics of learners of varying ages and skill levels, the learning process, and, of course, the dance material itself. There are currently few texts that can assist in this regard. Texts on dance teaching largely focus on pedagogical issues such as curriculum and lesson planning. There is a need for information about the fundamentals of motor learning and motor development as they apply to dance teaching and learning.

Dance educators have traditionally taught as they were taught – a substantial reliance on past practice. With the emergence of the movement sciences, the field of dance education has developed significantly in recent decades. It may now be appropriate to examine past teaching practices to determine whether the movement sciences can advance teaching and learning in dance. This book is the collaborative effort of two dance educators who have many years of experience in teaching dance in a variety of settings, and who wish to share their knowledge of motor learning and motor development to optimize the teaching techniques of others.

This book has four unique features. The first is its focus on integrating the relevant knowledge from the fields of motor learning and motor development with dance teaching. This text should provide those who educate and are educated through dance with a conceptual framework for understanding dance teaching and learning. Traditionally, dance teachers have been reluctant to explore texts in motor learning and motor development. Perhaps they find the current books to be too theoretical, with few connections to the practice of dance teaching. This book may be the first to bridge the gap between the movement sciences and dance; it integrates motor learning and motor development theories *with* the dance material. We hope that this information will allow teachers to make informed decisions on their behavior in the dance class and thus will help to prepare the future generation of teachers.

The second unique feature of this book is its focus on the learning process in the dance class. Throughout these chapters, a clear emphasis is placed on a learning model applied to dance skills. The model's three stages – the attempt, the correct, and the perfect stage – describe the cognitive operations that the learner goes through as he proceeds from the presentation of the new skill to its correct performance.

As a third unique characteristic, the text examines the learners' capabilities and limitations. The learning model is applied to the three typical categories of dance student: the young beginner, the adult beginner, and the experienced dancer. The information provided in these pages should afford a better understanding of the optimal learning environment for all students, regardless of age or skill level. This book should answer many questions, among them: How do I know that the dance skills I selected are appropriate for my students? Why is it difficult for an adult beginner to execute this skill? When is a demonstration most appropriate? What strategy can a learner use to memorize a sequence of steps? Are my verbal instructions confusing?

The fourth significant feature of the book is that it can be easily applied across dance forms. The proposed dance vocabulary can fit any dance form, as it utilizes basic categories of dance skills with no specialized terms. Concepts and theories are illustrated through practical examples across dance forms, and focus on learning problems common to all dance forms.

This book contains two sections and twelve chapters. Section One, "Foundations of Effective Dance Teaching," introduces the philosophy of the book, the dance material, the learning process, and the characteristics and needs of the learners.

A generic vocabulary to describe dance skills, as well as a skill analysis model applicable across dance forms are presented in chapters two and three. Chapter four introduces a learning model for dance. Chapters five, six, and seven address the beginner adult, the child, and the experienced dancer. Section Two, "Applying the Foundations to Dance Teaching," integrates learning and development theories into meaningful practice. Chapter eight describes the role of the teacher, and chapter nine suggests ways to select dance material. Instructional methods are presented in chapter ten, and chapter eleven covers feedback appropriate in the dance class. Finally, chapter twelve offers recommendations for future directions in dance education.

This book is intended as a reference book and a text for present and future teachers who are committed to quality teaching and learning. It invites all those in the field of dance to share in the joy of good dancing, good teaching, and good learning by exploring new approaches based on the principles of motor learning and motor development. This is not a "how-to" book but rather a blueprint for individualized optimal dance learning and teaching.

Dance and the Movement Sciences

This book examines one specific aspect of the study of dance – the teaching and learning of physical dance skills. The content of a well-rounded dance curriculum can and should include other dance experiences beyond skill training, such as exploration, improvisation, composition, observation, and performance. While we acknowledge the value of these experiences in the overall dance education of the child or adult, we focus on a more fundamental issue – how individuals learn the physical or technical skills involved in dance. Through an understanding of how individuals learn, we attempt to provide insights on how to teach. Effective teaching leads to the effective learning of dance skills.

Current books on dance teaching do not typically include the concepts learned in the movement sciences. Current literature in the movement sciences focuses largely on laboratory analysis of discrete motor skills or on sport skills. This makes the valuable lessons learned by this branch of science much less accessible to dance educators. To our way of thinking, this creates a gap in the knowledge required for teaching dance. There is a need for texts that combine educational concerns such as teaching dance and foundational perspectives found in motor learning and motor development theories. The combination of motor learning and motor development makes it possible to examine dance skill learning in children as well as adults and in novices as well as experienced dancers. In the discussion that follows in these chapters, concepts found in these fields of study provide theoretical support for dance teaching methods.

Motor learning is an area of study concerned with how movements are learned as a result of practice or experience. It takes into consideration factors that determine skilled motor performance. Motor learning includes concepts such as: the nature of motor skills, internal processes involved in learning, stages of learning, conditions of practice necessary for learning, and the nature and effectiveness of feedback. The theoretical basis of motor learning draws heavily from cognitive psychology, specifically the study of cognition, perception, information processing, attention, and memory.

The principles and processes affecting motor learning are applicable to all human movement. They can apply to any motor skill, including dance skills. This book addresses motor learning theories and principles critical in learning dance skills. For example, it is important for the dance teacher to understand the cognitive capabilities of learners, their ability to perceive visual, auditory, and kinesthetic information, and to plan the execution of the dance skill. Teachers must also understand the impact of feedback on learning. Instructional methods such as verbal instruction, demonstration, and feedback are examined from an information processing perspective. These constitute a part of the knowledge base required to promote optimal teaching and learning in dance.

Motor development is the study of changes over time as influenced by maturation and experience. It includes the study of the processes that underlie the observable changes in motor skills such as physical growth, changes in perception and cognition resulting from the maturation of the central nervous system, and changes due to the child's movement experiences. The focus is on understanding the interaction of biological factors and experience in skill acquisition. Of particular relevance for this text is an understanding of the information processing limitations of children that make them different from adult learners.

Dance skills cannot be acquired until the learner has gained some proficiency in fundamental motor skills. Dance skills are highly specialized and complex variations or combinations of simpler motor skills. It is important, therefore, to understand how and when the building blocks are acquired in a logical progression of skill acquisition. The teacher of dance must appreciate how maturational limitations or lack of experience may restrict which dance skills a child can learn.

Our discussion will be primarily focused on five dance forms: ballet, modern, jazz, folk, and creative dance. These forms are rarely discussed together in one book on dance teaching. However, it is our intention to break down some of the barriers in dance and address all teachers of dance regardless of form.

The first three forms represent the three major performing dance forms that also include formal technical training. In most secondary and post-secondary institutions, at least one or all three forms are available to teenagers and adults. Outside the school setting, in a studio for example, these forms are available to children as well. Folk dance and creative dance are often represented as more appropriate alternatives for children and are included in the elementary school curriculum. Sometimes these continue to be offered in high school and beyond.

The term "folk" dance is used as a generic term here, as representing the most typical dance form offered in the elementary school system. For older students, a more general term might be "social dance" as it may incorporate folk dance, ballroom dance, square dance, line dance, as well as the latest popular dances.

Some teachers may claim that the focus in teaching folk and creative dance is not specifically on the acquisition of dance skills since the skills are often basic. Instead, the focus is on developing cooperative social skills, facilitating personal expression, or simply, spontaneous play. Do these belong in a book on skill acquisition? Creativity and self-expression are not necessarily in contradiction with skill acquisition. Dance experiences are viewed as education in an art form.[1] As such, "skill" learning is part of the performing aspect of the study of dance as art as opposed to dance making and dance assessing. Performing one's dance skillfully and not just with expression, therefore, becomes important. Rather than viewing "skill" and "creativity" as dichotomous goals, we could view them as a continuum with the teacher placing more emphasis on one or the other goal.

A choice of goals also applies to folk dance. While some teachers choose to focus on recreational group interaction, others expect a high level of technical skill. Across the five different dance forms, teachers may place a different emphasis on the physical activity that is carried on in a class and set different levels of skill to be achieved. The difference in emphasis should not prevent us from analyzing the physical activity or examining the learning process in these dance forms. A child who experiments with spinning alone on the playground and a teenager trying to master a pirouette in a class are both engaged in learning turning skills.

The frame of reference for this book is the dance material that makes up the typical technique class (ballet, modern, or jazz) taught to amateur students of a relatively beginning skill level. Of course we acknowledge that a "technique" class is not the sum of what would be involved in training in a particular dance form. A modern dance curriculum, for example, could consist of a body conditioning class, a technique class, an improvisation class, a composition class, as well as a repertory workshop. Our focus, however, is on the teaching of dance skills. When discussing folk dance and creative dance, the focus will again be on the beginning student in a recreational or educational setting acquiring basic dance skills.

The idea for this book originated from a presentation made by the first author at the Canadian-American Dance Research Symposium, at the Canadian Association of Health, Physical Education and Recreation Conference, Kingston, Ontario, 1991. The complexity model and the learning model presented in these pages were developed for undergraduate kinesiology classes and have been adapted to dance teaching. We have applied the principles described in this book in our daily teaching of dance and have found them to be effective in facilitating the learning process in our students. We hope that present and future dance teachers will find in this text a valuable resource that provides useful tools for promoting effective teaching.

Reference

1.   Smith-Autard JM: The Art of Dance in Education. London: A&C Black, 1994.

Part One

The Foundations of Effective Dance Teaching

Marliese Kimmerle

Obstacles to Teaching Dance Skills

  Inappropriate Dance Material

  Ineffective Teaching Methods

  Isolation Between Dance Teachers and the Movement Sciences

  Isolation Between Teachers in Various Dance Forms

Solutions – Need for a Knowledge Base

  The Dance Material

  The Learning Process

  The Learners' Capabilities

Goals for Teaching

The Role of the Effective Dance Teacher

Chapter 1

Effective Dance Teaching

Teaching dance involves much more than knowledge of the dance material. A successful teacher makes good decisions about what to teach and how to teach it to a specific group of learners. The decisions a teacher makes when preparing a dance class are invariably based on his knowledge in three areas: the dance material, the learning process, and the learner's capabilities. An introductory ballet class with young beginners will differ greatly from a class composed of adult beginners. Although the lesson content may not be substantially different between one class and the other, the teaching methods are likely to differ considerably. In contrast to young beginners, older beginners have accumulated experience in a variety of motor skills and have developed learning strategies that they will be able to draw upon and use during the dance class.

A successful teacher, therefore, makes good choices about the learning material and environment for each group of students. An environment conducive to optimal learning is one in which the students are challenged, motivated, and successful. A positive learning climate is created when the teacher selects appropriate material to teach in the lesson and uses appropriate teaching methods during the lesson.

Why is this role so important? A teacher's main objective is to facilitate student learning. The goal of good teaching is, ultimately, to develop independent learners. Independent learners are consciously aware of their responsibility toward their own learning; they contribute by paying attention to what is being said and shown, and by attempting to produce correct movements. These students feed from their past experiences and progressively build upon those experiences. Teachers who select material that is too difficult or too easy, or who employ inappropriate teaching behavior, may adversely affect students' motivation to continue learning.

So, what are the major problems that must be overcome to teach dance skills effectively?

Obstacles to Teaching Dance Skills

The major problems in teaching dance skills are: inappropriate dance material, ineffective teaching methods, isolation of dance teachers from advances in the movement sciences, and isolation between teachers of various dance forms. The first two problems may be caused, and subsequently alleviated, by the last two problems.

Inappropriate Dance Material

It is imperative that the content of a dance lesson be suited to the needs and capabilities of the learners. Technical skills that are too advanced for young students or that are too simplistic for the experienced learners frequently result in the learner experiencing frustration and anxiety, in the case of the former, or boredom, in the case of the latter. How does the teacher know that the material is too complex or too easy for a group of students? This question will be addressed in the chapters on the dance material and the learners' capabilities.

Ineffective Teaching Methods

Imagine a teacher who has difficulty providing clear verbal instructions, a correct demonstration, or specific corrections. Experienced dancers may be able to overcome poor teaching techniques, but ineffective teaching methods will surely cause significant difficulties for beginners. How does a teacher know what methods are most appropriate for a specific group of students? This question will be addressed in the chapters on the learning process, the learners' capabilities, and the instructional methods.

Isolation Between Dance Teachers and the Movement Sciences

Dance instructors traditionally teach the way they have been taught. Can we not improve upon that situation? Tradition may not necessarily be a strong argument for continuing to use a specific teaching method. How does one respond to a problem that reoccurs with the same technique year after year? Where does the teacher turn for ideas? Knowledge is power: the more a teacher knows about dance, the learning process, and learners' capabilities, the more power he has to ensure that both individual and program expectations are realized.

Some dance teachers may have inadvertently isolated themselves from movement science research. While the movement sciences have traditionally given attention to sports investigations, there is now a strong body of research related to dance. Numerous examples of these studies are to be found within this text. Advances in the movement sciences, especially motor learning and motor development, must find their way into the dance classroom. Empirical knowledge in these fields of study can benefit teaching and learning dance skills in the same manner that it has for sport skills. The integration of motor development and motor learning theories into the applied field of dance instruction will ultimately promote better teaching and learning strategies.

Isolation Between Teachers in Various Dance Forms

The dance world can be a closed world at times, with textbooks, teacher training, and professional dialogue limited to a particular dance form. While crossovers between ballet, modern dance, and jazz teaching have become more frequent, there is still a gap between a focus on professional technique training and educational and recreational teaching, as well as between these three dance forms and folk dance and creative dance. While there are certainly some unique learning challenges in each dance form, there are also many similar teaching problems that transcend these boundaries. It is important that dance teachers, regardless of the form they teach, find ways to share their knowledge.

Solutions – The Need for a Knowledge Base

There are two possible solutions to the aforementioned problems: either maintain the status quo, or provide tools to fix the problems. The first solution implies continued conformity to traditional curriculum practices. The second solution is what this book is all about: we must equip dance teachers with the knowledge necessary to solve these problems. Knowledge about dance, the learning process, and the learners' capabilities is the tool that will allow teachers to make intelligent decisions in the classroom.

An effective teacher is someone who has a good grasp of foundation knowledge, and someone who can apply this knowledge to the classroom. Foundation knowledge includes three components: the dance material, the learning process, and the learner's capabilities. Application knowledge consists of transforming foundation knowledge into dance material, instructional methods appropriate for a particular group of learners and for a particular dance form. This text provides the foundation and application knowledge required for effective teaching in dance.

The Dance Material

Most dance teachers have a good understanding of the dance form they teach. Based on their own technique-performance background and teaching experiences, teachers know the skills and skill progressions that must be included in the curriculum. However, it is also important to be able to assess the complexity of one skill over another and to modify a skill so that it is appropriate to a specific age group. This knowledge is critical to an appreciation of the difficulty of dance skills, which in turn will help teachers select age and skill appropriate material. The dance material is presented in chapters 2, 3, and 9.

The Learning Process

The second component, seldom explored in traditional books on dance teaching, is the learning process. Motor learning theory provides an appropriate framework for describing how humans learn; there is a series of internal processes that the learner proceeds through that allows him to learn, produce, and accurately repeat a skill. These processes vary depending on the experience and age of the learner as well as the complexity of the skill to

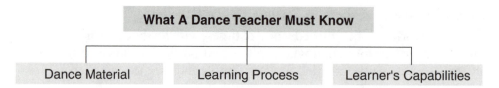

Figure 1.1
The knowledge required for effective teaching in dance.

be learned. It is important for the dance teacher to understand the learning process in order to make effective choices in his teacher behavior. Chapter 4 discusses the learning process in depth.

The Learners' Capabilities

The third component necessary for effective teaching is knowledge about learner capabilities. People of different ages present a unique set of mental and physical capabilities. Motor development and motor learning theories can assist in understanding what makes young beginners different from older beginners and what makes beginners different from experienced learners. Teaching material and methods may vary depending on the age and experience of the students. Chapters 5, 6, and 7 examine this component. Figure 1.1 presents the knowledge base required for effective teaching in dance.

Goals for Teaching

Having briefly introduced the foundation knowledge base required for effective dance teaching, we propose solutions to these problems. Dance material can be inappropriate because it is too easy or too difficult for the students. This situation can be corrected when the teacher knows his students' particular limitations and capabilities. Dance material may be inappropriate because it is presented in a non-logical progression. This can be addressed by a teacher who knows how to analyze dance skills and build skill-learning sequences that progress from simple to more complex skills. Therefore, knowing the dance material and the learners' capabilities is the solution to the first problem.

The second problem, inappropriate teaching methods, can be solved by understanding the learning process and capabilities of the learner. Understanding the complex mental processes a learner goes through when faced with a new skill should entice the teacher to plan ahead so that, not only are verbal instructions clear and to the point, but demonstrations and corrections are specific as well. The principles and processes affecting motor skill learning are in no way limited to sport skills. They apply to any motor skill, including dance skills. Dance teachers must understand the cognitive capabilities of their students: their ability to perceive visual, auditory, and kinesthetic information during the dance class, and their ability to use this information to plan and execute dance skills. Teaching behaviors such as verbal instruction, demonstration, and corrections are addressed from an information processing perspective, thus emphasizing the importance of considering student capabilities when deciding which instructional methods to use.

A major goal of this text is to address the third problem: isolation between dance teachers and the movement sciences. The foremost responsibility of dance researchers is to share their expertise in a particular field of study with dance practitioners. It is critical that researchers find ways to integrate theory with practice. Without this step, advances cannot reach those who teach and learn dance. Therefore, there is a pressing need for texts that integrate dance teaching and foundational perspectives grounded in theories of motor development and motor learning. It is our hope that this text will facilitate the mandate of dance teachers, regardless of their students' age and background, and regardless of which dance forms they teach.

In order to address the fourth and last problem, the isolation of teachers in various dance forms, it is important to break down some of the barriers that have created this isolation. By using a generic terminology to describe the dance material and by providing tools for skill analysis, this book presents a unique feature: it can apply to any dance form. This book is intended for all teachers of dance, regardless of what idiom they teach. There are similarities in dance material between dance forms, but even more importantly, and the major focus of this book, the human learning process is unquestionably the one common similarity no matter what the subject being taught.

Learning dance skills takes place in a specific progression, regardless of what is being taught. Additionally, all students come to the classroom with a baggage of experiences and with learning abilities specific to their age. They are, therefore, a large part of the equation. Therefore, all three components – the dance material, the learning process, and the learners' capabilities and limitations – are integrated to facilitate the role of all dance teachers, regardless of the dance form. Recognizing these common problems may help us make significant progress in becoming more effective teachers. What does it mean to be an effective teacher of dance?

The Role of the Effective Dance Teacher

Important aspects of teacher competency are knowledge of the subject area, commitment and management of student learning, and reflective assessment of teaching practices.[1] An effective teacher, therefore, is one who builds and nurtures an environment conducive to optimal learning. The knowledge base provided in this book will assist teachers to fulfill this role. This text does not promote or defend a particular teaching style, as there are probably many ways to teach effectively. Rather, this book argues that the teacher who understands the dance content, the learning process, and student capabilities is more likely to select appropriate material and teaching methods than one who has limited knowledge of these components.

Good teaching may be examined at three levels: what goes on prior to, during, and after the dance lesson. Before the dance lesson, the teacher has three roles: understand the knowledge base, evaluate the dance material and student capabilities, and select the dance content and teaching methods (Fig. 1.2).

The second level of effective teaching focuses on the teacher's role during

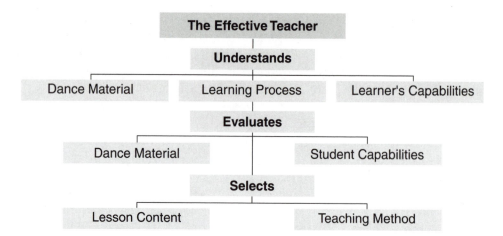

Figure 1.2
The role of the effective teacher prior to the dance lesson.

the lesson. This level entails the teacher's ability to manage the learning environment, that is, present the skill, observe and assess student behavior, make instructional changes if necessary, monitor student practice, present the new skill, observe, and so on. These roles are shown in Figure 1.3. Note that during a lesson, the role of the teacher vacillates between presenting the skill and monitoring students' responses. This is repeated for every skill introduced. Therefore, the first four steps are repeated several times during a lesson. Effective teaching in the classroom is not just a "bag of tricks." The effective teacher is able to respond to emerging situations with the appropriate action at the right moment, in the right amount, and of the right quality.[2]

In addition to preparing a sound lesson and managing the learning process during the lesson, an effective teacher has one more role to fulfill. This final role is to reflect back on the lesson and assess whether or not the lesson objective was achieved. If students have learned the intended dance skills, the lesson objective was met. If the teacher is not satisfied with the quality of learning and performance, then something must be changed before the next lesson: either the content or the teaching method.

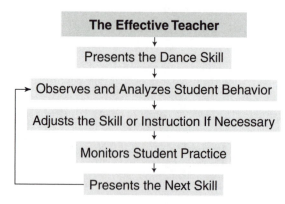

Figure 1.3
The role of the effective teacher during the dance lesson.

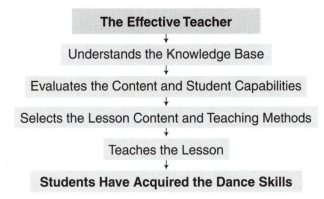

Figure 1.4
The role of the effective teacher throughout the learning cycle.

Considering that the outcome of effective teaching is skill learning, a successful lesson is one that leads to skill acquisition. The last model presented in this chapter (Fig. 1.4) integrates all the critical parts of the puzzle of teacher effectiveness: the teacher's role before, during, and after the dance lesson. Fulfilling this role successfully is, of course, directly related to the teacher's knowledge base and her observational skills.

A learning cycle may be either short-term (the lesson) or long-term (the semester, the year). Figure 1.4 might represent either a short-term or a long-term learning cycle. Regardless of the length, effective teaching culminates in successful learning, as evidenced by students having fulfilled the lesson objective. They have learned the dance skills and improved the performance of these skills. In the long-term learning cycle, learning abilities will also improve as a result of effective teaching.

A final point concerning the model in Figure 1.4 is that it may be discussed from two perspectives: a top-down perspective, or from the bottom up. Effective teaching originates from the teacher's knowledge (top-down) and results in skill acquisition. On the other hand, skill acquisition (bottom-up) is possible only with careful planning by knowledgeable teachers.

Despite the importance of advances in the movement sciences in the teaching of motor skills, the dissemination of this knowledge in dance teaching continues to be slow. The intent of this chapter has been to familiarize the reader with a general view of these advances and their contribution to the knowledge base in dance teaching. We suggest that good teaching in dance is dependent upon the relationship between the teacher's foundation knowledge base and his application knowledge, or ability to adjust to the students' learning capabilities. Perhaps not one theory or approach will ever be sufficient to fully understand the complexity of dance teaching and learning.

References

1. National Board for Professional Teaching Standards: *What Teachers Should Know and Be Able To Do*. Washington, DC: NBPTS, 1994.
2. Siedentop D: *Developing Teaching Skills in Physical Education,* (2nd ed). Mountain View, CA: Mayfield Publishing Company, 1991.

Marliese Kimmerle

The Communication Problem in Dance

The Function of Dance Skill Analysis

Terminology

　Movement

　Motor Skill

　Dance Skill

　Dance Techniques

Levels of Dance Analysis

　Level I: Body Action

　Level II: Components

　Level III: Context

The Complexity of the Dance Material

　Simple to Complex Dance Skills

　Simple to Complex Context

Chapter 2

How to Analyze the Dance Material

T he starting point of our knowledge as dance teachers is the material we teach. Depending on the age and skill level of the student and the dance form to be learned, there is a large range of skills that can be taught. Teachers in each dance form have their own repertoire of skills, including those personally acquired and those available in dance texts and curricula. Not all dance teachers speak the same language however. In order to fully understand and appreciate the skill learning process, we first need to standardize the way we discuss and analyze dance skills to ensure that we are all on a common ground.

The Communication Problem In Dance

When we try to define, classify, and analyze dance skills, we encounter a language barrier between the teacher of dance and the researcher of movement, between teachers of different forms of dance, and between the professional dancer and the dance educator. The lack of a common language separates traditional ballet teachers from modern dance teachers and creates a gap between technique teachers and teachers of creative dance. The increased scope of dance material available and the wide variety of dance training methods further exaggerate this problem.

The lack of a shared language leads to a lack of dialogue between dance educators and movement scientists who cannot understand why dancers have to use their own special movement language. Attempts to apply movement science research to dance teaching are difficult when biomechanical or motor learning skill classifications such as "discrete, axial movement" or "serial weight displacement" are used on the one hand and labels like "plié" or "barrel turn" on the other.

Communication has been hampered by confusion in the way dance and movement language is used and a similar language problem exists between teachers of the various dance forms. An open dialogue about the common problems of learning and teaching dance skills between dance teachers in different dance forms is difficult when the terms are French and English,

> Lack of a shared language leads to communication problems.

when ballet terms have been codified by 400 years of dance traditions while a new jazz skills may have been invented last week. There may not even be agreement on what is considered a dance skill and what is not. There seems to be no universal terminology that encompasses the variety of movements taught to dancers in the different dance forms, nor is there a clear dividing line between those terms that refer only to the physical actions that a dancer performs and those that describe the dynamics, style, or the aesthetic characteristics of those actions in a particular dance form. The task of skill learning then becomes a problem specific to a particular dance form and not a common problem of motor learning across dance forms.

The scope of the dance material to be covered creates additional problems. Historically, the development of ballet technique gave us a language of body positions, arm and leg gestures and steps, all standardized in reference to the four corners of the stage. In the 20th century a broad range of dance material has been added from modern dance and jazz. This material not only includes an expanded repertoire of body positions and steps but also new words to describe the range of motion possibilities in unique stylistic and dynamic variations. How do we capture these in a description of "skills?"

An individual student and future dance teacher searching for training in dance may find that in a modern dance or jazz class, the technique is not standardized but depends on the instructor's background. The student may end up as a disciple of a particular school of training such as Graham or Humphrey-Limon in modern or Giordano or Luigi in jazz. These approaches at least have documentation of the techniques.[1-5] Dance training in recent years, however, has become more eclectic and a student may sample from a variety of plates to make up her own menu of technique. Many of these new dance skills are not yet documented and may not be readily understood in a written format. The physical training of a dancer might also include gymnastics, martial arts, aerobics, and the latest street dances. The future teacher may therefore have a large repertoire of skills at her disposal without necessarily having a unifying structure.

While dance technique, performance style, training method, and language have continued to expand in modern, ballet, and jazz dance, many educators have rejected a technique approach to teaching children's dance. Rather they have promoted an educational dance, creative dance, or movement education approach. This approach is based on the movement analysis model developed by Rudolf Laban and translated into educational curricula in dance and physical education.[6-9] The philosophical distance between ballet, modern, and jazz teachers on the one hand and teachers of creative dance on the other is vast, thus reinforcing the communication problem. Is it appropriate to call what children learn in creative dance "dance skills?" How are movement themes different from dance skills? Is a competent mover different from a skilled mover?

Any attempt to make a comprehensive and exhaustive list of what to include under the label of "dance skills" may be futile, as would any attempt to make all teachers of dance adopt one uniform vocabulary. Despite the difficulty inherent in finding a universal dance language, it is critical that dance teacher find a common ground to share and understand dance skill acquisition. The isolation of teachers in different dance forms and the language barrier between dance teachers and movement science researchers often interferes with sharing knowledge and increasing our understanding about learning and teaching dance skills.

> It is critical that dance teachers find a common ground to share and understand skill acquisition.

A generic system of description and classification applicable to all dance forms is proposed. This system must be based on functional movements common to all dance forms, must identify the unique characteristics of each dance form and provide a way to analyze skills along a continuum of difficulty or complexity. Finally, the vocabulary must be understood by dancers and movement scientists. If we are to reap the benefits of research in the movement sciences to help us be better teachers of dance skills, we need to be able to clearly describe the physical skills that are being taught in a dance class. The rest of this chapter outlines such a skill analysis system. We turn first to the function of such a system.

The Function of Dance Skills Analysis

We can take it for granted that any teacher of dance has acquired a collection of dance skills, but she must also thoroughly understand the material she teaches. Although it is certainly possible to teach a dance class by following the skills as they are listed in a curriculum guide, syllabus, or dance text, that by itself is not a guarantee of successful or effective teaching. It is critical to understand the nature of these skills, their difficulty, and the relationship of one skill to another in order to select appropriate material for the age and skill level of the dance student and to guide that student through a progressive learning process.

The starting point for that understanding is to be able to describe and classify skills. An effective teacher must understand the material she teaches and the skill analysis process will help her to:

- Recognize the biomechanical categories of dance skills,
- Understand the range of skills in her particular dance form,
- Know the basic skill content of a good dance lesson,
- Identify and analyze the level of difficulty of specific skills,

- Select age and skill appropriate material for a class,
- Observe what component of the skill gives a student difficulty,
- Organize a logical progression of skills, and
- Recognize the commonalities and differences between dance forms.

We start the analysis of dance material by clarifying the use of terminology, introducing three levels of analyzing skills and identifying the complexity of the dance material.

Terminology

In an attempt to classify dance material, several term must be described: movement, motor skill, dance skill, and dance techniques. Each of these will be briefly explored.

Movement

The term "movement" is too broad and confusing for classification purposes. The use of the term by dance teachers is ambiguous and has little or no common definition across dance forms. "Movement pattern" may be used to describe any sequence of skills. A movement may refer to an action invented during improvisation, for which there is not an appropriate skill label. Teaching a child "to move" may be used to describe the acquisition of body control or precision of form in a particular skill. When is what we see a "movement" and when is it a dance "skill?"

Movement or motion has a different meaning for the movement scientist. Movements are categorized as flexion, extension, abduction, adduction, and rotation. If one wishes to examine the mechanics of producing efficient movement in dance, such as how to turn or jump effectively, it is necessary to analyze the movements involved, examine the spatial position of body parts from beginning to end, and to measure the timing and force production during the movement. That level of motion analysis has been carried out for a number of skills[10] and is useful for understanding the mechanics of specific skills. However joint movement analysis is too narrow to serve as an overall classification system and is not particularly helpful in furthering our understanding of dance skill learning.

Because the term "movement" has such varied uses in dance, movement and motion will be used in this text in an anatomical and biomechanical sense only. When it is necessary to describe what the body is doing in a dance skill, a number of functional categories of body actions will be used as the basic building blocks, such as the actions of jumping or balancing on one leg. Each of these actions consists of a number of joint motions, but these will not be the units of analysis.

Motor Skill

The term "motor skill" is the basic term used in motor learning and motor development literature. This term refers to a learned action or series of actions such as the skills of running, reaching and grasping, or balancing on one leg. There are many different ways of categorizing motor skills. Motor skills can be gross or fine motor, consist of single or multiple joint actions, be discrete, serial, or continuous, and be open or closed.[11,12]

The reason for this type of categorization in the movement sciences is that it recognizes the different types of motor skills, allows for comparisons between skills, and, relevant for this book, it allows one to examine the learning process in different skills.

Under this classification, dance skills generally are multiple-joint, gross motor actions that are discrete and/or serial and occur in an environment that is closed, that is unchanging and predictable (unlike the continuing adaptation required in performing sport skills). For example, a développé requires the coordination of many joints in simultaneous movement of the arms and leg while balancing on one leg, stabilizing the hip, and maintaining a continuous smooth sequence of motion. Dance skills are not one-joint, fine motor, or open skills. All dance skills are motor skills; many dance skills are highly complex skills. Describing dance skills solely as "motor skills" and placing them in these categories obviously does not do justice to the artistic nuances of dance, nor does it represent the totality of a dance skill. It simply gives a neutral starting point to begin to examine skill learning.

In the motor development literature, motor skills are further categorized as fundamental and specialized skills.[11] In the course of normal human development, we first acquire fundamental motor skills as the foundation for the later learning of specialized skills in games, gymnastics, and dance that build on these basics. The simple motor skill of jumping becomes a straddle vault in gymnastics or a stag leap in dance. Fundamental skills are classified according to their function in daily life, such as stability skills (stabilization of the head or trunk, balance, and body management skills), manipulative skills (movement of the limbs in handling objects), and locomotor skills (transporting the total body from place to place such as running, jumping, hopping). Each provide quite different learning challenges. These divisions are typically used in examining the progressive development of skills in children and form the prerequisites for skill acquisition in dance.

Dance Skill

Dance skills (like gymnastics and game skills) fall into the category of specialized skills that are combinations or adaptations of these motor skills in a new and more difficult context. Individual actions are combined; correct form as well as spatial and temporal precision become important. Dance skills, therefore, are complex versions of fundamental motor skills such as running, jumping, hopping, leaping, balancing on one foot, and controlling the motion of the arms and legs. A tour jeté in dance, a vault in gymnastic, and a spike in volleyball all involve specialized, more complex versions of jumping, even though their goal is quite

Figure 2.1
In contrast to a young child, an older child has stability on one leg and can perform a passé correctly.

different. Balancing on one foot is a basic motor skill. A passé involves a particular arrangement of foot, knee, and leg to produce a specific dance example of a balance skill. A young child beginning to dance may still be struggling with the simple action of trying to balance. With maturation and experience, she masters the balance problem and can then perfect the correct form required of a passé (Fig. 2.1).

Dance Technique

"Dance technique" is an umbrella term referring to the sum of dance skills taught and is a term typically used in ballet, modern, and jazz. It may also be used to differentiate the skills associated with a particular dance form, for example, modern dance technique versus ballet technique. The term "technique" is also used to separate the more structured skill development part of a dance class from the improvisation or composition parts of a class where students may invent or select their own dance material.

The term "exercises" has not been included here under the content of dance material. Clearly, dance students, like athletes, need to prepare their body to perform – to stretch and strengthen their muscles and to condition themselves aerobically. The warm-up and conditioning exercises that a dancer may engage in are not unique to the dance world. Therefore, common exercises like sit-ups, straddle stretches, running on the spot, and many others will not be covered under our discussion of dance skills.

From the perspective of this book, we will be focusing on specialized dance skills, which are complex, multi-jointed actions, performed in a variety of contexts. We need an analysis system that will help us categorize and describe these skills and identify what makes them complex so that we can understand the learning problems during skill acquisition.

Levels of Dance Analysis

We propose an analysis that takes place at three levels. The first level addresses what specific **body action** is being performed. The second level focuses on how the action is performed. Body actions take place in

Body Action   +   Component   +   Context

Figure 2.2
Three levels of analysis of the dance material.

and through space, in time, with varying degrees of force or muscular tension. This level of analysis is labeled **components**. Dance skills are seldom performed in isolation, however. They typically are combined in a sequence, involve other people, and are performed to music. The third level of analysis, therefore, examines the situation in which the dance skill is executed and is labeled **context**. The relationship of these three levels is illustrated in Figure 2.2

An example of the three levels of analysis can be illustrated with a développé. This action involves a balance on one leg while the other unfolds in the air. This action can be done with different movement qualities based on the use of time, space, and force components. It can be practiced as a single skill, fully supported at the barre, or in the context of a long adage sequence in the center paired with another dancer. Each of these three levels will now be examined in some detail.

Level I: Body Actions

A dance skill consists of one or several body actions. A plié consists of the motion of bending and straightening the knee while a waltz consists of three distinct steps. A list of all possible dance skills would be an insurmountable task. While such an undertaking may be an interesting vocabulary exercise, it would not help in describing the acquisition of dance skills. It would emphasize the differences in skills rather than the common learning problems.

Instead, we offer a condensed classification based on the functional category of the body actions involved. All dance students need to learn to control the alignment of the total body, to shift into a new balance in a different direction or on to one foot, to gesture with the arms or the free leg, to turn, jump, travel across the floor, and combine these actions together, regardless of the dance form they are studying. While there are clearly distinct features that distinguish a chaîné turn in ballet from a barrel turn in jazz, both skills require the maintenance of alignment through the center of the body, control of rotation through the position of the arms, and spotting. These six categories represent the biomechanical challenges that are inherent in the dance skills one performs (Fig. 2.3).

These action categories are ordered from static to dynamic. They are not mutually exclusive. Controlling the center can be considered as a skill by itself, for example, a pelvic contraction, curling or uncurling of the spine, or a plié. However this action is also inherent in performing all

Body Actions

Control of Center

Changing Base

Arm and Leg Gestures

Rotation

Elevation

Locomotion

Figure 2.3
Six functional categories of body actions.

other dance skills. Correct body alignment must be maintained in order
to perform controlled movements of the legs, a turn, or a jump and maintain correct weight transfer in locomotor movements. Similarly, a port
de bras can be learned as a separate action to develop control and place-

Table 2.1   Sub-categories of Body Actions

Control of Center: stationary
  Alignment of the total body
  Weightbearing on two feet
  Stabilization of pelvis/shoulder girdle with moving limbs
  Isolation of pelvis/shoulder movement
Changing Base: Balance
  Shifting balance to one foot
  Shifting balance to toes
  Stepping into a new balance
  Losing balance: fall
  Regaining balance
  Transition to and from the floor
Arm and Leg Gestures:
  Isolating and controlling arm and/or leg movements
  Coordinating arm and/or leg movements
Rotation:
  Direction change
  Turn on two feet
  Turn on one foot
  Turn in the air
  Traveling turn
Elevation:
  Take-off on one or two feet
  Land on one or two feet
  Horizontal and vertical flight
  Flight with changing body or limb positions
Locomotion:
  Locomotor patterns of walk, run, skip, hop, leap, jump, slide
  Combination of several patterns

ment of the arms. However, most turns, jumps, and traveling actions involve either a moving or a carefully positioned arm.

The proposed classification is cumulative, and represents the increasing complexity of action sequences that build in a dance class during a final combination or routine. A number of sub-categories are included in Table 2.1 to show the variety of skills that can be included in each of the six action categories.

Do these categories apply across dance forms? There is no doubt that one can clearly observe differences in the look of the body actions as one walks past a modern, ballet, and jazz class. These differences may be as basic as the body and limb positions emphasized, as we can see from this description of ballet: "the harmonious, perfected order and geometry of absolute body lines, the need for precise positions of head, body, arms, feet and directions to face."[13] In a jazz class, in contrast to the clean, geometrical centered body alignment of ballet, the body may be intentionally misaligned such as a pelvic release, a shifting of the rib cage, and the use of flexed wrists.[14] In some modern classes, we might not find any held body positions at all. The focus instead might be on continually shifting from one action to another.

If we look beyond the differences between styles and labels, and examine the body actions in a technique book, we would likely find that the six categories of skills are similar. That is, all beginning dancers, regardless of the dance form, need to learn the basic body actions in

Table 2.2   Class Content of Body Action in a Creative Dance and Jazz Dance Class

Class Content: Body Actions

Creative Dance Class	Jazz Class
Control of Center How large a circle can you draw with your hips without moving your feet?	Hip isolation, right, left, forward, backward
Changing Base Stand on one leg, and see if you can draw a large circle with your free leg	Développé to front, side, back, side
Arm Gestures Draw large circles all around your body leading with your hands	Start in high 5th, lower hands to jazz second
Rotation Use your arms to start your body spinning and to stop it	4th position parallel preparation into a bent leg inside pirouette turn
Elevation Show me the difference in jumping as high as possible and as far as possible	Run, run leap
Locomotion Run in a large circle, make is smaller and smaller until you come to a stop in the center	Diagonal jazz runs from corner to corner

isolation and then in combination.

A careful comparison of the following dance tasks in a creative dance and a jazz class for example (Table 2.2), shows that students in both classes are learning skills in similar categories of body actions, although the open-endedness of the tasks and the skill complexity are different.

Simply describing what actions the dancer is performing does not totally capture the skill. The quality of the movement is missing. The list of skills does not capture the essence of a creative dance or a jazz class and our classification system is incomplete.

Level II: Components

We need to add the components of space, time, and force. Dance skills cannot be explained only on the basis of the body action and the starting and ending positions. All dance skills are performed in three-dimensional space, take up time, and require a specific combination of muscular forces or tension. A dance skill is defined as a combination of body action and specific movement components (Fig. 2.4).

The particular combination of time and force is what dancers call movement quality. Qualitative differences produce the incredible variety of dance skills, stylistic and aesthetic qualities, and unique features that differentiate one dancer from another. It is the conscious manipulation and combination of these movement components, such as the release and capture of energy, that is characteristic of a Limon class, or the held energy in the trunk and the geometrical placement of arms and legs in classical ballet, that produces the richness of our dance vocabulary. Differences in movement quality produce the remarkable variety we see when a class is attempting to perform a dance skill in unison. Movement qualities provide the unconscious movement signature that each individual brings to a dance class. Students typically have preferences for certain time and force combinations in movement. Some students are comfortable learning sequences of held poses with slow, sustained transitions between skills while others enjoy the sudden bursts of energy as new actions are initiated at break-neck speed in a dynamic combination. Skilled dancers must learn to work through the full range of these qualities.

> Any dance skill is a combination of physical actions and the space, time, and force components.

Figure 2.4
A dance skill is a combination of a body action and specific movement components.

How the action is performed in space is also a critical feature of the skill to be learned. Where in space does the leg extend in second? How low should the body be in a jazz run? What air pattern should the arms trace in a port de bras? What is a clear diagonal position of the body? The spatial orientation is a critical part of the form, of the skill and must be learned along with the time and force characteristics of the action.

> The selection and emphasis of different movement components is the greatest difference between dance forms.

Any dance skill is a combination of the physical actions involved and the space, time, and force components. Sometimes these elements are fixed, thus an integral part of the skill. When learning a waltz step for example, the footwork, body posture, floor pattern, accent, and rhythm pattern are fixed. Other types of skills can be performed with any number of manipulations of these variables as can be seen in the following example.

Walking, a simple body action, is a weight shift from the ball of one foot to the heel of the other with a fairly predictable time and weight pattern. It can be manipulated for a variety of expressive purposes. It is the differences in stride length, tempo, and the force of the heel strike, along with the amount and type of motion in the rest of the body that allows us to identify the personal idiosyncrasies of someone's walk, or to distinguish the pitter patter of little feet, the shuffle of an old man, the clunk of a pair of work boots, or the clikkity clack of high heels.

The ability to manipulate movement quality at will is part of the dance training. A dance student has to learn to consciously produce an exaggerated stride length, to slow down the pace and perform a smooth, gliding weight shift in a modern dance walk. A dance walk done as a promenade in ballet slippers has quite a different quality from a bent knee lunge walk in jazz. The aggressive use of the hands and the counter tension in the body characteristic of jazz[14] are dramatically different from the sustained quality of a traditional port de bras pattern (Fig. 2.5). It is

Josie Hazen

Figure 2.5
The use of the hands and body in jazz is quite different than in ballet.

in the selection and emphasis given to different movement components that we see the greatest difference between dance forms. It is in this facet that we would recognize the style of the dance form.

Each dance form has its own preferred movement quality and therefore it is a particular challenge when a student shifts to a new dance form. The discomfort felt by a ballet student in forcefully contracting and releasing the pelvis, swinging the trunk, or throwing the arm into space in a modern dance class might take many lessons to overcome. A reviewer of the early history of modern dance expressed it this way:

> Each system required a re-siting of the body, an investiture of breath, balance, and bones, a particular response to time, an arranging of limbs in unfamiliar ways. If it fit your body, you would want to master it; if it felt alien, you might push your body into its forms with fanatical discipline and never really learn it.[15]

In a traditional folk dance class where correct performance of the steps and styles of different countries is emphasized, there is likely to be little variation or experimentation in space, time, or force characteristics since the finished dances are fixed. In some modern, ballet, and jazz classes a specific body action is taught with built-in dynamics; for example, in a Graham technique class, the dynamics of contraction and release are an integral part of the beginning spine curving skills. In other classes there is a lot of experimentation with different patterns of timing, spatial orientation, and force application. In a creative dance class, it is more likely that class content will focus on exploring one or more of these movement components with the specific body action being left up to the student. A typical task might be: "Design a rhythm pattern of slow and fast beats. Now find a locomotor patterns to go with it," or "See how many locomotor patterns you can do in a diagonal line." Understanding the particular space or time concept is the focus of learning in this instance and not the perfection of a specific body action.

Although we can describe and explore the space, time, and force components illustrated in Table 2.3 separately, all three are part of any dance skill. While it is possible, for example, to hold an isometric contraction and not visibly move the body in space, the body has a particular spatial design and the action has duration. If we teach a leg or arm swing, the skill already has a specific temporal pattern of tension and relaxation of particular sets of muscles and follows a pendular pattern in space.

In a teaching situation, we often isolate these components or emphasize one over another in order to help a student learn a skill, or to vary the skill practice. For example, a développé can be practiced by instructing students to focus on: extending the leg from the knee joint; drawing a line with the foot in a right forward diagonal; trying for a sustained timing on the way up and the way down; throwing the leg in the air quickly, and then floating it down slowly; or focusing on what muscles

Table 2.3   Detailed Description of Movement Components

Movement Components

Time:
  Duration of the movement, short/long
  Speed of the movement, slow/fast
  Acceleration/deceleration
  Rhythmic characteristics of the movement
  Temporal relationship of one body part to another

Space:
  Orientation of the body or parts while stationary in space
  Body orientation while traveling
  Body shape/design
  Level and direction of movement through space
  Pathway in air, on floor

Force:
  Amount of muscular force applied
  Pattern of tension and relaxation in muscles

to contract and what muscles to relax. Focusing on a different component creates a unique look and feel to the skill and may help the student with particular performance problems.

Dance skills then consist of one or several body actions performed in three-dimensional space with a particular combination of time and force characteristics. However, dance skills are not usually presented or performed in isolation.

Level III: Context

The third level of analysis is the situation in which the dance skill is performed in a combination or finished dance. Although a skill, when first learned, may consist of a single action such as a two foot jump performed in silence or to a regular beat while remaining on one spot, this is not how dance skills are usually performed. When mastered (and often long before), a dance skill is integrated into a sequence with other skills, performed in a complex spatial pattern to music and in synchrony

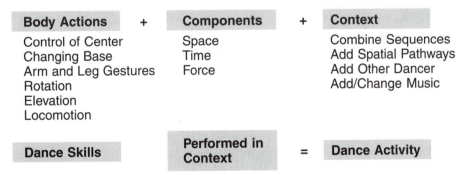

Body Actions	+	**Components**	+	**Context**
Control of Center		Space		Combine Sequences
Changing Base		Time		Add Spatial Pathways
Arm and Leg Gestures		Force		Add Other Dancer
Rotation				Add/Change Music
Elevation				
Locomotion				

Dance Skills	**Performed in Context**	=	**Dance Activity**

Figure 2.6
Putting the dance skill in a context creates the dance activity.

with other dancers. That is the context of the dance skill (Fig. 2.6) that can now be added to our model. The goal in dance skill acquisition is to be able to competently perform those skills in a variety of contexts. Similarly, an athlete is not considered skilled until she can successfully use her throwing, hitting, or catching skills in a game situation. Dance skills are initially learned in isolation, a fact particularly true for beginners. However, the ultimate goal is for those skills to be performed in a real dance context. It is, of course, this aspect that produces the most difficulty during learning.

> The goal in dance skill acquisition is to be able to competently perform dance skills in a variety of contexts.

Each dance form provides a slightly different context for the learner. However, learners experience similar difficulties across dance forms. Sequencing a series of dance skills, moving in a particular pathway through space, learning to work with different tempi and different types of music, and adapting to different partner and group relationships are common difficulties that exist in all dance forms.

There are now three levels of description that can be applied to any dance task, the physical action, the movement components, and the context. When we combine these three levels, there is an obvious degree of complexity and we can now more clearly identify the difficulties inherent in learning dance skills.

The Complexity of the Dance Material

These potential difficulties are summarized in the Complexity Model introduced in Figure 2.7 and shown in detail in Figure 2.8. This model was originally developed to show the progressive difficulty of fundamental to specialized skills and has been adapted for use with dance skills.[16] The difficulties can be divided into those inherent in the skill itself (body action and movement components) and those in the context in which the skill is performed.

A plié is a simpler skill than a développé, requiring no balance challenges. A hop done alone by a child meandering around a gymnasium is a relatively simple skill, but performed while holding hands with a partner in a folk dance combined with other dance steps in time to musical accompaniment is a fairly complex task. We have to remember that the

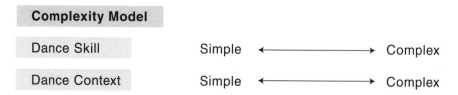

Figure 2.7
Introduction of the Complexity Model.

child or beginning adult has to learn not just a novel physical action but often to perform it in a novel and complex context. The teacher structures the level of complexity of the dance activity by choosing the skill and the context in which it is performed. The complexity of a skill can be decreased or increased by removing or adding one element. A skill can be taught slowly and then speeded up to normal tempo. The skill is learned individually and then a partner is added. A plié may be taught as a simple leg action or as part of a sequence with demi and full plié followed by a relevé, with simultaneous arm actions. In a modern dance class, there may even be a trunk or head isolation combined with the arm and leg.

> The teacher structures the level of complexity by choosing the skill and the context in which it is performed.

This process of selection is ongoing in any dance lesson, and is often done unconsciously by the experienced teacher as she automatically adapts to the level of the class or challenges her more skilled pupils. However the ability to make appropriate choices is a critical skill that must be learned by beginner teachers, and the Complexity Model is presented as a useful framework or checklist for making these selections. The elements are on a continuum; those on the left are more simplistic and those on the right are more complex. The addition of any one element increases the difficulty. By the time one reaches the locomotor combination, the folk dance or the dance study at the end of a class, one has usually included all of the elements. A more detailed examination of simple and complex skills and context is illustrated in Figure 2.8.

Simple to Complex Dance Skills

The dance skill category includes the elements of difficulty of the physical actions and the movement components that are built into the skill. Each of the individual elements adds another level of difficulty. A brush or tendu as it is typically taught in a modern, jazz, or ballet class, can be used as an illustration here. Although, on the surface, a brush may appear to be a relatively simple leg pointing action, it also consists of a simultaneous shift of balance to one foot while stabilizing the pelvis and controlling the position of the trunk. It is a leg gesture involving a sequence of joint motions that have a precise end point in space to the front, side, or back, and is performed within a specific time frame. The teacher may also add a circling pattern of the arms to the leg action and increase the balance problem by performing the skill on half toe or requiring a held balance. The skill is now quite complex.

"Simple" therefore is a relative term. The majority of dance skills are complex actions. One category in which they might be considered "simple" is that they are gross motor skills, that is, they involve total body movement, or movement of large body parts such as arms and legs. Fine motor skills are limited to the actions of small muscle groups such

Complexity Model

Dance Skill

Simple ←————————————→	Complex
Gross Motor	Fine Motor
Single Joint	Multiple Joints
Static (axial)	Dynamic (locomotion)
One Action	Several Actions
	Simultaneous
	Sequential
Free Movement in Space	Spatial Demands
Minimal Control	Control/Precision
Self Paced	Temporal Demands

Context

Simple ←————————————→	Complex
Single Skill	Sequence of Many Skills
Single Direction	Spatial Pathways
Solo	Adjusting to Others
	Match Other Dancers
	Others Dictate Movement
No Music or Set Tempo	Music/Changes in Timing

Figure 2.8
The complete Complexity Model.

as those of the hands. In dance, only the gestures of Indian or Hawaiian dancing would fall into this category. The only other category of skill complexity, where we might look for simple dance skills, is in single actions of one joint. However, these are generally only found in the warm-up, where bending, stretching, and rotating single body parts are used to increase range of motion and to improve body awareness. We can therefore identify most dance skills as complex and therefore likely to cause some learning difficulties.

> We can identify most dance skills as complex and therefore likely to cause some learning difficulties.

How much learning difficulty will be encountered depends on how many and how quickly elements of difficulty are added. In most dance classes, skills are not performed one at a time. Beginners in a folk dance class may initially be asked to perform a single kick or jump, but will almost immediately be asked to repeat the action in a long sequence. In a creative dance class, the students may be asked to travel anywhere in the room, at their own pace, with little demand for temporal or spatial precision. Within that same lesson, they will likely be asked to structure and refine the locomotor pattern. In most modern, ballet, and jazz classes the initial presentation of the skill already includes a specific spatial pattern, timing, and force characteristic, even for beginners. An example of a task may be, "Do a triplet turn starting with your left foot, accenting the first count."

The Complexity Model has focused on difficulties involved in learning dance skills and not on anatomical or mechanical difficulties. In addition to the categories listed, there is no doubt that some skills are simply more difficult to perform, due to the nature of the body action itself (the mechanics involved). For example, a 360° turn on one leg is more difficult to perform correctly than a three-step walking turn due to a combination of the spatial precision required, momentum, and muscular control over the moving limbs. Also some skills are difficult to perform for physiological reasons related to body structure, strength, or flexibility. A full split or maximum leg extension is difficult due to physical restrictions. The application of the model, therefore, is to evaluate skill complexity and hence learning difficulty.

The series of photographs of the développé illustrates increasing skill difficulty by adding movements in other joints and changing the balance demands (Figs. 2.9 through 2.11). We can also see the introduction of an additional difficulty by changing the context in which the skill has to be performed, from solo to synchronized with other dancers.

Simple to Complex Context

The difficulties in context depend on the amount of adjustment the learner must make in her movements and the number of restrictions under which the skill must be performed. These include the combination of one skill with another, a specific floor pattern, the adjustment to other dancers, and dancing to accompaniment. The difficulty is cumulative: each added element creates more difficulty.

A simple context is one where the student controls her own actions and there are few restrictions on how the skill is performed. She dances alone in her spot in the room, at her own pace, and does not have to continually readjust her body position nor deal with other people intruding on her space. Much of the class work in a creative dance class involves open-ended tasks and the only restriction imposed is the need to be aware of other individuals moving in proximity. In a more traditional technique class, it is usually the floor warm up, barre work, and the first time introduction of a new skill at center that are presented in such a simple context.

> The difficulties in context depend on the amount of adjustment the learner must make in her movement and the number of restriction under which the skill must be performed.

As students become more skilled and the class work progresses, center and locomotion combinations, lengthy routine sequences, and even full-

Josie Hazen

Figure 2.9
A développé as a simple
skill in a simple context.

Josie Hazen

Figure 2.10
A more complex
développé in a simple
context.

Josie Hazen

Figure 2.11
A complex développé in a
complex context.

length dances are learned. The context is now more complex as the dancer
is no longer performing the skill on one spot, but has to move across the
floor and reestablish her balance and her postural alignment over each
new base. After a skill is learned, it is combined with other skills in a

combination, so the newly learned traveling turn is performed with two leaps at the beginning and a balance pose at the end. These rather dramatic changes in complexity take place in most advanced dance classes. However they occur somewhat rapidly, even with children and beginners. In a typical folk dance class for example, children may start by practicing hopping by themselves on the spot, and end up performing a schottische step with a partner, moving in a circle with other couples to new music by the end of the class. The addition of directional changes and specific floor pathways, even without partner work, may present problems. Young children may be comfortable walking or skipping in time to the music until introduced to right, left, forward, backward, and traveling around in a circle in a folk dance.

When partner and group work is added, the complexity increases again. In most classes one first learns to execute solo skills. Due to space restrictions, performing an individual skill without encroaching on others' personal space is an initial adjustment. Other dancers are present in close proximity and as they all move, synchronization and adaptations are necessary in the direction and size of movement, for example, when performing leg gestures at the barre. When locomotor patterns are introduced, the adaptation becomes more complex. Synchronization of a group in performing unison movements while following a prescribed floor pathway is typically required in a final combination in a ballet, modern, or jazz class (Fig. 2.12). Picture the chaos the first time beginners are asked to come from the corner performing a sequence, two abreast and waiting four counts for the couple ahead of them. If the whole group is doing the same action, the adjustment is manageable. It may be as simple as adjusting the length of one's stride and the position of one's arms. Eventually however it may involve a whole routine choreographed with a variety of complex partner and group patterns.

The complexity can be increased further when some individuals perform different actions, at different times. In other dance skills, it is necessary to react or respond to what others do, for example, to follow one's waltz partner when he decides to turn or being in the right spot at the

Figure 2.12
Synchronization with the group adds difficulty to a simple locomotor skill.

right time to intercept the partner flying through the air in a pas de deux. These adaptations are more complex in that one has to anticipate and adjust to the partner (or the group) in planning one's own actions.

Accompaniment in the class provides the final context difficulty. Some form of accompaniment is usually present as soon as a new skill has been demonstrated and the students have practiced it a few times. This may be as simple as the teacher's voice providing the general duration of the action or matching one's movements to a very complex rhythmic pattern. Different dance forms tend to provide different challenges in accompaniment. The novice ballet dancer must learn to perform skills to a precise phrasing of accompaniment, an integral part of the skill from day one, but it is usually a very consistent pattern with a strong underlying beat. While similar accompaniment might be used in a modern class, the dancer may also be asked to move to a percussion instrument that emphasizes the dynamics of the movement, move to irregular phrased music, use her own breath phrasing, or even work in silence counting in her head. A jazz class may be accompanied by live percussion that may include syncopated rhythms and two or three simultaneous rhythms. A child in a creative dance class may be encouraged to develop an individualized rhythm pattern to accompany her own movement, or to respond to word sounds and meanings in poetry.[17]

A major difference between creative dance and the three technique forms lies in who is in control of the elements of difficulty. In a creative dance class, the movement tasks given by the teacher are generally very open-ended (e.g., "Find a way to turn while you are in the air"). The learner, therefore, is the one who chooses the difficulty of the physical action attempted and the way the movement is performed. In a standard ballet, modern, or jazz class on the other hand, the physical actions are clearly defined and the student is expected to copy the body actions and the dynamics precisely, regardless of her particular skill level or anatomical limitations. If the aim of the class were to produce identical skills, then the movement environment would be fairly predictable. The difficulty of the dance skill itself might be high, but the adaptations to the environment would be minimal. Everyone would be moving the same arm and leg and traveling in the same direction. In a creative dance class, on the other hand, much more adaptation may be required to accommodate the greater variety of movement choices made by others. The process of improvisation may produce a rapidly changing environment with the need to adapt position, speed, or size of one's movement or pathway to the execution of spontaneous movement by adjacent dancers. Working in a less structured class therefore is not necessarily easier than in a structured class.

Summary

In summary, this chapter has provided a system of analyzing dance skills that can be used in any dance form to identify the type and difficulty of the dance material and to build logical progressions. In the next chapter, this model will be applied to the problem of organizing the dance material in a lesson and in a dance unit.

References

1. McDonagh D: *Martha Graham: A Biography*. New York: Praeger, 1973.
2. Lewis D: *The Illustrated Dance Technique of José Limón*. New York: Harper & Row, 1984.
3. Stodelle E: *The Dance Technique of Doris Humphreys*. Princeton, NJ: Princeton Book Co., 1978.
4. Giordano G: *Anthology of American Jazz Dance*. Evanston, IL: Orion, 1975.
5. Luigi, Kriegel LP, Roach FJ: *Luigi's Jazz Warm Up: An Introduction to Jazz Style and Technique*. Pennington NJ: Princeton Book Co., 1997.
6. Preston-Dunlop V: *A Handbook for Dance in Education,* (2nd ed). London: Macdonald and Evans, Ltd., 1980.
7. Logsdon B, Barrett K, Ammons M, Broer M, et al: *Physical Education for Children: A Focus on the Teaching Process,* (2nd ed). Philadelphia: Lea & Febiger, 1984.
8. Stanley S: *Physical Education: A Movement Orientation,* (2nd ed). Toronto: McGraw-Hill Ryerson Limited, 1977.
9. Wall J, Murray N: *Children and Movement: Physical Education in the Elementary School,* (2nd ed). Madison, WI: Brown & Benchmark, 1994.
10. Laws K: *The Physics of Dance*. New York: Schirmer Books, 1984.
11. Gallahue DL, Ozmun JC: *Understanding Motor Development: Infants, Children, Adolescents, Adults,* (3rd ed). Dubuque, Iowa: Brown & Benchmark, 1995.
12. Schmidt RA, Wrisberg CA: *Motor Learning and Performance,* (2nd ed). Champaign, IL: Human Kinetics Publishers, Inc., 2000.
13. LaPointe-Crump JD: *In Balance: The Fundamentals of Ballet*. Dubuque, Iowa: Wm. C. Brown, 1985. p. 9.
14. LaPointe-Crump J, Stanley K: *Discovering Jazz Dance: America's Energy and Soul*. Madison, WI: Brown & Benchmark, 1992.
15. Siegel MB: Art, aspiration and the body: The emergence of modern dance. *In:* Bird D, Greenberg J (eds): *Bird's Eye View: Dancing with Martha Graham and on Broadway*. Pittsburgh, PA: University of Pittsburgh Press, 1997, p. xv.
16. Kimmerle M: Motor development and the dance curriculum: A selection of developmentally appropriate activity. *In:* Murray N (ed): *Children's Dance: Beyond Activity*. Reston, VA: Canadian Association for Health, Physical Education, Recreation and Dance and the National Dance Association, 1997.
17. Boorman J: *Dance and the Language Experiences with Children*. Don Mills, Ontario: Longman Canada Ltd., 1973.

Josie Hazen

Making Choices in Different Dance Forms
Making Choices in Body Actions
Making Choices in Components
Making Choices in Context
  Skill Sequences
  Pathway in Space
  Other Dancers
  Accompaniment

Chapter 3

Organizing the Dance Material

A skill analysis system can aid the teacher in analyzing the difficulty of any specific dance skill or completed dance. The next step is to apply this analysis to the examination of problems encountered in the selection and organization of dance content in a class and in a dance unit. This chapter offers some general guidelines and identifies some potential problems in making choices of content that apply across dance forms. Differences in these choices due to the nature of the dance form studied are also identified. We do not offer a prescription or a uniform solution. We recognize that there are different requirements and traditions in different dance forms. The guidelines are general, outlining some of the choices that teachers have available, with the hope that they will make intelligent choices.

We begin with an overview. In a typical class, regardless of dance form, age and skill level, students should be exposed to the six basic actions, learn to control the amount of force they use, control their movement through space, in time, and learn how to translate individual skills into sequences with other people in a culminating activity. The number, type and difficulty of body actions chosen, the movement components emphasized and the context in which they are presented, will, of course, vary from class to class, from teacher to teacher, and from one dance form to another. Figure 3.1 summarizes the material presented in Chapter 2, and represents the choice of content for a typical class. The teacher chooses the particular body actions to be reviewed that day and what new actions will be taught. Each action will be performed with the specific dynamic quality the teacher has chosen. At the end of the class both new and old skills will be combined in some type of culminating activity.

Across a dance unit, if the lessons are well planned, the skills chosen will become more difficult, students will perform them more proficiently, and

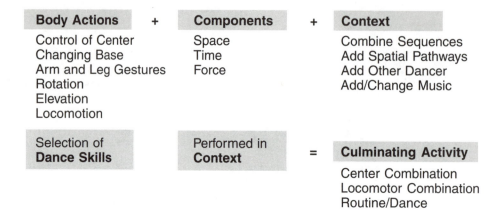

Figure 3.1
Content of a typical class.

their repertoire of skills will enlarge. They will have explored a full range of dynamics and the combinations they learn will become longer and more complex.

In order to accomplish this progression the teacher makes choices, for each class and for the total unit. These choices are not just about which leg or locomotor skills to work on, but also how those skills will be presented, that is, selecting the specific dance task or activity for that day. The lesson focus may change daily; for example, there may be a focus on arm actions or footwork in all the skills one day, the next day the focus may be on movement quality, or partner synchronization, or musical phrasing. The choices are made by teachers in all of the dance forms; however, they may be affected by the teaching tradition and the standard syllabi or curriculum of the specific dance form. Making choices in body actions, components and the difficulty of the skill context presents some common problems across dance forms, but there are also innate differences due to the dictates or special nature of the dance form.

> Across a dance unit, the skills chosen will become more difficult, students will perform them more proficiently, and their repertoire of skills will enlarge.

Making Choices in Different Dance Forms

Throughout this chapter, reference will be made to traditional practices and/or stylistic demands in the different dance forms that will influence teacher choices. It would be useful therefore to summarize some of these differences. Table 3.1 highlights some of the differences in emphasis between dance forms. Ballet has been used as the starting point. Although some of the skills will be similar in modern and jazz, the descriptions focus on some of the ways in which the

Table 3.1 Differences in Emphasis Across Dance Forms

Body Actions	Components	Context
Ballet		
Vertical spine and head	Focus is on medium/high level	Predictable skill sequences front/side/back
Centering around spine	Predictable spatial design of	Predictable group floor pathways
Poses with held arms,	arms and legs in space	Unison motion with many dancers
gesturing legs	Largely frontal view of body	Standard criteria of skill performance,
Static positions alternate with	Clear body designs in space	little or no individual variations
locomotion, jumps and turns	Tight space restrictions at barre	High level of musicality expected, precise
Focus on alignment and momentum	Strong verticality	synchronization with accompaniment
in many jumps, turns	Even metric phrasing	
Stress on amplitude, flexibility	Static use of strength or	
Footwork in ballet shoes	explosive strength in jumps	
	Many sustained held positions	
	Body design and line more	
	important than dynamics	
Modern		
Curling, uncurling of spine	Freer use of space	Emphasis on movement sequences, flow
Head may be off center	Unconventional and	of one movement into the next
Centering in pelvis	asymmetrical body designs, 3D	Less predictable floor pathways
Free flowing limbs and trunk	Rapid level changes	Unusual phrasing and rhythmic patterns
More total body movements	Uneven, non-metric phrasing	Some tolerance for individual variations
More emphasis on moving	introduced	adjusted to body structure
rather than holding poses	Dynamics may supersede focus	
Footwork in bare feet	on space	
	Large range of dynamic variations	
	Importance of the breath	
	The use of body weight, working	
	with gravity	
Jazz		
Body actions based on both	Strongly linear in both	Many different actions combined in long
modern and ballet but add:	body design and floor pattern	sequences
Lower weight, pelvis and knees	Explosive dynamics	Arms and legs coordinated in unusual ways
Pelvic, shoulder, rib cage	Fast tempo	Close proximity of many dancers
isolations	Many rhythmic changes	Complex spatial pathways with frequent,
Oppositional motion between	Use of all 3 levels	rapid direction and level changes
body parts	Use of syncopation	Unison group work
Few held positions, largely	Rapid weight shifts	Complex rhythm patterns, often
locomotor		polyrhythmic
Weight on bent legs		
Hand gestures		
Folk		
Total body held, upright posture	Medium level, seldom	Many repetitions of same step
Arms in stylized gesture or	in air or on floor	Predictable skill combinations
natural movement	Circular pathways or lines	Frequent but predictable floor pattern changes
Minimal arm/leg gestures	Metric tempo	Need to adjust individual spatial pattern to
Largely locomotor actions	Limited dynamic range	coordinate group pattern of dance
Adapt to different footwear		Unison skills with group,
(e.g., high heels, boots)		Mirror, leading and following with partner
		Predictable tempo and phrasing of music
		Often fast tempo
Creative Dance		
Full range of actions	Loosely structured spatial	Individual choice of skill combinations
Open-ended skills rather than	arrangement	Variability in skills performed require
copy precise skills	Large dynamic range	awareness of others spatial pathway
Individual variation and	Structured exploration of	A variety of partnering/group relationship
invention encouraged	space/time/force components	Less emphasis on unison, more coordination
		challenges of different skills
		May need to adapt to unusual accompaniment
		use of voice, percussion instruments

Josie Hazen

Figure 3.2
Modern dance techniques
require that the dancer use
the floor.

skills differ. A reminder is appropriate here. The descriptions are a characterization of a typical class taught to beginning students and are not necessarily representative of the art form as performed on stage by experts. The descriptions are of necessity somewhat stereotypical. The list is by no means comprehensive, nor can it possibly represent all the variations found in each form. This is particularly true of modern dance, which may include the most variability. The modern dance descriptions represent traditional modern dance techniques such as Graham, Humphrey-Limon, or Cunningham and may not apply to the improvisational forms of modern dance. The chart does demonstrate however, that the three-level skill analysis can be applied to identify some of these differences.

Making Choices in Body Actions

Some common problems in making body action choices will first be outlined. These are the neglect of some categories of body actions and an emphasis on routine building rather than skill development. The six basic body action categories: controlling center, changing base, arm and leg work, turning, jumping and traveling (*see* Fig. 3.1) are skills that should be part of the total dance program at any age or skill level regardless of dance form. It is not unrealistic to expect that some skills in each area could be covered in each class. It has been suggested that as many as 20 technical exercises can be presented in a dance class.[1] A common problem is that some areas of body actions are neglected. The main content in both a class and in a term may consist largely of the first three categories of body actions and the last three are neglected. The assumption appears to be that beginners primarily need to work on alignment, balance, and leg work while stationary, and are not ready to move dynamically, that is, learn loco-motor skills, until they have perfected the basics. How long will that take? Until the end of a term? While it is true that initial learning of many skills must take place while stationary, basic skills may not automatically transfer to traveling.[2] The consequence of this neglect is a dancer who has poor dynamic skills. Often you see a dancer who can confidently and competently move into static poses, but has great difficulty when he has to move across the room. Locomotor skills need to be practiced from the beginning in order for the student to understand what happens when he has to continually adjust alignment and shift

> A common problem is that some areas of body actions are neglected.

weight. Locomotor skills cannot be simply added on at lesson five, nor should they only be given five minutes at the end of a class.

A similar omission occurs regarding jumping and turning. Many beginners have few opportunities to learn and practice these skills. While many jumps and turns are complex, and some have safety concerns, there are also many simple skills in both categories. Beginners need to experience the feeling of turning and jumping, attempt to sort out how to apply force, control momentum, and orient themselves in space. Beginners, regardless of age and skill level, can cope with a three-step turn, a push turn, a pivot turn, and jumps or leaps with minimum height and simple body shapes. It is extensive experience with these and similar simple skills that teach some of the basic mechanics of these skills, not hours of work on static alignment alone.

This focus on static work can be exaggerated even more for leg gestures and balance skills, when the major part of class takes place only at the barre or sitting or lying on the floor where balance is greatly assisted. This is essential in the beginning when correct positioning of the leg and isolation of specific muscles is not well understood. However, learning to control center is not mastered simply by

Josie Hazen

Figure 3.3
Beginners can learn many
simple jumps.

standing still. It is an ongoing process that must also be learned dynamically. The amount of material that transfers from stationary skills to traveling may be limited.[2] A study of university modern dance students suggested that dynamic alignment is quite different from static alignment and that dynamic balance without support requires different neural mechanisms than balance at the barre.[3] A guide for teachers is suggested:

> "It may therefore be more useful to give dancers information and images to use while they are in motion in the class, rather than to spend great amounts of time correcting placement while dancers are standing motionless at the barre or in the center."[4]

The first set of problems, therefore, revolves around the extent to which the different body actions receive attention in class, and how early in a unit they are introduced. A different problem is the balance of time given to learning and practicing basic actions versus time spent on learning dances. In all dance forms, one ultimately combines skills and it is important for students to connect movements to each other. However, we will see in Chapter 4 that sufficient time must also be devoted to practice in order to acquire skill. Some teachers focus much of their time on teaching combinations or building routines, particularly if the goal of the course is to take part in a recital at the end of the term. Teaching individual skills may be neglected as students are trying to cope with complex contexts. This is similar to the concern expressed by some educators, parents and researchers that children in youth sports spend too much time in competition and not enough in sport skill development.[5,6]

Besides these shared organizational problems, there are also differences in the selection of body action content simply due to the tradition of a particular dance form. This will affect the degree of choice the teacher has. What would likely differ would be:

- The emphasis given to particular categories reflected in the amount of class or term time,
- Whether each body action category is covered in every class,
- Stylistic variations in how these actions are performed, and
- The degree of open-ended, individualized performance of skills versus standardization.

In a ballet class preparing students for syllabus exams, there is a precise order of skills designated for each part of the class and each level, a structured progression from one level to the other and room for teacher choice perhaps only in the combinations. The teacher, therefore, may not have any choice regarding skill content taught.

Some modern techniques such as Graham also prescribe a fairly structured set of skills to be performed in each class. In other modern dance techniques, the teacher might follow a set order of warm-ups, center alignment and leg skills and then select jumps, turns and locomotor skills and combinations from any number of skills in the students' repertoire or have the students invent new actions. A set structure is also found in many jazz classes, such as Luigi or Giordano styles,[7,8] but as in modern dance, an individual teacher may choose to make up his own eclectic mix of skills.

In a creative dance class, the teacher may choose to cover each action category in different lessons spread out over several weeks. On a particular day the whole lesson may be spent on jumps; working on the five basic jumps, focusing on take-offs, landings and body position in the air, emphasizing horizontal and vertical pathways, having each child perform his own variation of body shape in the air and perhaps coming up with a partner action-reaction jumping sequence. The following lesson might deal with turning.

All folk dances involve locomotor skills and the other five body actions play a supporting role, as they do not receive as much emphasis as the locomotor skills. Control of body center and correct weight shift are needed to maintain balance during rapid locomotor patterns. Jumping and turning are part of some energetic Russian and Israeli dances. Gestures of arms or legs are used to add the stylistic variations from one dance to the other, such as holding a handkerchief in a Greek line dance, clapping of the hands, knees and leather pants in a Bavarian Schuhplattler. The nature of this dance form, therefore, puts more emphasis on one of the six categories.

There is no one common rule applicable across all dance forms regarding the amount of time or number of skills to be covered in each area in each class, nor how early in a program they need to be introduced. A competent dancer, however, must have a foundation of some skills in each area. To leave a beginner at the end of his first dance course without exposure to an area and to limit that student to largely static skills leaves him poorly prepared for his next exposure, which should build on basic skills in each of the six categories of body actions.

> There is no one common rule regarding the amount of time or number of skills to be covered in each area in each class.

Just as there are choices to make regarding the specific body actions to be developed in a lesson, or in a whole dance unit, there are also choices regarding the components of space, time, and force.

Making Choice of Components

In each of the forms, as students practice their dance skills, they will be asked to vary the tempo of their movements, learn to reproduce different rhythm patterns and accents and learn to recognize musical phrasing. They will be asked to pay attention to the orientation and design of their body and limbs in space while standing and moving, learn to travel freely forward, backward, sideways and diagonally. They will learn to contract and release muscular tension and vary the dynamics of their movements. Exposure to these variations in movement components, therefore, must be part of the daily and unit content.

> Exploring movement components adds variety, allows for progressions and provides an understanding of stylistic variations.

Exploring the movement components can serve a number of different functions. One function is to add variety to the day-to-day skill practice; a second is to allow for progressions from simple to more complex versions of the same skills and a third is to provide students with an understanding of stylistic variations of skill performance in their dance form and provide some choreographic tools.

In order to become skilled in alignment, balance, gestures, rotation, elevation and locomotion, students must repeat these basic actions again and again in subsequent lessons. Initially, with novice dancers, the teacher may select the simpler aspects of time, space and force. The actions are usually performed one at a time, slowly, to an even 4/4 meter. The skills are learned facing the front of the room, the action is in one direction. This simplifies the skill so the student can focus on the action itself. It will take many repetitions to perfect the skill, and motivation to continue practicing is important. Boredom is avoided when students can practice the same skill in a different way by varying the spatial pattern and the dynamics.

Students must gradually be introduced to more complex skills. Continually adding new skills may be too difficult and frustrating for the

Table 3.2   Triplet Variations

Basic Body Action
  Step, step, step
Variations in Body Action
  Emphasize down, up, up, plié and relevé
  Add arm gestures
  Add trunk, or head inclination
Variations in Components:
  Start even 3/4 meter, accenting 1, shift to 6/8
  Shift to uneven 2/4, slow, quick, quick
  Do forward, then try backward, sideways
  Do a forward 360° turn
  Change accent, initiate turn on 2nd count
  Emphasize covering distance on the second and third step
  Focus on lightness, skimming across floor

student, but they need to be challenged to improve their skills. This can be done by staying with the same skills for several lessons but adding motions of the arms, trunk or head, performing the skill to the side and back of the body, traveling sideways and backward instead of forward, speeding up the timing, putting an accent into the movement, or trying to hold a position of stillness and then suddenly release it. Not only have these variations increased the difficulty of the skill, but it is now a more adaptable skill that can be used in many different dance styles and be performed to different music. An examples of a triplet is provided in Table 3.2 to illustrate skill variations in both content and components.

The choices made and emphasis given to different movement components provide the greatest differences between dance forms. It is in this area that we would get much of the "style" of the dance form. In a ballet class, there may be an emphasis on holding positions in stillness, traveling with lightness and learning to work in precise spatial pathways. In a modern class, one could be learning to hold on to a forceful isometric contraction or learn to release in a fall and recovery. In a jazz class one might practice transitions between skills requiring explosive energy and smooth, fluid motion. As students become more familiar with the specific dance form studied, they will also learn what are the typical spatial patterns and dynamics emphasized.

Apart from emphasizing different space, time, and force components, the teacher also has a choice of how to present these components. Some dance teachers present the body actions and specific components simultaneously. In a Graham technique class, for example, the contraction and release dynamics are an integral part of the beginning spine curving warm-up exercises. In a Limon class, fall, weight, recovery, rebound and suspension are an integral part of the technique.[9] For other teachers, in other forms, it may be more desirable to present a neutral body action first, and then have the students experiment with the variations produced by manipulating time and force components. There is no one set criterion for how to perform the skill. What may be more important for that teacher is to develop adaptable skills that can be performed with any number of qualitative variations.

Making Choices in Context

The final option the teacher has is to plan a culminating activity for the skills learned in each class. This is where the teacher takes the student from skill training to "dancing." Just as sport skills must eventually be practiced in a learning environment that is game-like,[10] so individual dance skills must be combined and performed to music with other dancers. In a modern, ballet, and jazz class, this will likely consist of a center and/or a locomotor combination. The combinations may also be part of a routine or a piece of repertoire with parts

Table 3.3   Examples of Culminating Activities

Ballet	Center adage performed in unison with class
Modern	Triplet combination with partner, mirrored in direction
Jazz	32 count entrance to "One" from Chorus Line
Folk Dance	Teton Mountain Stomp
Creative Dance	Partner study based on circular pathways

added on each day, culminating in a finished dance at the end of the term. A folk dance class usually ends with a performance of the dance, while in a creative dance class the lesson might end with showing a group dance study in front of the class. Samples of these culminating activities are provided in Table 3.3.

Each dance form provides a different context for the learner. However, by the end of each class, and certainly by the end of the unit, all students should have been exposed to the four key aspects of dance context presented in Figure 3.1. They will have learned to sequence a series of dance skills, travel in a variety of pathways through space, work with different tempi and different types of music and adapt to different partner and group relationships. The complexity of each of these will vary to provide a suitable learning experience for the age and skill level of the student. The teacher has many choices to make in context. These options are described in the following, along with some of the differences in context found in the different dance forms.

Skill Sequences

The skills learned in the class are combined with other material learned in previous classes. Combining skills teaches transition, weight shift and the maintenance of smooth flow from one skill to the next to create a seamless movement phrase. Table 3.4 illustrates sample combinations from a jazz and a creative dance class. Although the actual dance activity is quite different, the challenge of making a smooth transition is common to both examples.

A number of choices face the teacher. Initially he has to decide how much competence is required in individual skills before the students

Table 3.4   Examples of Skill Combinations

Creative Dance	**Jazz Dance**
Center Combination	
Draw a circle with your hips, let it go into your arms and then into your whole body	Two step-bends to right side with hip and shoulder isolations, add pirouette turn and reverse pattern to the left
Locomotor Combinations	
Combine the following into a phrase in any order: traveling, a turn, a balance pose, a jump	Three jazz runs, leap, repeat, tour jeté, tabletop bent leg arabesque, leg swing through to front

are asked to combine skills. It is a question of finding a balance between focusing largely on practicing individual skills, which may become boring and frustrating to the student, and focusing too much on routine building at the expense of skill development. The teacher also has to decide on the length of the sequence and the difficulty of the individual components. He has to decide whether the combination will be done both on the right leg/side and the left. Transferring a locomotor combination to the other leg/side going across the room is a common practice in most dance classes. Here students at least have some thinking time to make the mental switch as they wait their turn on the other side. Immediately connecting a combination from one side to the other increases the complexity considerably and is quite difficult for beginners.[11] Finally the teacher has to decide whether the combinations are cumulative from class to class, with additional components being added every day or whether short independent combinations are taught each day.

> The teacher decides whether the combinations are cumulative, or whether short, independent combinations are taught each day.

Pathways in Space

Once skills are combined, their spatial patterns must also be learned. Performing dance skills involves becoming aware of the room space you are dancing in, as well as the floor and air patterns your movements make. While beginners start by trying to focus on the actual body actions, eventually they also must be able to mentally step outside themselves, see themselves perform the skill and be consciously aware of the patterns their movements make. They are dancing through space, not just moving joints and taking positions. This can be as simple as being aware of the diagonal path of a locomotor pattern through the studio space or as complex as remembering all the different floor patterns in a choreography. The idea of making pathways as you move can be introduced as part of the space component of locomotor skills, however, the concept of spatial pathways really becomes important when skills are combined in a culminating activity. When one is part of a group in a routine, it is not enough to simply learn whether one travels to the right or the left but also to be aware of the spatial design of the whole group performing the choreography.

> Performing dance skills involves becoming aware of the room space as well as the floor and air patterns your movements make.

In folk or ballroom dance, this awareness of spatial patterns of the individual and the group is essential as one progresses from learning a specific step to learning the formation of a particular dance. The introduction of the typical floor patterns is usually done early in a folk dance unit, since the students are likely to learn a complete dance each day. In a creative dance class, there are generally no pre-set floor patterns, although being aware of the patterns made by one's actions is certainly an important aspect of learning. A culminating study in a class may in fact be introduced by asking the students to design an interesting floor pattern and then choosing the skills that suit the pattern.

Other Dancers

A culminating activity almost always involves other dancers. The activity the teacher chooses may require several or only a few adjustments to others. The interaction with other dancers may vary with the dance form and consist of several different types. Students must learn to perform identical skills in unison and coordinate the performance of different skills with a partner or group. Identical movements can further be divided into unison, canon, mirror, leading and following variations.

> Students must learn to perform identical skills in unison and coordinate the performance of different skills with a partner or group.

Unison partner or group work requires that all dancers perform the same skills at the same time and move in the same direction. The chorus line is a clear illustration. Dancers hold the same body position, reach the same extension in arms and legs at the same time, and travel through space at the same speed with the same sized steps. The difficulty comes in adjusting one's own range of motion to that of others and dealing with a very restricted amount of space between dancers. In the early stages, this may simply require matching one's steps with a partner in a locomotor combination across the floor at the end of the class. A more complex unison problem involves the whole class performing a series of steps with frequent direction changes in a folk dance, or a chorus line jazz routine with heads, legs, and canes at the same angle. Performing group skills in unison while following a prescribed floor pathway is seen in a final ballet, modern or jazz combination in most classes and may require a series of changing, complex partner and group patterns.

Canon may be one of those group patterns. Canon is another example of identical skills, but with a time delay. The dancers still perform the same skills, but one (or a groups of dancers) starts and is followed after varying time periods by the next dancer(s). The additional difficulty is a clear understanding of timing in order to wait the required number of beats.

Mirroring involves reversing the body part or direction of move-

Figure 3.4
Unison group patterns require dancers to match their actions in space and time.

Figure 3.5
In a technique class, students are often required to mirror the movement of the teacher.

ment in a combination. It may be the same action performed side-by-side, or facing a partner and moving the right arm or leg while he moves his left, or stepping backward while he goes forward. This variation can be used to add complexity to skill combinations in a technique class. Mirroring is an essential component of folk or ballroom partner work.

Leading and Following is an example of mirroring typically seen in folk and ballroom dance. In most folk dance steps, following is a fairly simple instance of mirroring as the man polkas forward starting with his left foot and the woman starts backward on her right following a prescribed spatial pattern. In ballroom dance, the adjustments needed to lead and follow become more complex. The steps may be prescribed, but the order of steps and the spatial pattern are decided on the spot by one of the partners. The man needs to clearly signal any change in step or pattern, and the woman needs to be alert to subtle changes in hand or shoulder position to instantly react, or even anticipate the next action. Additional problems are due to the need to make close physical contact throughout the mirrored steps. Not all partner patterns, however, require only the reversing of steps. A more complex partnering occurs when two people perform entirely different skills.

Partner coordination of different skills requires more complex adjustments, as one must predict where one's partner will be in space and time. This is typically seen in duets where one dancer balances, spins or jumps. The partner may be required to apply appropriate force to initiate or stabilize the skill and also to be in the right place so that he can catch her arm at the right time as she comes out of a turn, or her whole body in a jump. This must be fine tuned to a high skill level in a traditional pas de deux or in the intricate partnering of Latin or swing dance. Many of these skills are not appropriate for a beginning dancer. However, simpler partnering skills may be introduced in a culminating activity; for example, in a folk dance, one partner may continue to waltz forward while the other twirls under his arms to finish in a closed dance position.

All of these partner or group variations provide options for increasing complexity. For advanced dancers it is likely that a final choreography will include all of them. Beginners are likely to be challenged at least with partner and group unison, and possibly some mirroring combinations.

Accompaniment

There is usually a specific rhythmic pattern and tempo in the performance of a dance skill, whether it be the even beat of a march, a 3/4 metre for a waltz step, the syncopated rhythm of a jazz pattern, or a breath phrase for a modern dance contraction. Sometime the steps have been learned only to verbal counts, but ultimately they will be performed to some kind of accompaniment. The teacher chooses what, and how difficult the accompaniment will be. For the beginner during the early learning stages it is suggested that repetitive music with a clear, easily recognizable, underlying beat be used. As the student progresses, he will be expected to perform the skill to different metrical and non-metrical accompaniments and to more complex musical phrasing.

Different dance forms may provide different challenges here as will the preferences of individual teachers. Typically, accompaniment of some sort is used throughout the skill part of the lesson, so individual skills will already have been learned to a specific phrasing and tempo. For the culminating activity the teacher may select a different piece of music and individual skills may have to be modified or performed with different dynamic qualities. This will require new adjustments as the skills are combined.

Table 3.5   Developmental Level of Locomotor Skills

Fundamental Skills	**Specialized Dance Skills**
Learn weight shift, rhythm, and correct form	Combines stylized/rhythmic variations of fundamental skills
Walk, run, hop, leap, jump	Dance walks, triplets,
Slide, gallop, skip	Step ball change, jazz runs
	Waltz, polka, two-step
	Pas de chat, chassé

Summary

In summary, we can see that the teacher has a large choice of options of dance material in body actions, components and context that he can use to plan variations for his classes to avoid boredom and also to build logical progressions of difficulty. Locomotor skills can serve as a good example of some of these possibilities. Table 3.5 shows developmental progressions. For novices or young children, the skills chosen would be the fundamental versions of locomotor skills. Initially the focus may be on understanding the characteristic weight shift and rhythm pattern of each. More experienced children or adults would be ready to learn specialized locomotor skills found in the different dance forms. Table 3.6 shows how these fundamental or specialized skills could be varied throughout a dance course for different skill levels by changing the body actions involved, the movement components or the context.

In this chapter, we have examined the common organizational prob-

Table 3.6   Variations of Locomotor Skills

Choose Body Actions
   Correct footwork
   Focus on proper mechanics: ankles, knees, hips
   Emphasize correct weight transfer, take-off, landing
   Explore body position: typically vertical, but can have trunk and head variations
   Change arm actions: usually in opposition, but can be held
Choose Components
   Vary rhythmic characteristics
   Speed up the tempo
   Perform sideways and backward, not just forward
   Emphasize horizontal distance or height
   Practice light landings
   Change movement quality
Add More Complex Context
   Repeat skill many times, e.g., series of leaps across the floor,
   Combine several locomotor skills, e.g., step-hop, step-hop, run, run, leap
   Combine with turns, falls or stationary poses
   Develop a locomotor combination to a musical phrase
   Follow a particular floor pattern
   Work in unison, canon, mirror, sequence with partner or group

lems across dance forms and some of the differences in selecting dance material for a lesson and a dance unit. It is not practical to suggest uniform rules across all dance forms. There are, however, general guidelines that apply to most. These are:

- The order of body actions in a dance class normally follow the order presented in Figure 3.1.
- All categories of body actions should have been presented by the end of a unit.
- There are sufficient examples of simple skills in each body action category, that it is possible to cover selected skills in each category in each class, even for beginners.
- There should not be an over-emphasis on static work to the detriment of dynamic skills.
- Manipulation of space, time and force components should be used to create variety and progressions.
- Culminating activities are an important component of the class where students can experience dancing.
- The choice of context variables in culminating activities is vast, and allows for challenges and adjustments for any skill level.

In the next chapter, we turn away from the details of skill analysis and class structure to examine the learning process of acquiring these skills. This is followed by an examination of the different categories of learners. We will return in Chapter 9, to the questions of selecting specific dance material that suits the needs of a particular learner.

References

1. Lord M, Chayer C, Girard L: Increasing awareness of your strategies for teaching dance technique. Impulse 3:172-182, 1995.
2. Skrinar M: Selected motor learning applications to the technique class. *In:* Clarkson PM, Skrinar M (eds): *Science of Dance Training.* Champaign, IL: Human Kinetics Publishers, Inc., 1988, pp. 269-277.
3. Krasnow DH, Chatfield SJ, Barr S, Jensen JL, Dufek JS: Imagery and conditioning practices for dancers. Dance Research Journal 29(1):43-64, 1997.
4. Krasnow DH, Chatfield SJ: Dance science and the dance technique class. Impulse 4(2):162-172, 1996.
5. Gallahue DL, Ozmun JC: *Understanding Motor Development: Infants, Children, Adolescents, Adults.* Dubuque, IA: Brown and Benchmark, 1995.
6. Magill AM, Anderson DI: Critical periods as optimal readiness for learning sport skills. *In:* Smoll FL, Smith RE (eds): *Children and Youth in Sport: A Biopsycholsocial Perspective.* Dubuque IA: Brown and Benchmark, 1996, pp. 57-72.
7. Luigi, Kriegel LP, Roach FJ: *Luigi's Jazz Warm Up: An Introduction to Jazz Style and Technique.* Pennington, NJ: Princeton Book Company, 1997.

8. Giordano G: *Anthology of American Jazz Dance*. Evanston, IL: Orion, 1975.
9. Lewis D: *The Illustrated Dance Technique of José Limón*. New York: Harper and Row, 1984.
10. Rose DJ: *A Multilevel Approach to the Study of Motor Control and Learning*. Boston: Allyn and Bacon, 1997.
11. Kimmerle M: Lateral bias in dance teaching. Journal of Physical Education, Recreation and Dance 72(5):34-37, 2002.

Panagiota Klentrou

A Learning Model

A Learning Model for Dance Skills
　　Stage One – Attempt Stage
　　Stage Two – Correct Stage
　　Stage Three – Perfect Stage
Progressing Through the Stages of Learning
　　Combination One - Jazz Inside Turn (8 Counts)
　　Combination Two - Jazz Phrase (32 Counts)
　　Combination Three - Jazz Dance (80 Counts)

Chapter 4

How a Student Learns Dance Skills

As you watch your students try to correct a skill after you gave verbal corrections, and see some repeating the skill exactly the same incorrect way, do you ask yourself why? Do you understand why they have not corrected their errors or why a beginner has difficulty remembering a long sequence of steps? A good dance teacher must possess knowledge, not only of the dance material, but also of the learning process in order to teach effectively. Motor learning theory stresses that it is imperative that teachers possess a thorough understanding of human movement.[1] The study of human movement includes cognitive and neurological functions underlying motor learning and development. Dance scholars recognize the benefit of the field of motor learning in dance; it provides information about ways in which motor skills are produced and controlled, and about teaching and performing these skills.[2-4]

This chapter introduces the learning process and how that process changes over time. Although the learning model proposed in this chapter can apply to any age group, it will be presented in a generic fashion. Chapters 5, 6, and 7 will focus on how the learning model adapts to the needs of the three most common types of learners: the novice adult, the child, and the experienced learner, respectively. The underlying framework of the model is grounded in motor learning theory. It is hoped that this chapter will help the reader recognize why it is imperative that dance teachers understand how people learn.

A Learning Model

At the beginning of the semester, you have students who struggle with basic dance skills. Over the semester you notice an improvement in the control of these skills, and at the end of the course, a number of these students can execute specific dance skills relatively well. They have learned the skills. Motor learning can be defined as "a set of processes associated with practice or experience leading to relatively permanent changes in the capability for movement."[5] The key words in this classic definition are *processes*, *practice*, and *relatively permanent changes*. The processes are those internal cognitive activities that take place between watching the demonstration and performing the dance skill. In motor learning, these processes are:

- Input, identifying the stimulus;
- Processing, selecting a response; and
- Output, executing the motor skill.

A motor skill cannot be learned without practice; practice is, therefore, a critical factor for learning. How does the teacher know that a student has learned the skill? The only means by which the instructor can determine this is by observing the student's motor response. Learning has taken place when the student is able to repeatedly produce a correct skill.

Although factors such as motivation and fatigue may interfere and cause poor performance, they do not affect learning. For example, when your students have repeated a strenuous sequence of steps several times at the end of the lesson and are tired, their performance may be poor. This is not an indication that they have not learned the sequence. Their performance at that time may be poor, but when they come back the next day, they are able to execute the dance sequence well. We can, therefore, say that they have learned the dance skills.

Over the years, a number of learning models have been proposed.[5] A learning model is basically a visual chart used to describe how we believe the brain works during learning and what changes take place in the learners' behavior as they master skills. Early models were initially developed for mental tasks and have been adapted to motor tasks in the laboratory. Their direct application to real life learning in the gymnasium and dance studio is somewhat difficult. The most general approach to learning stems from an information processing framework in which the learner is viewed as a processor of information. A simplified information processing model (Figure 4.1) consists of three stages: the demonstration (input), the learner's mental activities (internal processes), and the motor response (output).

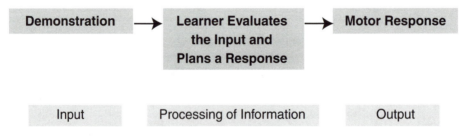

Figure 4.1
A simplified information processing model.

The input is the new skill demonstrated or described to the learner. During the internal processing of the input information, the student must figure out what the demonstrated movement was, and what to do in order to imitate the skill. She attempts to answer questions such as: How did the action begin? What did the legs do? Were the steps to the right or left? or When and how long did the right arm move? These questions are processed, and a decision is then made to select and initiate an action that resembles the demonstration. The overt action represents the output. It may or may not match the demonstration, depending on students' experiences and learning abilities (these will be described in the next chapter).

A Learning Model for Dance Skills

Dance skills are basically learned the same way other motor skills are learned. It has been suggested that learning a dance skill begins with the presentation of the skill and ends with its replication immediately or several hours, days, or months later.[6] We have taken the key concepts of models proposed in motor learning, and translated them into a model consisting of three stages and 11 steps. The learning model proposed here includes the attempt stage, the correct stage, and the perfect stage. The model takes the learner from initial learning to mastery of dance skills. It has proven to be a useful tool in the authors' classes. The model's stages parallel the three classic motor learning stages – the cognitive, associate, and autonomous stages – which were proposed several decades ago.[7] The attempt stage represents the learner's first exposure to the new skill. The correct stage covers the practice time needed for the learner to self-monitor the execution of the skill. Finally, when the learner can execute the skill with minimal conscious attention, she has reached the perfect stage. The three-stage model is presented in Figure 4.2.

As previously mentioned, it is important to keep in mind that, although these stages account for learning in general, a novice dancer will go through the learning process differently than an experienced dancer, and a young learner will behave differently than an adult. We will now walk through the three stages and describe mental processes and strategies that the beginner goes through when faced with a novel skill. Characteristics of each stage are discussed through a dance example, and the changes that take place with practice are described. Each step is presented linearly through a développé, a basic leg gesture found in the vocabulary of many dance forms.

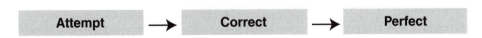

Figure 4.2
A model for learning dance skills.

Table 4.1   The Attempt Stage of Learning Dance Skills

Step
1. Pick up relevant cues
2. Form a mental image of the skill
3. Retrieve/construct a motor plan
4. Execute the skill

Stage One – Attempt

You are presenting the développé, a new dance skill, to your students. The learning process begins when the développé is verbally described and demonstrated. At that time, the learner is confronted with a problem: she must understand what the new movement is and figure out how to do it. This stage requires a great deal of mental effort as the learner attempts to grasp what the action is in order to be able to execute it globally. During this stage, the student goes through four steps: pick up relevant cues, form a mental image of the movement, construct or retrieve a motor plan, and execute the movement. These four steps are presented in Table 4.1.

Step 1: Pick Up Relevant Cues

The teacher executes a technically correct développé with the right leg, right arm in second position, en croix (action executed to front, side,

Figure 4.3
A challenge for teachers is to explain a skill in a way that the student will understand.

back, and side again). Relevant cues are what your students hear and see as the essential characteristics of the skill being described and demonstrated. This could be: Which is the supporting leg? What does the free leg do? Where does it go? Where and how does the action end? One student may be better at picking up the verbal cue "bring the foot slowly to the knee," while the visual cue of seeing the action may be easier for another. A beginner may be able to pay attention to only one portion of the skill, for example the first half of the leg action. Another student may, on the other hand, retain more cues such as the entire leg action, the timing, and spatial directions.

Another characteristic of beginners is that they tend to see and hear unnecessary cues. Students may be easily distracted by the model's clothing, hairstyle, the presence of another dancer right next to them, or noise coming from the back of the room. Beginners, especially young beginners, have poor attention capacity; they may not know which cues are important when watching a demonstration of the skill.

The first step of the model is clearly dependent upon students' perceptual abilities and experience. For example, a student who is a musician may easily detect the rhythm of the exercise; she would then be able to concentrate on other aspects of the demonstration. Likewise, a figure skater or gymnast may recognize that this is a one-legged balance skill. After she listened to the verbal instructions and watched the demonstration, what does the learner do with that information?

Step 2: Form a Mental Image of the Skill

The input or cues detected by the student (e.g., path of working foot along supporting leg, timing, or ending position of right foot) are now stored in memory and used to form a mental image of the développé. That mental image will then be used to plan the first attempt of a développé. For the student who is also a musician, the timing may be the most important cue for her internal picture of the développé whereas for another student, it may be the spatial configuration of the gesturing leg. With practice, the learner becomes better at detecting all the important cues and can therefore store in memory a more comprehensive image of the action.

> The cues detected by the student are used to form a mental image.

Step 3: Retrieve/Construct a Motor Plan

The student must now learn to repeat the action. The plan of action for the first try is based on the motor skills stored in the student's memory. As presented in Chapter 2, a one-legged balance is a fundamental skill that may not have been practiced, unless the student has studied gymnastics or figure skating. If she has experience in these sports, a motor plan for this action already exists and can be retrieved from memory while a new motor plan for the action of the working leg is added. However, the inexperienced dancer has to construct a rudimentary plan of action with the help of the instructor; this plan will be modified and improved with practice and feedback.

Step 4: Execute the Skill

The student is now ready to try her first développé. The motor plan activates the proper muscle groups responsible for the execution of that dance skill. The beginner will likely execute a rough approximation of the développé with uncertain weight distribution, poor body centering, and turnout stability.

In summary, the learner's main concern during the attempt stage is to form an idea of the task. The first attempts at the task, according to motor learning theory, are usually marked by gross error.[8] These errors are corrected during the next attempts, thus showing impressive gains in performance. As the student gains an understanding of the skill, she tries out several ways of doing it. This causes her performance to be inconsistent. For example, the first développé may be clumsy and awkward as the student concentrates on all the aspects at once; the next one may show a clearer working leg action but a poor body placement and shaky arm position. The third attempt may be quite good while the next one shows lack of stability, and so on. It is important to remember that these steps are not always linear. For example, you may have to describe and demonstrate the action several times before the students can form a mental image capable of a rough imitation of the skill. The characteristics of the first stage are summarized in Table 4.2.

> The learner's main concern during the attempt stage is to form an idea of the task.

How long does the student remain in the attempt stage? This stage may last from several minutes to several hours or days depending on the complexity of the skill as well as the learner's age and experience. A beginner might understand the développé in a few minutes, yet require lengthy practice before reaching technical perfection at

Table 4.2	Characteristics of the Attempt Stage of Learning Dance Skills
Intent	Understand the skill and execute a rough approximation
Characteristics	Inconsistency in performance
	Performance gains are significant
Duration	Few minutes to several hours depending on the complexity of the skill, and learner's age and experience

Gabrielle Laurence

Figure 4.4
When the student is able
to perform a rough ap-
proximation of the skill,
she is said to enter the
correct stage.

the perfect stage. On the other hand, a more complex action, for example a sixteen bar adage would of course take much longer. Essentially, when the learner is able to roughly perform the new skill, she
is said to enter the next stage.

Stage Two - Correct

During this stage, the learner concentrates on refining the skill by
selecting more effective ways to do it. The
emphasis is now on more efficient performance. With practice and proper feedback,
the image of the skill becomes more accurate
and the learner is better able to detect and
correct her errors. A more precise mental representation serves as reference for error detection. Clearly, the beginner is not ready for

> In the correct stage,
> the learner
> concentrates on
> refining the skill.

this, as she does not fully comprehend the skill yet. The skill will be
refined through the teacher's proper feedback. The student's goal here
is to become more independent and able to process internal feedback
without relying on the teacher's corrections. This stage includes three
mental operations: monitor the performance externally or internally,
compare/reprogram the motor plan, and attempt the corrected skill.
These operations are outlined in Table 4.3.

Table 4.3   The Correct Stage of Learning Dance Skills

Step
5. Monitor performance externally/internally
6. Assess and reprogram the motor plan
7. Attempt the corrected skill

Figure 4.5
During the correct stage, the student often requires the instructor's assistance to feel the proper motion.

Step 5: Monitor the Performance Externally and Internally

During or immediately after Step 4, the student should be able to feel, based on proprioceptive information, whether the développé she just executed is correct. She is concerned with questions such as: Was my hip stabilized? Was my turnout sufficient? Did I shift my body weight to the supporting leg? In general, a novice is unable to detect and correct her own errors because she has not yet developed a mental image of correctness or a kinesthetic sense for the correct action. The beginner cannot tell whether the working or non-supportive hip is too high or whether the free leg is fully extended at the end of the développé. The second type of information available to the learner is extrinsic feedback, either verbal or tactile, provided by the teacher. Tactile feedback is when the teacher touches or positions a joint to indicate that the hip is too high or the knee not fully extended; verbal feedback is when the instructor gives these corrections verbally. External feedback is crucial during this stage.

Step 6: Assess and Reprogram the Motor Plan

The learner revises and resets the motor plan for the next execution of the développé. She thinks, "I must remember to keep a symmetrical turnout in both hips and not to lean on the supporting leg." The mental image of the skill is now modified with the teacher's feedback, and becomes

Table 4.4   Characteristics of the Correct Stage of Learning Dance Skills

Intent	Develop error detection/correction mechanism and improve the skill
Characteristics	Execution is more precise and technically correct Performance gains are gradual
Duration	Hours, days, weeks, years, depending on task complexity

Table 4.5   The Perfect Stage of Learning Dance Skills

Step
8. Practice with ongoing monitoring
9. Revise performance
10. Produce skilled movement
11. Combine skill with other skills, people, and music

closer to the performance goal. Once the mental image is modified, so is the motor plan, and this produces a movement different from the first attempts. The new motor plan aims to correct the errors detected in the first développé.

Step 7: Attempt the Corrected Skill

The new motor plan for the développé is activated, resulting in the execution of a more refined skill, one that more closely resembles the initial demonstration. The characteristics of this stage are shown in Table 4.4. In contrast with the first stage, this stage requires extensive practice and repetition, and therefore lasts longer. When the learner has refined the développé to the point that it is performed in a consistently correct fashion and she is able to self-monitor without feedback from the teacher, the learner has now arrived at the last stage of learning, the perfect stage.

Stage Three – Perfect

The beginner is now capable of performing consistently correct développés. According to the motor learning literature, students who have reached this stage do not think about the individual steps of the routine, for they have become automatic.[8] The role of the teacher dramatically changes as the student is able to detect and correct her errors; the teacher's feedback is more indirect, with more subtle suggestions to maintain quality of performance. The perfect stage (Table 4.5) includes four steps: practice with ongoing monitoring; revise the performance; produce a skilled action; and combine the skill with other skills, music, and people. Having reached this stage, the dancer can now pay attention to other aspects such as other skills, the accompaniment, and other dancers.

> At this stage, the learner no longer needs feedback from the instructor; she relies essentially on her own internal feedback.

Step 8: Practice with Ongoing Monitoring

When the dancer has reached this stage, there is no longer a need for demonstration, only revising and perfecting the skill. The skill is practiced until a perfect execution is programmed and produced. A perfect skill is the result of a perfect mental image of the skill. The length of this phase is related to the skill level of the learner as well as the complexity of the skill. Some students may never reach this level of competence due to physical limitations or cognitive capacities. The dancer has now gained the capability to detect and correct her own errors. Extrinsic feedback has been replaced by internal monitoring, and the dancer has developed a keen kinesthetic sense of the développé; she knows when the skill is technically correct and when it is not. The reference of correctness is fully internalized, therefore external help coming from mirror or teacher is no longer necessary.

Step 9: Revise the Performance

The dancer is able to make changes to the motor program in order to perform a technically correct développé. Small errors are detected rapidly. She is able to divide her attention between executing the skill correctly, and monitoring her ongoing performance.

Step10: Produce a Skilled Action

A consistently correct développé is now performed by the dancer. In other words, she goes on "auto pilot" and can execute the action without consciously attending to it. For example, once the heel is lifted off the floor, the foot extends automatically, and the turnout is second nature. The dancer's attention, no longer required during execution, can now be placed on other aspects of the performance such as the skills coming next or the position of other dancers.

Step 11: Combine the Skill with Other Skills, Music, and People

The dance skill is now executed within the typical dance context, meaning that it is performed as part of a sequence, with specific spatial pathways, to music, and with other dancers. The context of a développé may be an adage combination. When the dancer has reached this stage, she is able to plan, monitor, and perform technically correct skills with minimal attention demands. The last step of the learning model portrays the culmination, integration, and refinement of all elements included in the dance context. The dancer has now mastered the motor skill and concentrates on performing it within the larger dance sequence, and in synchrony with music and other dancers. The characteristics of this stage are shown in Table 4.6. Unlike the first two stages, there is no time line attached to the perfect stage

Table 4.6   Characteristics of the Perfect Stage of Learning Dance Skills

Intent	Bring the skill at the level of automaticity
Characteristics	The skill is mastered
	Performance gains are minimal
	Error detection/correction is mainly internal
Duration	Unlimited

Attempt

1. Pick up relevant cues
2. Form a mental image
3. Retrieve/construct a motor plan
4. Execute the skill

Correct

5. Monitor the performance externally and internally
6. Assess and reprogram the motor plan
7. Attempt the corrected skill

Perfect

8. Practice with ongoing monitoring
9. Revise the performance
10. Produce a skilled action
11. Combine the skill with other skills, music, and dancers

Figure 4.6
Detailed model for learning dance skills.

as it represents the culmination of extensive practice. By that time, the skill is soundly established in long-term memory.

In summary, the attempt-correct-perfect model represents the global process of learning a dance skill. The model, shown in Figure 4.6, illustrates an ongoing loop that can be broken into smaller loops during dance skill learning. The length of time required to learn and master dance skills depends on the learner's skill level and the complexity of the skill. For example, a simple skill (*see* Fig 2.8) may reach the perfect stage during one lesson, whereas a more complex skill may require several weeks. Likewise, a simple sequence of skills may be mastered in one lesson, compared to a choreography that may take several weeks to be completely mastered.

> The attempt, correct, and perfect model represents the global process of learning a dance skill.

How is that model useful in the practical world? When facing a class, the teacher should be able to place each student somewhere along these 11 steps, and should adjust her teaching accordingly. If students have reached Step 5 for one skill, the instructor will teach them differently than if they are at Step 9. As mentioned earlier, the proposed learning model should help teachers understand what goes on in their students' heads as they attempt to learn dance skills. It is also important to remember that students are constantly going from one stage to another, and that they are learning several skills at once. Imagine students learning a dance for the recital. They could very well be at the attempt stage for a new skill, at the correct stage for two, three, or more skills, while at the perfect stage for some other skills. In this regard, dance students are constantly learning and mastering skills.

Progressing Through the Learning Stages

Having presented the eleven-step learning model using the développé as an example, we will now walk through the stages with another dance movement, but this time over the course of a semester. In this way you will see the progression from learning a simple sequence of skills to learning a dance.

The dance example is a eight-count jazz inside turn, a combination of locomotion, balance, gesture, and rotation, described as follows: two steps forward (right, left), arms down, counts 1, 2; parallel passé with right foot, arms to chest, count 3; right foot steps into 4th, arms in 4th, right front, count 4; inside turn on right foot, (left foot in parallel passé), arms bent to chest, count 5; land in lunge, arms in 4th, count 6; and for counts 7, 8, repeat counts 5, 6. The sequence could be repeated on the other side, ending in the initial direction, and resulting in a 16-count sequence. Such a simple sequence of skills is common in dance classes with beginners, regardless of the dance form. The teacher could probably think of a number of variations she teaches in her classes. In a creative dance class, students could be asked to combine steps and turns to form an eight-count sequence. The eight-count sequence in a folk dance could be four steps forward and four steps backward, with hand clap on the 4th and 8th count. This example shows that even beginners have the opportunity to dance early in their training. They get to perform new dance skills within the context of dance, that is, they perform the skills within a sequence, with specific spatial pathways, with music, and with other dancers. We are now going to progress from the first combination, the eight-count sequence, to the second combination, a 32-count phrase, and finally to the third combination, a one-minute dance.

> Students need help from the teacher in dissecting the sequence, and pointing out repetitions.

Combination One – Jazz Inside Turn (8 Counts)

Since this is a sequence of eight movements, students must identify and memorize the movements in their first attempts. The instructor should help students dissect the sequence and point out that some of the actions are repeated, thus making the sequence simpler to remember. She might decide that students should only pay attention to the turn first, then the position of the feet, and finally add arm actions. The students go through the attempt, correct, and per-

Josie Hazen

Figure 4.7
Once mastered, a dance skill must then be integrated with other skills, performed to music, and in relationship to other dancers.

fect stages, and are finally able to perform the sequence correctly. Part of mastering the skill is paying attention to the specific space, time, and force components of the actions. Students learn to execute the sequence with the proper counts, spatial directions, and amount of muscular tension for each action. The time it takes them to reach the perfect stage may be one or more lessons. Keep in mind that not all students will reach that stage. It is possible that some students will not fully master the sequence before more steps are added.

The sequence becomes automatic when students can perform it without conscious attention. They have acquired an accurate mental image of the sequence and an efficient motor plan, and are able to adapt to changes in components that may be required (e.g., new speed/music, new direction, or change in arm gesture). The next step is to perform the sequence within a 32-count phrase.

Combination Two – Jazz Phrase (32 Counts)

The jazz inside turn is now being performed within a dance context, as part of a longer phrase of skills, and to music. As in the previous instance, students still must memorize skills, but this time, there are four times as many counts. The phrase may include four sequences of 8 counts, an isolation progression, a jazz walk combination, the jazz turn sequence, and perhaps the repetition of one of the three sequences. The new challenge is to learn what comes before and after the jazz inside turn. Presumably knowing the other skills in the phrase, the students now go through the perfect stage for the longer phrase.

> Dance consists of serial skills. With practice, learners develop strategies to memorize longer sequences.

Finally, after students have perfected this phrase, as they have perfected many other similar phrases, it is time to perform it at the right time within the entire dance, in unison or contrast with other dancers, at the proper location on stage, and to the music. In other words, they are ready for the culminating activity.

Combination Three - Jazz Dance (80 Counts, 60 Seconds)

This level clearly adds more elements of difficulty to the original jazz turn. The context is now complete, and the dancers must learn the entire choreography the way it will be performed on stage. The main challenge is to perform all dance skills and sequences accurately, with proper spatial configurations, in time to music, and in relation to other dancers.

When students perform in the concert at the end of the semester, they have mastered the complex dance skills that make up the dance. They have progressed through the learning stages and have perfected these skills. The process of skill learning and mastery takes time. At the end of the semester, students are different than they were at the beginning. They have acquired a greater repertoire of dance skills, better learning strategies, greater memory and attention capacity, and more confidence in regulating their own learning. They are better movers and better learners.

Summary

Recognizing that there are individual differences, we can say that learning is influenced by two major factors: the learner's maturation level, and her experience in dance. Faced with the same novel dance skill, a child beginner may be quite different from an adult beginner. With practice, however, changes do occur in the learner's capabilities to process information. These factors will be addressed in the following chapters.

References

1. Abernethy B, Kippers V, Mackinnon L, Neal RJ, Hanrahan S: *The Foundations of Human Movement*. Champaign, IL: Human Kinetics Publishers, Inc., 1997.
2. Overby L: Principles of motor learning applied to the teaching of dance technique. Kinesiology and Medicine for Dance 14(1):113-118, 1991.
3. Minton S: Research in dance: Educational and scientific perspectives. Dance Research Journal 32(1):110-116, 2000.
4. Gray JA: Dance education in the future: Trends and predictions. Journal of Physcial Education, Recreation and Dance 61(5):50-53, 1990.
5. Schmidt RA, Lee TD: *Motor Learning and Control: A Behavioral Emphasis* (3rd ed). Champaign, IL: Human Kinetics Publishers, Inc., 1999, p. 264.

6. Puretz S: Bilateral transfer: The effects of practice on the transfer of complex dance movement patterns. Research Quarterly for Exercise and Sport 54(1):48-54, 1983.
7. Fitts PM, Posner MI: *Human Performance*. Belmont, CA: Brooks/Cole, 1967.
8. Magill RA: *Motor Learning: Concepts and Applications* (6th ed). Boston: McGraw-Hill, 2001.

Gabrielle Laurence

Physical Capabilities

Repertoire of Dance Skills

Learning Abilities – Information Processing Abilities

   Perceptual Abilities

   Attention Capacity

   Memory Capacity

   Error Detection and Correction Capacity

Chapter 5

The Novice Adult Learner

There are basically two categories of learners, beginners and those who are experienced. Each category may consist of either young or adult learners. Experienced teachers know that beginners possess a number of capabilities and limitations that are different from those of experienced students. Learners possess innate abilities, a maturation level, previous movement experiences, and a level of motivation that predispose them to a certain degree of performance proficiency.[1] Therefore, the role and behavior of the teacher should vary to accommodate the learners' needs, as it is his role to help students develop strong problem-solving skills and ultimately become independent learners.

It is reported that adult beginners in dance represent a significant portion of the overall population enrolling in dance studios and schools.[2] What is so special about adult beginners? Adult beginners, ranging from age 18 and up, may be found in dance studios, recreation centers, and dance programs in schools. This chapter explores the physical capabilities, repertoire of dance skills, and learning abilities of the novice adult in the dance class. Although we recognize that there are individual differences that affect the learning and performance of dance skills, general traits that characterize the adult beginner can be identified. This chapter discusses these characteristics and how they influence learning.

Physical Capabilities

Motor development literature suggests that physical capabilities consist of health and performance-related components, and fundamental motor skills, and that these components prepare an individual to learn a motor skill.[3,4] Health-related components consist of muscular strength and endurance, cardiovascular endurance, joint flexibility, and body composition. These influence the ability to function daily at an acceptable level. On the other hand, performance-related abilities such as speed, agility, power, coordination, and balance are required to meet

Gabrielle Laurence

Figure 5.1
The novice adult's most
serious challenge is to
transform basic locomotor
skills into specialized
dance skills.

the demands of quality motor performance. Some dance educators stress the importance of health-related components in the training of ballet performers[5] while others emphasize both health and performance-related components in dance training and performance.[6]

By virtue of their age, adults taking dance classes for the first time have reached mature physical growth, and therefore, have refined their coordination, balance, flexibility, agility, muscular and cardiovascular endurance, and muscular strength. Depending on their participation in regular physical activity, these adults may have been able to maintain these abilities at a relatively good level. On the other hand, adults who have led a more sedentary lifestyle might lack body control, overall co-ordination, and balance.

Locomotor, manipulative, and non-locomotor skills are the basic categories of fundamental motor skills.[3] Sports and dance use loco-motor and non-locomotor skills, whereas manipulative skills are specific to sports. In theory, adults have mastered all fundamental skills to a reasonable level of proficiency. To some extent, they can skip, hop, run, leap, bend, stretch, swing, and turn. However, some adults may not have performed these skills since childhood. Therefore, the dance teacher will encounter large individual differences in how these skills are performed.

The advantage the beginner adult has over other beginners is that he has developed a good repertoire of fundamental skills. The novice adult's most serious challenge is now to learn specialized dance skills. This means a new way of balancing and coordinating body parts to produce special-ized forms of locomotion and non-locomotion (e.g., a jazz walk with hip and arm gestures, or a specialized jumping turn). The adult's body must now be trained to move within the context of dance. A third aspect in which novice adults differ from other categories of learners is their repertoire of dance skills.

Repertoire of Dance Skills

Of all the factors described in this chapter, a repertoire of dance skills is the one that is practically nonexistent in beginners. The novice adult simply lacks experience in dance and therefore lacks the concomitant skills. As demonstrated in the discussion in chapter two, dance skills are complex; they are performed sequentially, with specific timing and spatial restrictions, and in relationship to others. To help understand the link between the two classifications of skills, fundamental motor skills and the six categories of body actions found in dance are presented in Table 5.1. Keep in mind that all locomotor and non-locomotor skills are found in dance, and that all axial movements are part of control of center. For the purpose of clarity, each of the six body action categories has been linked to a single term of the fundamental motor skill classification.

> Novice adults' greatest advantage over other beginners is that they have accumulated a good repertoire of fundamental motor skills.

Adult beginners who are knowledgeable about how their body moves should be able to transfer their knowledge to a new set of skills. These individuals are likely to possess good overall coordination. Through movement experiences, a novice adult has acquired thousands of mental images and motor plans of fundamental motor skills. These mental representations are used to guide new learning tasks, resulting in greater physical capabilities for dance skills in adults than younger beginners. For example, an adult beginner who has acquired a good sense of dynamic balance over the years through a variety of motor experiences may be able to tackle a dance skill requiring dynamic balance more efficiently than one whose balance skills are weak.

Table 5.1 Fundamental Motor Skills and Dance Body Actions

Fundamental Motor Skills	Dance Body Actions
Stability	
Axial Movements	Control of Center (alignment)
Bend-stretch-turn	Rotation
Twist-swing-gesture	Gesture of arms and legs
Balance	Changing base (balance)
Locomotor Skills	
Walk-run-gallop-jump	Locomotion
Leap-hop-slide-skip	Elevation
Manipulative Skills	
Throw-catch-kick	
Trap-strike-bounce	

Some students may never reach a highly proficient level of balance, coordination, or ease in their jumps or turns, because they lack in physical capabilities. It is up to the instructor to set the highest possible learning and performance goals for all students, regardless of skill level. An appropriate strategy for teaching dance to inexperienced adults may be to capitalize on motor skills they have mastered, and highlight similarities between these skills and the novel dance skills.

As presented in Chapter 2, dance skills include six categories of body actions. Due to the complexity of most dance skills, however, the adult beginner is faced with learning a new vocabulary of actions, or a new way of moving. For example, proper body alignment centering is a basic dance concept the novice adult may struggle with at the beginning. Having to perform movements to music may be another novelty for a novice learner. In this regard, all beginners may be similar in that they must acquire a new vocabulary of skills specific to dance. The fourth and last category that differentiates beginners from experienced learners is their cognitive learning abilities.

Learning Abilities – Information Processing Abilities

The learning process described in the previous chapter indicates that, in order to learn skills, individuals must possess basic cognitive capabilities. Learners must be able to process information (e.g., perceive, attend to, and retain information in memory) in order to plan and execute movements, and to detect and correct errors in their performance. Although individual differences exist in the capability to learn, motor learning research suggests that beginners differ from experienced learners in their ability to process information from their body and from the environment.

> Beginners differ from experienced learners in their limited ability to process information from their body and from the environment.

Beginners tend to have limitations in their ability to perceive, attend to, and retain information. They also lack in their ability to detect and correct their movement errors.[1,3,7] These cognitive functions are, of course, critical in the learning process. Although information-processing abilities are at a premium across all stages, they are most crucial during the attempt stage while the correct stage capitalizes on the ability to detect and correct errors.

When novice adults are first learning a dance skill, they tend to be overwhelmed with information. Although they are beginners in dance, adults have accumulated an impressive amount of experiences learning a variety of motor skills. They have, in essence, already learned how to learn and as such have acquired some strategies for remembering information. We all have learned rehearsal strategies such as

Gabrielle Laurence

Figure 5.2
With proper guidance,
beginners will develop
strategies to detect and
correct their movement
errors.

repeat instructions or steps in our head, and these strategies consequently help us remember what we are supposed to do. The limitations most relevant to learning dance skills center around the difficulty of coping with a large amount of information coming from different body parts and from the environment in a short period of time.

The learning model presented in Chapter 4 is based on the concept that the learner is a processor of information similar to a computer. This process begins with the perception of the input, the demonstration, and ends with the production of an output, which is the skill. In addition to perceptual abilities, the novice adult must be able to make sense of the information presented in the demonstration. This means that he must know what to look for, what to pay attention to, what to store in memory, and what to imitate.

Most dance skills require the simultaneous and/or sequential action of many body parts and the integration of visual, kinesthetic, and auditory cues. In this regard, the main difficulty a beginner adult faces is that, due to his lack of dance experiences, his ability to process relevant information may be slow. The fact that he has virtually no dance images in memory creates uncertainty on the part of the learner as the try to grasp exactly what it is they should be looking for. With proper guidance, the beginner will develop perception, attention, memory, and error detection/correction strategies that will enable him to process only relevant aspects of the demonstration, and to ignore unimportant cues. The study of perception, attention, memory, and error detection/correction is vital to understanding information processing in dance learning and performance.

> With proper guidance, the beginner will develop perception, attention, memory, and error detection/ correction strategies...

Perceptual Abilities

All voluntary movements depend upon some form of perceptual activity. Perception is the process of gathering and interpreting sensory information from the body and the environment.[3] Sensory information coming from the body is called kinesthetic sense, whereas sensory information coming from the environment is perceived through visual, auditory, olfactory, gustatory, and tactile receptors. Of these six sensory receptors, the most relevant to dance skill learning and performance are the kinesthetic, visual, tactile, and auditory systems.

Experts in motor development argue that the quality of motor performance depends on the accuracy of the learner's perception of the stimulus, and his ability to interpret this information into a series of coordinated actions.[3,4] For example, the student's capability to imitate a eight-count dance phrase of turn, step, jump, and arm gesture depends on his ability to perceive each of the four components, interpret them in the proper order and context, retain all this information in memory, and finally repeat the phrase. Has he seen what each body part did during the turn? Which direction? Was the step sideways or forward? On which foot? What type of jump? Where were the arms during the jump? Landing on which foot? Referring back to the learning model, the learner's perceptual abilities are crucial during the attempt stage, as they initiate the learning cycle.

> Strong perceptual skills are crucial in the attempt stage, as learners try to pick up relevant cues.

The development of perceptual abilities takes place through body, spatial, directional, and temporal/rhythmic awareness.[3,4] Body awareness, often referred to as body schema or body image, is basically the internal representation or map of body parts, their location, function, and relationship to each other. Body schema is innate, and may be refined with maturation and experience.[8] The beginner adult has developed a mature global body image. With experience, this body image will be refined to suit dance skills. Proper alignment in dance requires a clear mental image of the body's structure (e.g., its three axes and planes of motion).

Spatial awareness is knowledge of how much space the body occupies, and the body's relationship to external space and objects. The ability to interpret and organize visual information is necessary to understand the spatial configuration of dance skills, the dancer's own and other dancers' location, and motion in space. Directional awareness is the ability to identify two distinct sides of the body (laterality), and to project the body within the dimensions of external space (directionality). The fourth movement awareness component, temporal awareness, is the ability to perceive time or rhythm, a perceptual skill most crucial in dance. Kinesthetic information comes from within the body. Temporal information is perceived from the external environment.

Kinesthetic Abilities

Movements that require that a position be maintained or conscious controlled movement of a limb to a particular point in space depend on the individual's ability to use kinesthetic information efficiently.[8] This is the case in dance. Kinesthetic awareness, the conscious sensation of movement and body position, is critical in the acquisition of motor skills.[4,8] This form of sensory information reaches consciousness via proprioceptors located in the stretch receptors in the muscles, the Golgi tendon organs, the sensors in the joints, and the vestibular apparatus. These sensory receptors provide information about the location, direction, and speed of movement of body parts. For example, they tell the dancer that his free leg is fully extended, or that his arms are correctly positioned à la seconde. In general, kinesthetic awareness is poorly developed in novice adult dancers, as it is highly specific to dance skills. Critical in error detection and correction, kinesthetic abilities develop with age – with maturation of the central nervous system and with experience.

> Critical in error detection/correction, kinesthetic awareness develops with maturation and experience.

The ability to maintain equilibrium, or balance, depends on information from the vestibular apparatus. The "successful performance of virtually all motor skills depends on one's ability to establish and maintain equilibrium."[4] Balance is probably one of the most important fundamental abilities in dance, and therefore a prerequisite for dance performance. Located in the inner ear, receptors in the vestibular apparatus yield information about the orientation and movement of the head. This information is critical in the perception of balance, or one's feeling of uprightness. In a modern dance class, for example, when performing a side tilt,

Gabrielle Laurence

Figure 5.3
Novice adult dancers' lack of dance images in memory makes it difficult for them to produce a correct position at first.

beginners must consciously override the natural tendency to keep the head vertical while the body tilts. Similarly, beginners have difficulty maintaining a horizontal head position when performing a table-top arabesque, while the ballet arabesque with head up is easier to maintain.

The novice adult requires assistance from the instructor to develop kinesthesis, as he is unable to fully detect and correct equilibrium or other types of movement errors. The instructor can help by asking students to concentrate on the feeling associated with a particular movement, in other words, pay attention to information coming from the movement itself.[8]

Rhythmic Abilities

Temporal or rhythm awareness refers to the ability to identify a temporal pattern or pattern of sounds, and to reproduce it through movement. Although it is not the intent of this discussion to provide a thorough analysis of rhythm, some basic elements linking rhythm to dance are important to consider.

Rhythm awareness represents a critical dimension in learning dance, as most dance skills are performed to music. Any discussion of dance without reference to music would seem incomplete. It is indeed difficult to dance with the absence of some form of music, or to listen to music without doing some form of physical action. All dance skills have a distinctive timing. A step hop, for example, has an even timing, the step and hop being equal in duration, whereas a skip has an uneven rhythm, the hop being shorter than the step. Typically, a dance skill is performed to a specific meter, rhythm, and tempo, whether the even beat of a 2/4 march, the 3/4 meter of a waltz, or the syncopated rhythm of a jazz pattern performed to percussion. Rhythm is therefore an inherent part of dance skills, regardless of whether they are performed to music or not.

> The ability to hear and interpret rhythmic patterns is part of learning and performing dance.

Most dancers, choreographers, and teachers consider rhythm a crucial element in dance training and performance.[9] The ability to hear and interpret patterns of sounds is part of learning and performing dance skills. Among the basic elements of rhythm, those that seem most relevant in dance training are the beat, accent, meter, duration, rhythmic pattern, and tempo; these are presented in Table 5.2. Clearly, dance students must acquire a basic understanding of these elements in order to develop rhythmic abilities.[10]

In order to become proficient movers, dance students must develop two types of rhythmic abilities: perceptual and motor. Perceptual rhythmic abilities allow an individual to detect, identify, recognize, discriminate between, and analyze elements of rhythm as he listens to a musical piece. Motor rhythmic abilities include a motor reaction to or translation

Table 5.2   Basic Elements of Rhythm for Dance Training

Beat	Temporal unit of a musical piece or pattern of movements. In a 4/4 measure, the beat is one quarter note.
Accent	Stress on one beat. Normally the first beat of a measure is stressed.
Meter	The basic structure of a musical piece or pattern of movements. A 3/4 meter indicates that there are three beats per measure, and that one beat equals one quarter note.
Duration	The length of a sound or movement. The longest duration is the whole note, followed by the half note (twice as short as the whole note), quarter note, eighth note, and so on. The quarter note represents a walking step, while a running step is represented by an eighth note.
Rhythmic Pattern	Grouping of two or more durations or accented and unaccented durations. A simple rhythmic pattern could be two eighth notes and one-quarter note.
Tempo	Rate of speed of a musical piece or pattern of movements. A moderate tempo would result with the quarter note played at the rate of 80 times per minute.

of rhythm through movement, such as producing, reproducing, or illustrating a rhythmic pattern through movements of the body.

Current literature in rhythm studies suggests that untrained individuals tend to accurately imitate simple rhythmic patterns, those made up of short and long durations, the long duration being twice as long as the short duration.[11] This suggests that beginners should have no difficulty performing and recognizing dance phrases of walking and running steps, or movements with a 2:1 ratio. Conversely, dance skills with more complex rhythms, for example rhythms with a 3:1 ratio, may be more difficult to perceive and reproduce.

Perceptual skills require more in depth information processing than reproduction skills. In other words, it is relatively easy to imitate a rhythmic pattern by clapping hands or stepping. It is, however, more difficult to identify or describe the structure of a pattern, because this requires recognition of the beat interval, and the precise composition of each beat in the pattern.[12] We also know that individuals with no musical training tend to hear sounds that are closer together as part of a group, whether that rhythmic group is accurate or not.[13] For example, a skip (comprised of a step and a hop) placed on the first beat of a 4 beat pattern is likely to be perceived to arrive on the second beat because the short part, the hop, is closer to the second beat than it is to the step. However, recent empirical evidence suggests that specific training may eliminate this tendency.[12]

> Perceptual rhythmic abilities require more in-depth information processing than motor rhythmic abilities.

What does this mean for the adult learning dance? The natural tendency to group sounds in a certain way may also indicate a tendency to program motor patterns in a similar way. This is because movements tend to be programmed according to one's perception of the stimulus. In dance technique, timing is often precise. Therefore, specific training will help beginners accurately perceive the timing of movements, which will allow them to prepare accurate motor plans for their movements. The dance instructor must help beginners understand rhythm so that their perceptual skills are accurate. Accurate perceptual skills are critical in the attempt stage of learning, especially when students watch a demonstration and are trying to pick up relevant temporal cues. The timing of a skill is one of the relevant cues required for a successful execution of the skill. Timing is also one of the components used to analyze the complexity of a skill, as suggested in Chapter 2.

The timing of dance skills is not always something that comes naturally to all students. You have likely come across students who have great difficulty identifying the meter of a piece of music because they cannot hear the accented beat. These perceptual skills are learned, and therefore must be taught. There may be a presumption that, because students practice and dance with live or recorded music, their rhythmic skills will develop. Research indicates that this may not be the case.[9] If we want students to know precisely on which beat of the measure a leg gesture or landing is to occur, we must teach them. If we want students to be able to discriminate between even and uneven rhythm, we must explain the difference to them, and provide opportunities for them to learn to recognize these differences and to translate them into dance steps. Perceptual and motor rhythmic abilities related to dance are summarized in Table 5.3.

Finally, a temporal awareness concept important in dance is the synchronization of movements to music, known as temporal anticipation in motor learning theory.[1] Basically, synchronization requires anticipation of when the beat will arrive and anticipation of when the muscle groups should be activated for the movement to occur at the time of arrival of the beat. The main temporal cue that will help students anticipate the beat is the instructor counting the exercise, as it specifies meter and tempo. The accompaniment, of course, provides the continuous temporal cues throughout the exercise.

Processing information takes time. From the time the plan of action, for example, to step on the right foot on count one, has been determined

Table 5.3 Perceptual and Motor Rhythmic Abilities for Dance Training

Perceptual Abilities	Motor Abilities
Identify the beat, accent, meter	Clap or step the beat, accent
Recognize the meter, pattern	Illustrate the pattern with movements
Discriminate between durations	Translate the durations into gestures
Analyze the rhythmic structure	Perform a 2/4 meter with locomotion

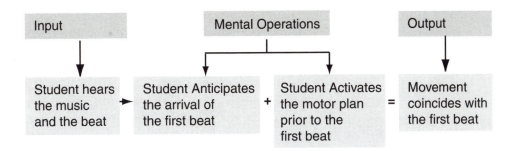

Figure 5.4
The synchronization process.

to the time the right foot makes a step, time has elapsed, perhaps a few milliseconds. The dancer must therefore anticipate when the beat will occur so he can activate the motor plan soon enough to ensure that the physical action will coincide with the beat. The process of synchronization in dance is summarized in Figure 5.4. As in many types of movements, the dance student performs the mental operations leading to synchronization while executing other movements. The student is planning the next movement while one is being carried out. With practice, these mental operations take place without conscious attention.

There is no guarantee that the beginner will learn these mental operations by himself, they must be taught. The ability to anticipate the exact time of arrival of the beat and to synchronize action to music develops, as any other perceptual and motor skill, through conscious attention and guided practice. The best way teachers can help students anticipate is by providing clear and accurate preparation counts.[14] This aspect is expanded in Chapter 10. In a recent study with ballet students, experienced instructors confirmed that one of the most common rhythm-related problems with senior ballet students was that they were often late in their timing.[9] Lack of precision in timing indicates that students are unable to anticipate the beat, or do not pay attention to what they hear. This problem may be alleviated by focusing students' attention on the temporal aspect of dance skills early in their training.

> Dance instructors must train students to develop sensitivity to rhythm early in the learning process.

The central nervous system of the novice adult has matured; his perceptual systems are fully developed. However, lack of specific dance experience limits his ability to perceive kinesthetic, spatial, and temporal components of dance skills. When analyzing the perceptual characteristics and demands of dance, it becomes clear that all perceptual modalities are integrated and thus participate in the planning of a successful action. The next question is: How can the beginner pay attention to the relevant information when watching a demonstration?

Attention Capacity

In the literature on motor development and learning, attention is considered the core of information processing.[3,7] Attention is one of the key components in learning and performing motor skills. Attention is the ability or the capacity to consciously attend to an event. It is said to be limited, meaning that we can only attend to one thing at a time. Attention is also a serial capacity: we can do one thing, then another, and so on. Finally, attention is a selective process. It can be trained to concentrate on some information and ignore other information.

The implications of these properties of attention are numerous. A beginner's capacity to pay attention to information can be easily exceeded if too much activity is presented at once. Asking the beginner to pay attention to several aspects of a demonstration, or giving him too many corrections at once is, therefore, not recommended. The teacher can help beginners pay attention to one or two specific elements of a demonstration by pointing out these elements to them prior to the demonstration. The instructor is basically telling them to only pay attention to these points, and to ignore the rest. Another example of attention capacity overload, regrettably common in the dance studio, is when the instructor expects beginners to execute an action and, at the same time, pay attention to verbal corrections. It is clear that their limited capacity is exceeded in that situation. Teachers must, therefore, be selective in what they ask their students to do.

> A beginner's capacity to pay attention to information can be easily exceeded if too much activity is attempted at once.

With practice and experience, students develop strategies that enable them to do more than one thing at a time. Once a skill is learned, it requires less attention, thus freeing some attention to focus on another

Josie Hazen

Figure 5.5
The teacher can help beginners pay attention to one or two elements of a demonstration.

skill. One advantage dance has over many sports is that it consists mainly of closed skills. This means that there are very few external distractors for the dancer to worry about, as opposed to team sports that consist of open, thus unpredictable skills. Closed skills are easier to learn, as they impose less demand on the learner's attention capacity. However, because dance consists of serial skills, they can be quite taxing on the learner's ability to memorize them.

Memory Capacity

Memory is the ability to retain and retrieve information. The learner's ability to mentally represent a dance skill is related to experiences stored in memory. As with the ability to attend to information, memory capacity is critical in the formation of a mental image of a new skill, which takes place in the attempt stage of learning.

Short-Term and Long-Term Memory

Both short-term memory and long-term memory are important in learning dance skills.[1] Short-term memory, called the working memory, is the system used when the student watches the demonstration and tries to remember it long enough to repeat it immediately. A good description of how this memory system works is given in the following dance example:

> Suppose you have just watched a dancer perform a sequence of dance movements and you must perform that sequence, which is a common occurrence in instruction and dance audition situations. Working memory processing activity would be involved because you must keep in memory the visually presented sequence of movements and translate that visual information into motor performance. Involved in this translation process would be retrieving from long-term memory the movement information required to carry out the sequence.[15]

Just how much information can a novice adult remember? Work in cognitive psychology indicates that short-term memory has a limited capacity. An individual can only remember seven plus or minus two items at a time. If not rehearsed, these items will stay in short-term memory approximately 60 seconds.[16] The limited capacity of short-term memory has significant implications for beginners, especially when attempting to learn long sequences. With appropriate strategies, however, novice learners can increase their memory capacity, and thus memorize more than seven discrete items of information.

How does information flow from short-term to long-term memory? Items that have been mentally rehearsed following a demonstration are passed on to long-term memory. Long-term memory is the storage space for information or skills that have been well learned. It has no limit in terms of the quantity of information that it can retain or duration of its retention. The entire spectrum of skills that have been well learned over the years is stored in long-term memory.[1] Once it has reached this storage space, information stays there. Imagine going downhill skiing or riding a bicycle for the first time after 15 or 20 years. If these skills were mastered then, you should have no difficulty performing them again after a brief rehearsal time, even bringing your performance level to what it was when last performed. In practical terms, this tells us that a beginner's greatest handicap is his lack of dance experiences stored in long-term memory. This handicap can be seen in their inability to integrate the time, force, and space components all at once. Consequently, novice adults require more demonstrations and more practice than experienced dancers.

> Novice adults' greatest learning handicap is their lack of dance experiences in long-term memory.

Although active throughout the entire learning cycle, information processing abilities may be most crucial during the attempt stage. There is a distinct link between the memory systems and constructing a motor plan for the new skill. An important function of the motor plan is to search and recall from short-term and long-term memory the past dance experiences closest to the new skill. For example, a loss in balance during a pirouette would be stored in memory. On the next attempt, the student makes an adjustment based on that stored information. Without short-term memory to recall prior performance, improvement would be difficult.

Recall and Recognition Memory

According to the Schema theory of motor skill learning, there are two types of memory, recall memory, and recognition memory.[7] Recall memory is the ability to remember and retrieve from long-term memory a skill, movement, or step that has not been demonstrated. Recall memory is said to be more complex than recognition memory because it requires that the learner reconstruct a motor plan from memory and execute the movement. Recognition memory, the simplest form of remembering, is the ability to recognize that the new skill is the same as or different from a particular skill learned the previously. Both memories are limited in beginners, as they have virtually no mental representations of dance movements stored in long-term memory.

Short-term and long-term memory systems are in operation, not only during the attempt stage, but also during the correct and perfect stages. With practice, the beginner will be able to modify and refine motor plans, and, as a result, produce skilled movements. Figure 5.6

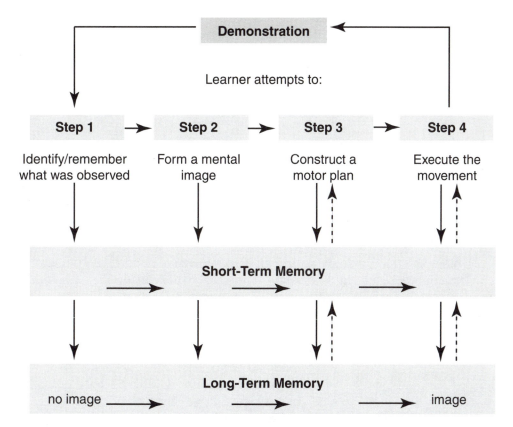

Figure 5.6
The role of short and long-term memory during the novice adult's attempt stage.

illustrates the role of short-term and long-term memory during the novice adult's attempt stage.

Chunking Strategies for Learning

How can the instructor help a beginner increase short-term memory capacity? We all know that it is possible to memorize more than just a few steps with practice. Through a retention strategy called chunking, individuals can memorize large amounts of information by increasing the size of one item, thus grouping or chunking initial elements together into one large item. Take for example a professional dancer who has acquired an extensive repertoire of dance skills over the years. At will, this dancer can retrieve any one from long-term memory, practice it once or twice, and then perform it relatively well.

In contrast, a beginner attempting to learn a four-minute choreography would likely struggle with small items first. Under proper planning and guidance, the instructor can facilitate chunking strategies during lessons, resulting in memorization of the entire dance. Take for example a choreography performed to a 4/4 music at a comfort-

Table 5.4   Effect of Practice on Chunking Strategy to Increase Memory Capacity

Novice Adult	One Item in Memory	Beat	Length
First week	One pattern of four actions	4	3 sec.
	One phrase of four patterns	16	12
	One segment of four phrases	64	48
	Two segments of four phrases	128	96
Twelfth week	One dance of six segments	384	288 (4.8 min.)

able tempo. Students would first memorize a pattern of four movements representing four beats. Then, probably during the same class, they would learn one phrase of four patterns (16 beats). The dance could expand to the first segment of the dance, consisting of four phrases (64 beats) during the next two lessons or so. Progressively, the students would memorize the entire dance made up of six segments, 384 beats, over four minutes long. The chunking technique for memorizing large sums of information is illustrated in Table 5.4.

> With practice in chunking, beginners learn to memorize larger amounts of information by increasing the size of one item.

Of course, we know that more practice is necessary to perfect and master the steps, and to perform the dance with fluency. Nonetheless, novice adults have managed to retain a large quantity of movements in memory. They have done so by grouping or chunking movements into meaningful units, and by progressively increasing the size of one unit. Chunking prevented them from overloading their memory capacity; it also allowed well-learned movements to be transferred to long-term memory. The next step is to learn to monitor performance by detecting and correcting errors in movements, the fourth cognitive ability required for dance learning.

Error Detection and Correction Capacity

As mentioned earlier, the greatest deficit beginners have is their lack of experience in dance. Without movement images stored in long-term memory, learners are unable to monitor their own movements. They cannot compare the information produced by the jump they just did with the feel of a correct jump, as they do not have the mental kinesthetic image of that feel in long-term memory yet. For the most part, beginners must rely on the instructor's corrections. Feedback provided by the instructor serves to develop a kinesthetic sense of what a correct and incorrect movement is.

Parallel to teaching beginners new dance skills, instructors must also teach them how to monitor their own movement performance. Students must learn to be sensitive to the total range of information produced by the movement. It can be kinesthetic (the feel of the correct leg action or shift in balance), visual (seeing the action of the leg in relation to the supporting leg), or auditory (hearing the sound of the foot brushing on the floor at a certain speed). For example, each time the learner executes a jump, its performance is compared with the mental image of that jump stored in memory. If no difference between the image and the performance is recorded, no error is detected. If the performance differs from the mental image, then an error is detected.

> Feedback provided by the instructor serves to develop a kinesthetic sense of the correct movement.

The instructor can help beginners by having them pay attention to these sorts of information coming from their movements.[1] One way dance educators can accomplish this is by asking them to describe the action, and what it feels like when it is done well. By asking them to talk about the movement, students are forced to consciously attend to what they are doing. And this, as it will be pointed out later, is part of the ultimate role of an effective teacher, to help students become independent learners.

A final point to make concerning error detection and correction abilities is relative to the specificity of the movement. Are slow and fast movements practiced the same way? Motor learning theory argues that specific strategies are required for slow and fast movements.[17] If the movement is slow, an adage movement for example, the learner has time to detect movement-produced information and use it to modify the movement. If, on the other hand, the movement is fast, a jump or sharp turn for example, the learner has no time to detect errors during the execution; instead, he must concentrate on preparing a motor plan that will produce the correct movement.

> In order to detect and correct their own errors, novice adults must learn to attend to kinesthetic, visual, and auditory information produced by the movements.

Summary

In summary, the novice adult is that very special learner whose physical and mental systems have fully matured. This learner has acquired good information processing abilities and a good vocabulary of motor abilities and skills. He is fully equipped to tackle a new type of motor skills. With no dance experiences in memory, the beginner adult's most challenging task is therefore to develop an eye and ear for dance skills, to get a sense of this very unique, and often complex way of moving. With experience, he will develop, in addition to a dance vocabulary, strategies to perceive pertinent information faster and more accurately, focus attention on specific aspects of the movement, remember more information more accurately, detect even the most subtle of errors, and finally correct these errors. When he has refined these cognitive abilities and strategies, the novice adult has probably become an experienced dancer.

References

1. Schmidt RA, Wrisberg CA: *Motor Learning and Performance: A Problem Based Learning Approach,* (2nd ed). Champaign, IL: Human Kinetics Publishers, Inc., 2000.
2. Gniady J: Ballet grows up. Dance Teacher, October 1999, pp. 86-91.
3. Gabbard CP: *Lifelong Motor Development,* (3rd ed). Boston: Allyn and Bacon, 2000.
4. Gallahue DL, Ozmun JC: *Understanding Motor Development: Infants, Children, Adolescents, Adults* (3rd ed). Madison, WI: Brown & Benchmark Publishers, 1995.
5. Hammond SN: *Ballet Basics,* (4th ed). Mountain View, CA: Mayfield Publishing Company, 2000.
6. Chmelar R, Fitt S: Conditioning for dance: The art of the science. Kinesiology and Medicine for Dance 14(1):78-94, 1991.
7. Schmidt RA, Lee TD: *Motor Learning and Control: A Behavioral Emphasis,* (3rd ed). Champaign, IL: Human Kinetics Publishers, Inc., 1999.
8. Rose DJ: *A Multilevel Approach to the Study of Motor Control and Learning.* Boston: Allyn and Bacon, 1997.
9. Côté-Laurence P: The role of rhythm in ballet. Research in Dance Education 1(2):173-191, 2000.
10. Côté-Laurence P: Development of rhythm literacy for dancers. *In:* Young Overby L, Côté-Laurence P (eds): *Dance Education: A Lifetime of Experiences.* Proceedings of the Focus on Dance Education Conference. East Lansing, MI, 1996.
11. Fraisse P: Rhythm and tempo. *In:* Deutsch D (ed): *The Psychology of Music.* New York: Academic Press, Inc., 1982, pp. 149-180.
12. Côté-Laurence P, Kerr R: The role of procedural knowledge in the perception of rhythmic patterns. Paper presented at the Canadian Society for Psychomotor Learning and Sport Psychology conference, Waterloo, Canada, October 2000.
13. Clarke EC, Krumhansl CL: Perceiving musical time. Music Perception 7(3):213-52, 1990.
14. Plastino JG: *The Dancer Prepares: Modern Dance for Beginners,* (4th ed). Mountain View, CA: Mayfield Publishers, 1996.
15. Magill RA: *Motor Learning: Concepts and Applications,* (6th ed). Boston: McGraw-Hill, 2001, p. 147.
16. Miller GA: The magical number seven, plus or minus two: Some lim-

its on our capacity for processing information. Psychological Review 63:81-97, 1956.

17. Schmidt RA, Wrisberg CA: *Motor Learning and Performance. A Problem-Solving Approach*, (2nd ed). Champaign, IL: Human Kinetics Publishers, Inc., 2000.

Gabrielle Laurence

Comparing Child and Adult Beginners

The Young and the Older Child

Physical Limitations Due to Growth

    Growth Spurt

    Proportion

    Bones, Joints and Muscles

Competency of Fundamental Skills

Experience in Dance Skills

Learning Abilities

    Information Processing

    Learning Strategies

    Perceptual Skills

    Motor Planning and Control

    Cognitive Skills

Chapter 6

The Child Learner

We have identified the capabilities underlying skill learning by a novice adult. Now we turn to the child. Developmental limitations of children restrict both the choice of dance material selected and the method of teaching, which must be adapted to their growing body structure and a developing brain. Both affect what, and how fast children will learn. While we acknowledge that there are gifted children who are skilled dancers at a very early age, this chapter is focused on typical children. We explore some of the differences that need to be taken into account when teaching dance to children instead of adults.

When we teach an adult class, identifying learning difficulties is fairly straightforward. However, when we see children performing dance skills poorly, we are left with many possibilities to consider. Why can't the children learn this skill? Is the skill performed poorly because the child:

- Did not understand what was required;
- Cannot remember all parts of the skill between the demonstration and the time she has to perform it;
- Cannot construct an adequate plan for the skill because she has little past dance experience and a poor mental picture of the skill;
- Knows what to do, but does not have the strength to do it;
- Knows what to do but cannot control her movement to do the skill correctly;
- Has the motor control to perform it, if only she knew what "it" was;
- Is not able to pay attention to feedback from her performance or from the teacher;
- Does not know that she has performed the skill poorly;
- Could perform the skill perfectly well if only she was allowed to do it slowly, or finally,
- Is not particularly interested in performing a skilled movement, but is simply enjoying the act of dancing?

All of these options are possible explanations. Some of them may be due to physical limitations; others are due to limitation in a child's ability to process information in the same way that an adult can. The child has a smaller knowledge base, cannot process all the information available from the perceptual system, or cannot do it quickly.[1-3] The first and last items on the list of options require a different explanation. They suggest that a child understands and thinks about dance skills differently than an adult.

Comparing Child and Adult Beginners

Our concern is to explore why a child may have difficulty learning a particular skill. Child learners share with novice adults a lack of experience. A teenager or adult, facing the first ballet class, will in some ways face similar challenges to an eight year old in the same situation. All must become familiar with a new movement vocabulary, remember a sequence of positions or steps, pay attention to precise details of body position, move through space and stay in time with the music. As novices to dance skills in general, or ballet skills in particular, children are venturing into foreign territory. The effect that lack of experience has on skill learning in a novice has been detailed in the previous chapter and is summarized in Table 6.1. It applies to both adult and child beginners.

However even at the attempt stage, and certainly in the correct stage, a child, particularly a young child, is not the same learner as an adult, nor is a five year old the same learner as a ten year old. If we want to understand the child attempting to become skilled in early dance experiences, we must take additional factors into consideration. Children have bodies that are still growing. Their anatomy (body proportions, joint structure, and muscles) is not yet mature and this will have an impact on their ability to perform. Similarly, their nervous system is not yet fully developed. As dance novices, children share the attention, memory, and error detection limitations (*see* Chapter 5) of novice adults. The child has additional limitations in the functioning of the perceptual system, in planning and controlling movements and in problem solving. These will dramatically affect how much and how fast the child can learn in comparison to an adult.

Table 6.1   Summary of Novice Adult Learner Difficulties

Learning Steps		Difficulties
Step 1	Observes movement/hears instructions	Does not know what is important
Step 2	Picks up relevant cues	Only gets a few details
Step 3	Makes mental image	Is incomplete
Step 4	Constructs a motor plan	Does not have one; adapts
Step 5	Performs the skill	Performs poorly
Step 6	Attends to feedback internal/external	Has limited attention

Marliese Kimmerle

Figure 6.1
The child learner is
physically and mentally a
different learner than the
adult.

Psychosocial or affective development also plays a role in contributing to the child's acquisition of skills. How children feel about themselves in general (self-esteem), their perception of their motor skills (perceived physical competency), as well as their ability to interact positively with fellow students and teachers also show developmental shifts. This directly or indirectly influences their approach to the learning situation. The effect perception of competency has on learning in general and participation in physical activity and sports specifically, has been well documented.[1,4] We will not attempt to review that literature here since the effect it has on learning dance skills is fairly similar to that documented in other areas of physical activity. The key point for dance educators is that if we hope to keep children involved in dance for a lifetime of enjoyable activity, we must ensure that we give them success-oriented experiences – the material we present must not exceed their learning capabilities. To do that, we must understand what their capabilities and limitations are.

The Young and the Older Child

A common practice in motor development texts is to divide perceptual-motor development into stages rather than attempting to describe what happens at each chronological age. One could attempt to discuss each age group, for example, the typical 6 year old, the typical 7 year old, and so on. There are good reasons for avoiding such a year-by-year timetable. Chronological age is not a good indicator of maturation.[4,5,6] While one can identify an overall developmental progression that appears to be age related, children also develop on individual timetables depending on their particular combination of hereditary characteristics and life experiences. These individual differences in development can produce as much as a two or three year range in a group of children of the same chronological age. This applies to the development of perceptual skills, cognitive skills, stage of maturity of fundamental skills, development of specialized skills and the age of puberty. In a second grade class with an average chronological age of seven, there may be children who, in their developmental age, range from five to nine years. It is therefore not enough for a teacher to know what to expect from the typical seven year old; the teacher must be aware of the range of possibilities as well as what developmental changes precede and follow this period.

It is therefore helpful to think of stages of development that describe the general progressions in each of the above areas. The preschool to high school age span can be divided into four stages: early, middle, late childhood, and adolescence (Table 6.2).

In order to simplify the discussion of the capabilities and limitations of the child learner, the end of the early and the beginning of the late period have been selected for comparison. The most dramatic period of perceptual-motor and cognitive development affecting dance skill learning is middle childhood. The contrast between the young child just entering school at 5 or 6, when she is likely to receive the first dance exposure, and the older pre-puberty child of 10 or 11 engaged in more focused dance skill acquisition is the most relevant for comparing learning capabilities and limitations. Although there are still dramatic physical changes occurring in adolescence that affect skill performance, the learning capabilities of teenagers are similar to those of adults.

> The most dramatic period of perceptual-motor and cognitive development affecting dance skill learning is between five and ten years.

Therefore we focus on the transition between the young child and the older child with an emphasis on the progressions in learning capabilities between the ages of five and ten years.

A review of developmental theory and an extensive timetable of perceptual-motor skill development is beyond the scope of this book. The reader is directed to a number of excellent motor development textbooks[1-4,7,8] that provide background to the summaries. We will focus here

Table 6.2   Stages and Ages of Development

Stage	Age Period
Early Childhood	2-6 years
Middle Childhood	7-9 years
Late Childhood	10-12 years
Adolescence	13-19 years

on those capabilities and limitations most relevant to the learning of dance skills. These include physical growth, maturation of fundamental motor skills, experience in dance skills, learning capabilities from an information processing approach, and cognitive development from a Piagetian perspective.

Physical Limitations Due to Growth

This text focusses on how children learn dance skills and, therefore, concentrates primarily on cognitive factors rather than biological or physiological aspects of growth and development. Discussions of physical fitness, training and conditioning, or injury prevention in children are omitted. This information is available in a number of sources.[9-11] However, some attention must be paid to growth patterns and anatomical development that determine the state of the body the child brings to the learning experience. This affects the teacher's selection of dance material and may limit the amount of progress the child can make. Therefore, we briefly highlight some pertinent aspect of growth.

Human body structure (height and proportion) reaches its mature state around 16 years for women and 18 for men,[9] although the exact timeline is dictated by genetic make-up. Adult learners enter a dance class with a "finished" body. Unless they undergo a dramatic weight loss or gain, they are familiar with their body. Not so for the child. The child is learning dance skills with a body that is structurally still immature and that continues to change, sometimes extremely rapidly (especially around the age of puberty). It is therefore important to consider, at least briefly, some important structural changes.

Growth Spurt

Children grow taller with age, showing a slow steady increase during middle and late childhood before the adolescent growth spurt. A child's height does not necessarily affect the acquisition of skills, although an extremely rapid period of growth may interrupt skill development. A growth spurt precedes puberty and starts around the age of nine in girls, peaking between 11 and 12; this is two years earlier than boys.[9] This growth spurt creates social problems as senior elementary or junior high classes attempt co-educational folk or social dance with girls who tower several inches over boys. It may also create some physical problems. At the start of the growth spurt, muscle growth has not caught up with the sudden growth in long bones. A highly skilled athlete/dancer may be particularly affected as she becomes tight and possibly risks injury and can no longer perform some of the skills with ease.[12,13] Teachers must be particularly cautious with stretching activities at this age.

Proportion

There are other more subtle aspects of physical growth and changes in anatomy, notably a change in body proportion. Anyone working with preschoolers will note that the body proportions are not yet adult like. The adult proportion of head to body (1/8 ratio) is not attained until about age 12; this may have biomechanical implications for motor performance.[2] A teacher in a movement program for toddlers and preschoolers will note that balance and stability are affected by the larger head proportion. This will affect the child's ability to run smoothly and perform dynamic balance tasks.

At the other end of the spectrum, the changes associated with puberty, including the growth spurt, and a shift in the amount of muscle mass and percentage and location of fat, create dramatic changes in proportion for both sexes.[4] Not only does this create a change in the individual's body image and often in self-concept, but it also dramatically affects the learner's "body sense." Learning dance skills is highly dependent on body awareness, and the ability to monitor and control precisely what the body is doing at any point is crucial. For males, the increase in muscle mass, particularly in the upper body, is an advantage for many movements that require strength, such as pas de deux lifts. For females on the other hand, the dramatic increase in fat deposits creating the female curves drastically affects the biomechanics of motion and the efficiency of force production by the muscles. Female gymnasts, skaters, and dancers are particularly affected since many of the skills they perform require efficient manipulation of the center of gravity and precise force production (such as jumps and turns and difficult balance poses).

> Changes in body size and proportion associated with puberty in females dramatically affect skilled performance.

For some elite athletes, these physical changes bring about a sudden drop in performance, or even a drop from competition as they attempt to adjust to their changing body. For the less highly skilled child, the effect of changes in body proportion and composition on performance may not be as drastic. Teachers should be aware that progress in skill learning may temporarily be disrupted or revert to an earlier stage as the growing child tries to adapt to her body.

Bones, Joints and Muscles

The bones in young children are not completely ossified, that is, they are still lacking in strength. The growth plates are still producing long bone growth well into adolescence.[9] This may be the reason that young girls are generally not encouraged to go up on toe, until the bones of the legs and feet are strong enough. The approximate age to begin safe pointe work is thought to be 12 years of age.[13,14] A highly skilled young dancer working on a syllabus with a group of adolescents may therefore be held back from toe work even though her dance skills are superior. Experimental studies are underway to find quantitative measures of strength and flexibility in the feet that may be used to help the teacher make the

Gabrielle Laurence

Figure 6.2
A highly skilled young
dancer may not be ready to
work on pointe.

decision as to when a child is ready to progress to pointe[15] and discussions of appropriate training techniques are available.[16]

The state and function of joints and ligaments and the degree of muscle strength also differs in children and adults and undergo changes with growth and maturation. All three affect the range of motion a child has at various joints, and the ability to hold a body position or to stabilize a body part. Readers interested in more details of pediatric physiology, including changes in flexibility and muscle mass with maturation, and the effects of training can consult developmental or pediatric sports medicine texts.[1,4,9-11]

Young children generally have more flexible joints than adults, and female children tend to be more flexible than males.[9,17] Flexibility decreases by the time a child reaches adolescence and is affected by the amount and type of activity. It has been suggested[2] that gender differences reported in childhood may be due to greater social acceptance of stretching exercises and the greater participation in dance and gymnastics by women.

The greater flexibility of young children presents some injury potential and is cause for some concern if certain skills are overemphasized. Children can more readily attain some of the exaggerated or acrobatic body positions in dance in comparison to inactive adults. However, they may not yet have developed the muscle strength to balance that flexibility and, without proper instruction, may be physically at risk. Flexibility in the back and the hip joint are of particular concern in both gymnastics and dance. Performing turnout correctly is of concern for adults dancers but should be even more carefully monitored in children, whose greater rotation at the hip must be balanced with strength work. Young dancers can sometimes be found spread-eagled on the floor in a full straddle, chest to floor, the envy of many an older student with less flexible hip joints. However, extreme range of motion is no guarantee that this same child will be able to hold a high leg extension while standing in a correct alignment without a pelvic tilt and a hyper-extended back. Similarly, an overzealous teacher may encourage a child to stand in an exaggerated turnout in second, which a loose hip joint permits, without at the same time working the muscles that stabilize the pelvis and prevent lower back problems. The risks of improper dance training for children has been publicized[13,14] and has had an impact on teaching practices. There is also an increasing body of literature available in sports medicine concerning the young athlete that is relevant to dance training and performance.[10,18]

> The greater flexibility of young children presents an injury potential if it is not balanced by strength work and correct teaching.

Competency of Fundamental Skills

Dance skills are specialized, complex skills, built on the fundamental skills of stability, locomotion, and manipulation. In dance, stability skills are the basis for correct body alignment and control while standing or moving, changing body shapes, changing directions or stopping, and are crucial to any skill involving support on one leg. Locomotor skills are the basis of all traveling dance steps and aerial work. Manipulative skills in a sports context refer to throwing, catching, and kicking skills. They are not seen in dance unless props are used.

Although terminology and time lines may differ slightly from one motor development or physical education textbook to another, these three groupings are the generally accepted descriptive categories of fundamental motor skills. Children learn to run, jump, hop, skip, kick, throw, and stand on one foot between the ages of two and six years in fairly predictable levels or stages of skill progression.[1,2,4,19]

If you know the age of the child, do you know what stage she will be in and can you assume that she is ready to perform a skip or a leap correctly? In theory, "children have the developmental potential to be at the mature stage of most fundamental movement skills by about age six."[20] In actual practice, they may or may not be there. Readiness to learn has been defined as: "the combination of maturation and experience that prepares an individual to acquire a skill or understanding."[21] For example, you can attempt to teach a young child that when you lift one leg off the ground you must tighten the other leg and that the arms must be used to counterbalance. The young child's nervous system may not be able to integrate information from both legs and arms and despite a best effort, the child will wobble and loose balance. The ability to progress is also

Gabrielle Laurence

Figure 6.3
Older children can perform
skipping skills with some
precision and body
awareness.

influenced by practice. Think of the girls you know who are immature throwers because they had little exposure to ball skills. Not all children reach the same level of competence in fundamental skills, and some never reach the mature stage of a skill.[4] Witness the number of male and female undergraduates who cannot skip properly, or who do not know the difference between a leap and a hop because they have had an overexposure to sports and a lack of dance and gymnastics in their earlier education. Therefore, you must expect individual differences in how far and fast children progress to be affected by slow maturation, poor instruction, or lack of practice.

> A child's readiness to progress in fundamental skills is influenced by both maturation and experience.

However, even if fundamental skills are at the mature stage and therefore technically correct, young children are still developing proficiency in these skills, such as moving as quickly as possible, developing amplitude, distance, or controlling force. A young child may be able to demonstrate the correct leg action in a leap. It is quite another challenge however to control the arms, perform three leaps in a row, cover distance, and leap in time to a musical phrase. It is reasonable to expect young children to perform these fundamental skills in a dance class, but not have much control over space, time, and force components, or be able to do the skills in a complex context. This progression from simple fundamental skills to more complex dance skills is presented in Table 6.3.

If children are taught dance skills before they have these basic competencies, and put into the complex context (sequences, pathways, music, other dancers) that is involved in some dance forms, they may be frustrated in their attempts to learn and skill acquisition may be hampered. While the issue of whether the specialized skills of ballet, jazz, or tap should be taught to young children is, on the one hand, a

Table 6.3   Skill Progressions with Age

Skills	Age
Acquisition of Fundamental Skills	2-6 years
Stability, body management	
Locomotor	
Manipulative	
Introduction to Specialized Skills	7-12 years
More proficient fundamental skills	
Combinations of fundamental skills	
Fundamental skills in complex context	
New dance skills	
Selection and Refinement of Specialized Skills	12 years to adult
Choose among dance forms, specialize	
(e.g., jazz dance skills)	

question of educational philosophy not addressed in this book, it is on the other hand an issue in skill acquisition. The child attempting to learn a pas de chat or an assemblé, who is not yet able to perform a simple hop, a skip, or a jump competently is likely to face difficulty.

The main activity focus of a young child should be on acquiring basic competency in fundamental motor skills.[4] Not only does this increase the child's perception of physical competency, ready to be challenged by more difficult specialized skills, but it also provides the knowledge base in the motor learning model. The construction of motor plans for more complex skills is based on the existence of simpler skills. While specialized skills can be introduced when the child appears ready, that should not be the main focus for the typical young child in an educational or recreational setting.

> The young child must develop competency in fundamental skills before progressing to specialized dance skills.

The conscientious teacher is often at odds with over-enthusiastic parents or children who want to begin the specialized skills of ballet or jazz at a very early age. One solution is to give the class a dance label but make the content fundamental locomotor and body management skills. This can be done in a dance-like setting with music while keeping the context simple (e.g., work at the child's own pace, freely in space, with single skills).

There are, of course, exceptions. Gifted children and child prodigies who have started to play the piano, play tennis, or take dance lesson at an extremely early age do exist. These children appear to have exceptional motor and cognitive capabilities and already have a broad knowledge base and a large vocabulary of skills at a very young age. However, the typical child in her primary school years will still struggle to acquire competency in fundamental motor skills.

Experience in Dance Skills

During middle childhood (ages 7 to 9) and late childhood (ages 10 to 12), a child is normally introduced to a variety of specialized skills in dance, sports, and gymnastic in or outside of school. The older child is ready to focus on dance skills but for the majority, dance skills will be novel skills. It is certainly possible that in a dance studio one might encounter ten year olds who have been involved in skating or gymnastics or even dance for five years. In a public school setting, however, it is far more likely that for most children this would be their first concentrated exposure to dance. Some of the children in their primary school years may have had an introduction to rhythmic activities, "exercises to music," simple folk dances, and perhaps some exploratory creative dance experiences based on fundamental skills. We would therefore consider them novice dance learners.

As presented in Chapter 5, previous experience learning motor skills in general, and the amount of practice will determine the extent to which new dance skills are learned and perfected. Ten-year-old children may by now have had several years of practice throwing balls, or jumping over objects. However, they will not likely have practiced a 360-degree turn, a stag leap, or a grapevine step. Some may never have seen these skills performed. The main focus will be on teaching them to perform the actions of the jump, turn, or step combinations, with some variations introduced in body design, in timing, and in dynamics. Since dance skills are not yet automated, children will have some difficulty coping with complexity in the context of the skill, such as moving to music, sequencing other skills, or dancing with other people. These can be introduced one at a time.

> Older children are ready to learn dance skills and be gradually introduced to the complexities of context.

Although it may be tempting to treat older children like beginner adults in terms of selecting "beginner" dance material, it is important to remember that older children are not yet mature learners and cannot be expected to react to instruction or to progress through skills in a similar manner.

Learning Abilities

Given a normal range of experiences and no nervous system abnormalities, most children should have a mature functioning nervous system by the age of 12. For most perceptual and cognitive skills, therefore, a child of 10 to 12 years is considered mature.[1,4] In terms of the capability for learning dance skills, the 12 year old may be considered an adult. However, the child, between five and ten years, is attempting to acquire skills with an immature nervous system and will face learning limitations. These limitations are in the amount and speed of information processing, the lack of learning strategies, and immature perceptual and cognitive skills.

Information Processing

Children share with novice adults the limitations of inexperience and, therefore, do not know what cues to look at as they observe a new skill. They also lack motor plans for the skill. They face additional problems as a result of an immature functioning brain. The major brain structures are present at birth so these limitations are not structural but rather func-

> The young child has difficulty processing a lot of information from her body and the environment quickly.

tional. Communication between parts of a child's nervous system is limited and slow. The child has difficulty processing a large amount of information from the environment and different parts of the body quickly. As a result she encounters difficulties in the three aspects of skill acquisition: input, processing, and output. The child has problems attending to and integrating input (such as instructions and demonstrations) as well as monitoring the body during motion. Processing input, that is, interpreting and remembering the details of what she saw and heard, and planning a response is limited. Skill execution will likely be poor with limited ability to detect or correct errors. Part of this difficulty is a result of the child's lack of learning strategies that adults are able to use to assist them with attention, memory, and error detection.

The difficulty of processing a large amount of information in a short time and integrating information coming from different parts of their body and the environment can be illustrated with an activity. Something as simple as clapping hands and tapping toes rhythmically may be quite difficult for five year olds.[22] If that has to be done quickly and in time to music, mixing auditory information with kinesthetic information makes this exercise even more difficult. Most dance skills require the movement of many body parts, and the integration of visual and auditory cues during instruction and demonstration.

For a variety of reasons, young children are slow to respond. Compared to a 10 year old or an adult, a young child is slow to react to a stimulus, and slow to initiate a movement response. A young child does not necessarily move slowly, but is inefficient in handling large amounts of information quickly.[1-3] This is particularly a problem when the child has to respond quickly to an external stimulus. The first grade teacher, who puts on lively fast paced music and asks the children to skip continuously around the room on the beat, may be disappointed in the result. A self-paced activity may be more appropriate, or simply slowing the activity down may allow the children to cope. For the five year old, the skill of skipping is not yet perfected. It is attention demanding and cannot be performed quickly. Children must control their movements in space to avoid crashing into each other. Young children have difficulty when an activity requires both speed and control. Performing skills quickly and accurately at the same time demands a high degree of attention and managing both skills in conjunction is something we expect of older children and adults.

Even when there is no time constraint, simply sorting through the overflow of information can cause difficulty. Picture a young child standing in turn-out. There is skill-relevant information available from the joints and muscles of the hips, legs, ankles, and feet, from the reflection in the mirror, and from the instructions of the teacher. There are also superfluous cues such as the other children moving in the room, their best friend smiling at them, and the view out the window. A young child cannot inhibit salient but irrelevant cues nor does she have the ability to identify which cues are important. If she is performing a complex skill, her attention will be focused on performing the skill. She will not have attention capacity available to monitor the sensory information that she is receiving about her body. Limited attention is allocated to these cues while the child is busy attempting a novel body position such as a turned out leg. This necessitates external feedback from the teacher, and possibly tactile feedback to help the child feel where her arm or leg is. If the child comes back tomorrow, she may have totally forgotten the new body position and make the same mistakes.

Learning Strategies

Although there is controversy in the motor learning literature regarding the extent of transfer of learning from one skill to another,[23] there is agreement that one "learns to learn." The experience of trying to acquire particular motor skills should teach individuals how to become better learners the next time they face a new skill.[24] The child's lack of experience is not limited to dance skills but also lack of experience learning many motor skills. The child has acquired few learning strategies to assist with attention, rehearsal, or retrieval of motor plans. The lack of "control" strategies, for efficiently storing, retrieving, and using large amounts of information is a major problem for children.[3,17]

> A major limitation for the young learner is the lack of learning strategies.

Novice adults, when they first learn skills, also tend to be overwhelmed with information. However, the average 20 year old has acquired strategies to sort through and remember information. In order to deal with too much information from the body and/or the environment, adults have learned attention-focusing strategies (e.g., "remember to look only at the ball and not at the tennis player," or "look first at the feet to catch the weight shift in the new dance step") to ensure that important cues are not missed. This is called selective attention.

Another strategy involves grouping or chunking several pieces of information into one. A slide, slide, rock back, rock front, becomes a lindy step. Visualization, labeling, and rehearsal are other strategies that help individuals become efficient learners. As the skill is demonstrated, one imagines a picture of the movement or says cue words such as "right, behind, right, touch." While waiting one's turn, the dancer repeats these cues. Such rehearsal aids correct reproduction since it keeps the steps in short-term memory between the time the student sees the skill and has to perform it.

Young children do not spontaneously rehearse. Their failure to use cognitive strategies has been attributed to lack of practice.[17] Children can be taught to use strategies around five years of age, begin to use them independently around 7 or 8, but do not make effective use of strategies until around age 11.[1,3] Remembering skill sequences is an essential part of most dance lessons. Therefore, rehearsal would appear to be necessary. In a study comparing five and six year olds to eight and nine year olds,[25] both groups were taught verbal rehearsal in order to perform a six skill sequence. Although the youngest remembered less than the oldest subjects, they too benefitted by remembering more skills in the correct order than a control group that received instruction and demonstration only. The older children, however, used a more systematic approach to rehearsal and had a greater variety and more sophisticated rehearsal strategies. This research suggests that young children should be encouraged to verbally, mentally, and physically rehearse skills.[25]

Is handling a lot of information quickly without the aid of learning strategies the only problem? Can the teacher solve the information processing limitations by simply talking slowly, teaching one action at a time, and making sure the children are sitting down and paying attention? Although these may certainly reduce distractions, simplify the input, and provide the child with time to figure things out, these do not solve all the problems. Learning dance skills also requires the ability to interpret verbal instructions and demonstration, translate them into a mental representation, and monitor our performance as we try to reproduce them. These processes are largely dependent on the maturation of perceptual skills, which show major shifts between the young and older child.

Perceptual Skills

Perception involves the ability to attend to, organize, and interpret information from the body and the environment. Perceptual skills initially allow a learner to translate what she sees and hears into a mental picture of what she is supposed to do and then to feel what, where, and how she moves as she performs the dance skill. The sensations received from sense organs are organized and interpreted in the brain based on our past experience. The ability to act based on that information is dependent both on the maturation of the central nervous system and motor experiences. The teacher can tell a child that her shoulders are up, but that does not mean she can feel it or contract the right muscles to fix it.

Gabrielle Laurence

Figure 6.4
Older children can take the teacher's perspective and recognize that she is moving her right leg.

A child's perceptual skills are shaped by the kind and amount of motor skills experienced.[8] Many children brought up in a physical activity program consisting largely of sport skills have underdeveloped kinesthetic skills. It is almost impossible to separate a child's motor problems from perceptual problems and therefore it is customary to refer to skill development as perceptual-motor development.

Similarly, it is difficult to separate perceptual skills from cognitive skills. A child's cognitive spatial mapping ability, for example, has to come into play to help her correctly identify and interpret spatial patterns and directional changes, such as when she performs a square dance. It is not simply a question of taking in the visual information. Similarly, the ability to do mental rotation of spatial images is an essential component of seeing the teacher's demonstration and recognizing that the images have to be reproduced on the opposite side of the body.

Table 6.4	Perceptual Skills Related to Dance
Kinesthetic Skills	Body schema Laterality Inter-limb coordination
Spatial Skills	Directionality Mental rotation Visualization of abstract spatial patterns
Temporal Skills	Control tempo (slow, fast) Identify rhythms Reproduce rhythms Respond to/synchronize with, external tempo, rhythm
Perceptual Integration	Integrate visual and auditory cues in demonstration Coordinate spatial and temporal patterns in dance sequences Coincidence timing

An in-depth description of the developing perceptual system and related cognitive skills is beyond the scope of this book. However, it is important to understand the most relevant aspects of perceptual development for five-year-old to ten-year-old children taking part in dance activities. Components of perceptual development relevant for skill acquisition in dance are summarized in Table 6.4.

Kinesthetic Skills

Kinesthesis is "the conscious sensation of movement and/or limb positions."[26] Kinesthetic skills help the learner determine orientation in space, what parts of the body are moving where, how quickly and with how much force. These skills are essential for performing skilled, controlled motions. Kinesthetic skills or, more commonly called body awareness, function to let the learner know that she is tilted or upside down, that she has raised the hip up along with the lifted leg, that force was applied suddenly to throw the leg into the air, but controlled to float it back down. In general, the problem in young children is not that the information is not available from their senses. The problem tends to be too much sensory information, due to an inability to attend to and pick out the important cues. If the cues are attended to, the child also must remember this information and to act on it. These body awareness skills show a fairly predictable progression during childhood with major developments between 5 and 10 years.[8] Teachers can assess the kinesthetic development of young children by looking at how well they are able to perform a number of simple skills that demand body awareness. With a child of four or five years of age, we might look at her ability to isolate and move individual body parts (e.g., flex and extend ankles, rotate shoulders or tuck the head in as the spine curls). By six or seven, we could look at dynamic balance, in changing directions and stopping, at the coordination of both arms in space and time, or the coordination of arms and legs in simple gestures or locomotor patterns. The child's ability to discriminate small degrees of movement is still limited.

> Kinesthetic skills help the student determine orientation in space, what parts of the body are moving where, how quickly and with how much force.

With maturation and practice, body awareness becomes more precise. One would expect an older child to make fine adjustments in placement and have better control of small degrees of motion. She should be able to keep a longer sequence in memory. Developmental research labels these skills as "kinesthetic acuity" and "kinesthetic memory." To evaluate acuity, the child may be asked to discriminate between two similar limb positions[22] or reproduce movements and positions exactly.[27] Both skills are required if an older child is studying ballet, modern, or jazz technique. To study kinesthetic memory, the child may be asked to observe a number of skills and then reproduce them all in the correct order. Body awareness skills important for dance for the 5- to 10-year-old age group consist of several components: body schema, laterality, and inter-limb coordination.

Body Schema

The motion of the body is interpreted through a "body schema" or conceptual body map that has developed from past movement experiences. This schema is innate and an inherent part of the central nervous system,[8] but is incomplete. Active use of the body helps to build a complete body schema, which is the basis of accurate motor planning. It is also needed as a reference point to compare what we do. A preschooler still has a poor body schema as demonstrated by the inaccurate representation of body proportions and the missing body parts seen in nursery school stick drawings of people. By age five or six, most children can correctly label and isolate movement of specific body parts.[8] They respond appropriately to instructions (e.g., to bend the knees, elbows, turn the head, shrug the shoulders in games such as "Simon Says" or "Head, Shoulders, Knees and Toes"). However, they may not be able to monitor and control these movements very well. For example, one can expect that a young child would understand the actions required in a plié but not be aware that she was rolling in at the ankles and tilting the pelvis. A ten year old on the other hand would be expected to be able to attend to the feedback from her body during the movement. Without a fairly complete body schema, one cannot develop body awareness.

> Young children can identify and move individual body parts, but cannot monitor or control the motion yet.

Laterality

Part of the development of a body schema involves the concept of laterality. This is the conscious awareness that the body has a right and a left side, and the ability to correctly use the right and left limbs in activities. Children as young as age three and four understand that they have a right and left side to the body, although their ability to use the right or left arm or leg on command is little beyond a 50 percent chance. The ability to correctly label and use right and left may not be well established until seven or eight years of age.[1,4,8] Therefore, even as late as kindergarten and first grade, the response to the singing game of "Hokey-Pokey," or any other lateralized activity, will find children confusing right and left, watching other children, or copying the teacher. A related difficulty is crossing the midline, that is, reaching with the right arm into the left body space. There are major improvements between five and seven years of age, although some children may still have difficulty as late as age 10.[8]

The concept of laterality is different from lateral preference or dominance. Children and adults typically have a preference for using one hand and foot over the other. Children will, for example, have a preferred foot for hopping and galloping.[7] For most children, this preference is well established by the time they enter school, although teachers might encounter the occasional ambidextrous child who does not have a preference. Current educational thinking respects the child's right or left preference for writing or gross motor skills. However, respecting their preference does not mean limiting movement experiences to the preferred side. From a dance point of view, it limits a child or adult to have one "illiterate" side.[28] Sufficient opportunity should be given to develop basic competency on the non-preferred side (e.g., the child learns to start off on the left as well as the right foot, and to turn counter-clockwise as well as clockwise). This contributes to the full development of the body schema and the child's spatial awareness. However, for a five year old, instructions may have to start with "the other foot" or "the hand with the red not the green ribbon."

> Children should be given opportunities to develop skills on both the right and left leg and move in both directions.

Inter-limb Coordination

Finally, the integration of information from various parts of the body is critical in dance skills. The integration of right and left arms and legs is needed for a simple hop as well as the more complex leg gestures with accompanying arm patterns in ballet, modern, or jazz. Children age five or six, for example, cannot competently perform skills such as jumping jacks,[22] which require the rhythmical coordination of both sets of limbs. Correct skipping with controlled oppositional arm swing is the last locomotor skills to mature.[4] Even older students who are competent in walking with an oppositional arm action, can forget this coordination pattern when asked to perform exaggerated jazz lunge runs for the first time. Inter-limb coordination shows major improvements between the ages of 5 and 10. This should be kept in mind when planning locomotor patterns in dance that require accompanying arm gestures.

Spatial Skills

When the child travels around the room, she has to not only be aware of what her body is doing, but also be aware of her own and other people's location and motion in space. She also must be able to identify the spatial pattern of the dance activity and copy it in her own body. These are not simply visual skills (such as visual acuity and depth perception). Seeing and tracking large, slow moving objects such as other people in a room are present in infancy. As they run in a classroom, kindergarten-age children can see walls and visually track other moving children. This

Marliese Kimmerle

Figure 6.5
When traveling around the room, a child must be aware of her own and other people's location and motion in space.

activity does not present a visual perceptual problem, rather it is a dynamic balance and stopping problem if the child is not paying attention and going too fast. Interpreting the visual world of dance is a question of comprehending spatial concepts such as right and left, mirroring, spatial pathways and abstract geometric patterns. These spatial concepts combine the child's kinesthetic skills with the cognitive skills of the concrete operational stage[29] and develop between seven and ten years of age. By age 10 the child will have acquired these spatial skills — directionality, mental rotation, and the ability to visualize abstract patterns.

Directionality

Directionality is dependent on some basic navigation skills and the presence of laterality. Navigation skills, also called spatial mapping, describe the ability to mentally construct and remember a spatial pattern or pathway. Young children are able to understand simple pathways (e.g., follow the leader in a straight line or a circle) because they have simple map making skills. They can, for example, remember which door leads to the dressing room and which to the gymnasium and what sidewalks to cross to get to school. They understand that one can travel to either side or go forward or backward, but

> Understanding the direction and spatial pattern of skills is difficult for the young child.

they do not have a clear understanding of these directions. Five year olds need "traffic cop" assistance from the teacher if a singing game or walking dance requires anything more complex than the whole group moving in single file or around in a circle. Where laterality represents the child's concept of the right and left side of her body, directionality refers to the understanding that people and objects are located and move in directions, such as right, left, forward, and backward. Directionality may mature as late as 9 years of age.[1,8]

Most dance skills are taught with a directional pattern. For example, a locomotor pattern, such as step-together-step is shown moving to the right. A five or six year old cannot automatically detect that the direction of movement is to her right and left or that the pattern in a dance is counter-clockwise. This explains the frantic mother or dance instructor at a parent's night with four and five year olds, signaling off stage, as three children move right and one goes left in a thoroughly rehearsed routine.

Mental Rotation

Mental rotation, another spatial skill is the ability to rearrange or reverse a spatial pattern that is seen. It requires the presence of perspective taking – the ability to see the world from another's perspective rather than from an egocentric perspective. In a dance class, the practical application involves the ability to distinguish between copying and mirroring actions when the teacher demonstrates with her back to or facing the class. It also includes the ability to transfer a pattern learned on the right to the left side. The child has to distinguish between:

- The teacher has her back to me, and I am going to use the same leg she uses, or
- The teacher facing me is using her left foot and I am going to mirror her and use my right foot, or
- We are now going to do exactly the same combination we just learned to the left.

These abilities are not developed in the young child; therefore, she may need physical assistance to comprehend which side of the body to use. By age 10, children can accurately identify the right and left side of the facing person.[8]

Visualizing Abstract Spatial Patterns

A further extension of directionality is the capability to visualize complex spatial patterns, remember them, and then reproduced them. This is generally not developed until the child has reached seven to ten years of age. Complicated square or folk dance patterns are usually not attempted until the child is capable of recognizing and remembering spatial patterns. A contributing factor is that young children are still largely egocentric; they cannot take an external perspective and see the world or objects from an objective perspective.[29]

Temporal Skills

The ability to hear and interpret patterns of sound is clearly part of performing dance skills. As we have seen in Chapter 5, this involves both perceiving of the sound pattern and reproducing it. It includes auditory perception as well as the understanding of elements of rhythm such as beat, accent, meter, duration, patterns, and tempo.[30] Children begin to respond rhythmically to music at an early age, as they sway, rock, and bounce.[31] As they approach school age, children's singing and movements become more rhythmic. Children can move to their own rhythm before they can adjust to someone else's rhythm.[19] The developmental stages of rhythmic perception and understanding have been well documented; for example, most six year olds can maintain a steady beat, can discern fast from slow, and long from short.[31]

> Young children can slow down and speed up in self-paced movements but have difficulty adapting to the external cues of music.

Timing also involves being able to continue movement at a smooth, consistent, regular pace. This is difficult for the young child who cannot monitor and control movement sufficiently to carry out continuous repetitive movements such as clapping, banging, tapping, or hopping.[22] There is a definite gender advantage at the early ages for females, but major improvements have taken place by age nine for both sexes. Asking a young child to "dance" along with the music using a specific locomotor pattern will likely not result in a skilled performance, although it may well be a very enjoyable dance experience for the child.

Children from five years old onward are able to discern differences in rhythm patterns, although they are not necessarily able to reproduce them accurately. The ability to respond to changing patterns (to be flexible in timing or to adapt to other people's timing in a coincidence timing situation) is not fully developed until the age of 11 or 12. Music used for a young child, therefore, should have a predictable, regular beat without sudden shifts.

Perceptual Integration

In presenting the kinesthetic, spatial, and temporal skills above, it quickly becomes obvious that it is difficult to separate the role of one perceptual mode from another. Many dance skills involve the integration of all three. Adults being taught a dance skill can simultaneously watch the teacher demonstrate the step and listen to the instructions while marking the body movements. When they perform a skill they can listen to the accompaniment while simultaneously attending to feedback to correct body position, and visually monitoring where other people are in the room in order to avoid collisions. Dance patterns require that one carefully match where one is in space at a particular time in relation to others.

Young children have a limited ability to integrate and process multiple perceptual cues. Major shifts in perceptual integration skills occur between five and seven years but continue to improve until age

11 or 12.[8] In addition, sensory-motor integration, or paying attention to perceptual cues at the same time that the child is attempting to perform a skill creates difficulties (e.g., the child hears the music and is trying to control her body in a continuous hopping action). This integration problem severely limits the selection of complex dance skills or context and the teaching methods employed for demonstration, instruction, and feedback.

Coincidence timing is a specific example of perceptual integration. The anticipation and relating of one's own movement to adapt to that of another moving person or object is called "coincidence timing."[22] This is an essential component of working with a partner in folk dance. A grand right and left in square dance, for example, requires that each child pay attention to the speed and spatial pattern of locomotion to match that of the person ahead of her, and the person meeting her from the other direction.

Motor Planning and Control

Motor planning involves the assembly or the retrieval of motor plans for action. On the first day of a new skill, a plan of action must be assembled. The child who has practiced a 360-degree turn for weeks should have a completed plan for the turn that can quickly be retrieved from memory. Motor control involves the smooth, precise, and efficient execution of the movement. It is dependent on having a correct plan in place, the ability to monitor one's movements, and the ability to isolate and contract the appropriate muscles.

As noted in Chapter 5, experience and practice result in a large repertoire of more complete plans. These plans consist of well-rehearsed, automated subroutines that do not require attention. For inexperienced adults or children, planning is incomplete, attention demanding, and slow. An additional problem for young children is the processing limitations described earlier that affect not only receiving perceptual cues coming in, but also planning and controlling what goes out. Five and six year olds have difficulty planning simultaneous or continuously repeating actions of many body parts (such as continuous hopping or skipping) and doing any planning or adapting while they are in the midst of movement.[22,27] Planning long sequences of movements and reproducing them in correct order is also a problem.[25]

> **Young children cannot plan long sequences and are not adaptable planners.**

Referring back to the complexity model in Chapter 2, young children can handle single movements with few body parts in situations where little or no adaptation to external situations is required. They cannot plan "on the fly" nor can they quickly select appropriate alternatives (e.g., quickly changing direction to avoid an oncoming child). The complicated continuous sequences of actions in a typical technique class would likely be beyond their capabilities.

The controlled execution of a skill improves with practice, but is also subject to developmental limitations. Two of the most important limitations are force control and associated movements. Both involve the regulation of the amount of muscular contraction. There are major improvements in this regard between six and ten years of age. Young children cannot regulate or monitor the amount of force they use, therefore control of distance, speed, and body position is poor.[2] Initially, children must learn when and how to apply force and make their muscles contract on command, for example to tighten up their stomach or buttock muscles as they stand, or lift a leg, to learn to push off the ground and tighten up the rest of the body in a jump. With practice they learn when to apply force, but they still have difficulty controlling how much. They use too much force and overshoot or too little and cannot hold a position.

> Young children have difficulty controlling the amount and timing of muscle contractions.

A related problem is isolating and contracting only those muscles needed for efficient action and inhibiting associated movements, that is, extraneous contraction of muscles not needed for the action. A young child learning to use scissors, for example, often makes facial grimaces at the same time. The inhibition of this overflow contributes to learning to control movement and shows major improvements between the ages of five and eight.[32] The fine tuning and regulation of muscular control is largely dependent on central nervous system maturation. This limitation produces clumsiness, lack of coordination, exaggerated movement, and the inability to isolate specific body parts. A dance class where exact placement, minute body adjustments, and sudden changes of dynamics are required will produce difficulties for young learners.

Cognitive Skills

So far, we have looked at limitations in learning due to an inefficient flow of information through an immature brain and a lack of learning experiences. We must take a broader perspective on learning motor skills. Developmental limitations also exist in children's understanding, their thinking skills, and their problem-solving abilities. We have already identified the connection between kinesthetic skills and cognitive concepts of space. Cognitive theories such as Piaget's[29] are typically used to explain how ideas, concepts, and thinking skills develop and how these might affect skill learning.

According to Piaget's theory of cognitive development in children,[29] there is a major transition in thinking skills around age seven. This marks the shift from the pre-operational thinking of the young child (2 to 6 years of age) to the concrete operational stage of the older child (7 to 11 years of age). This is a shift from egocentric, here-and-now, perceptual thinking to the ability to abstract. "What you see is what you get" and "I am the center of the universe" represent the perspective of a five year

Table 6.5   Cognitive Skills Involved in Skills Acquisition

Task Comprehension	Understanding goal of task Comprehend skilled performance
Metacognition	Taking perspective Self regulating, monitoring Planning alternative
Abstract Thinking	Reasoning, problem solving, strategy use Conceptualizing of space, time Understanding rules

old. She understands ideas and concepts by experiencing them. A kindergarten child understands the concept of a circle by drawing one, or by joining hands and walking along lines on the floor, not by listening to the teacher explain the geometry of circles. The key aspect of the concrete operational stage is that the child develops logical thinking skills. She is able to organize and structure her thinking and begin to visualize abstract concepts. A ten year old should, therefore, be able to listen to instruction to go clockwise, then counter-clockwise, in and out of the circle, visualize this in her head, and do the pattern of a folk dance correctly without having to walk through it first.

These developmental changes in thinking processes affect the capability to acquire dance skills in terms of task comprehension, metacognition, and abstract thinking. The newly acquired cognitive skills are presented in Table 6.5.

Task Comprehension

A teacher of adult students can safely assume that they understand that the goal of the class is to strive toward skilled performance. For a young child the goal may be quite different – indulging in the physical sensation of jumping, twirling, and falling, for example, and being totally uninterested in "correct" performance. This is not an information flow problem but a difference in thinking between a young child and an older child or adult. The awareness that there are standards of correct performance is characteristic of the concrete operational and not the pre-operational child. Young children may be aware that adults have expectations of correct behavior and want to please them, but when left to their own inclinations, they may not comprehend the need to strive for a particular end product. In addition to being limited in their ability to remember the details of the skill, lacking the motor control to execute them correctly and not being able to monitor the outcome, young children may not have the slightest interest in error detection and correction.

Metacognition

The term "metacognition" can be broadly defined as an awareness of our own thinking, the ability to evaluate our own actions, and adjust our behavior accordingly. In other words we are able to step outside of ourselves and see what we are doing. It includes capabilities such as self-regulation, perspective taking, and the ability to weigh alternative choices of action. The presence of metacognitive skills is a prerequisite to the child's readiness to detect and correct errors. One has to be able to watch the skill being done and listen to the "voice in the head." An adult or older child can say, "watch out, you are going too fast; at this speed you'll get out of control, slow down." This type of self-regulation is well beyond the scope of a five year old, but develops in the older child. By 10 or 11, one can certainly expect a dance student to evaluate how she performs a skill, changes what she is doing, and strives to improve.

> The young child is not able to self-monitor or regulate her actions.

A part of self-regulation is an awareness of one's own limitations in relation to the demands of the dance skill (e.g., "Last time I tripped when I did this. I'd better come to a full stop, so I can go the other way."). This critical evaluation of one's own performance involves the cognitive skill of perspective taking and is not simply the ability to interpret sensory feedback.

Another aspect of metacognition is adaptive problem solving and decision making, the ability to evaluate a situation and to choose among alternatives. This is based on the understanding that there are other options. A pre-operational child is not able to simultaneous consider many aspects of a problem, mentally represent a series of actions, or ponder possible outcomes. A young child tends to be inflexible, with a fixed plan of action. Adaptable planning is typically not seen until 10 years or later.[27] A young child has a rigidity of thinking and often repeats the same mistakes over and over again. The teacher may have to point out other possibilities of doing the skill for the child.

Abstract Concepts

Earlier we pointed out that interpreting sensory input is dependent on an understanding of some abstract concepts. The most obvious examples in dance are space and time concepts. These concepts develop from infancy, starting with object play and our exploration of our surroundings. Motor experiences serve to build a foundation of concepts to help the child interpret her experiences. The ability to visualize a spatial pattern or comprehend the phrasing of the music in a complicated jazz routine or a folk dance requires concepts of spatial mapping and rhythm constructs.

Summary

The dance teacher must be conscious of the developmental limitations of children in order to select appropriate dance material and teaching methods. This chapter has outlined the limitations that a growing body, the lack of past motor learning experiences, and immature perceptual and cognitive skills place on the skill acquisition process in children. A particular focus has been on clarifying developmental shifts in perceptual and cognitive processes between younger and older children.

Although they have been discussed separately, perceptual and cognitive skills are interrelated and neither can be separated from motor skills in the developmental process. These essential components of how humans learn are interdependent. Perceptual and cognitive skills are developed through motor activity, and skillful movement is dependent upon them. The teacher of children, particularly young children, must be aware of these limitations, and either remove expectations of extensive skill development to simply allow the child to enjoy the experience of moving, or be prepared to offer a lot of external guidance, instruction, and evaluation to the child to lead her toward improving performance.

When selecting the dance material for young and older children and setting skill achievement goals, the limitations of physical, perceptual and cognitive development outlined in this chapter must be kept in mind. Later, in Chapter 9, we present guidelines for selecting appropriate material.

References

1. Gabbard CP: *Lifelong Motor Development,* (3rd ed). Boston: Allyn and Bacon, 2001.
2. Haywood KM: *Life Span Motor Development*, (2nd ed). Champaign, IL: Human Kinetics Publishers, Inc., 1993.
3. Thomas J: Children's motor skill development. *In:* Thomas JR (ed): *Motor Development During Childhood and Adolescence*. Minneapolis: Burgess Publishing Co., 1984, pp. 91-104.
4. Gallahue DL, Ozmun JC: *Understanding Motor Development: Infants, Children, Adolescents, Adults.* Boston: McGraw-Hill, 1998.
5. Magill RA: *Motor Learning: Concepts and Applications*, (4th ed). Madison, WI: Brown and Benchmark Publishers, 1993.
6. Seefeldt V: The concept of readiness applied to the acquisition of motor skills. *In:* Smoll FL, Smith RE (eds): *Children and Youth in Sport: A Biopsychosocial Perspective*. Dubuque IA: Brown and Benchmark, 1996, pp. 49-56.
7. Payne VG, Isaacs LD: Human Motor Development: A Lifespan Approach. Mountain View, CA: Mayfield Publishing Co., 1995.
8. Williams HG: *Perceptual and Motor Development*. Englewood Cliffs, NJ: Prentice-Hall, 1983.
9. Malina RM, Bouchard C: *Growth, Maturation, and Physical Activity.* Champaign, IL: Human Kinetics Publishers, Inc., 1991.
10. Cahill BR, Pearl AJ: *Intensive Participation in Children's Sports: American Orthopaedic Society for Sports Medicine.* Champaign, IL: Human Kinetics Publishers, Inc., 1993.
11. Smoll FL, Smith RE: *Children and Youth in Sport: A Biopsychosocial Perspective.* Dubuque IA: Brown and Benchmark, 1996.
12. Leard JS: Flexibility and conditioning in the young athlete. *In:* Micheli

LJ (ed): *Pediatric and Adolescent Sports Medicine*. Boston: Little Brown and Co., 1984, pp. 194-210.

13. Howse AJG: The young ballet dancer. *In:* Ryan AJ, Stephens RE (eds): *Dance Medicine: A Comprehensive Guide*. Chicago: Pluribus Press, Inc., 1987, pp. 107-114.

14. Teitz CC: Sports medicine concerns in dance and gymnastics. Pediatric Clinics of North America 29(6):1399-1421, 1982.

15. Solomon R, Micheli LJ, Ireland ML: Physiological assessment to determine readiness for pointe work in ballet students. Impulse 1:21-39, 1993.

16. Barringer J, Schlesinger S: *The Pointe Book: Shoes, Training and Technique*. Princeton, NJ: Dance Horizons, 1998.

17. Thomas JR: Children's control, learning and performance of motor skills. Research Quarterly for Exercise and Sport 71(1):1-8, 2000.

18. Micheli LJ, LaChabrier L: The young female athlete. *In:* Micheli LJ (ed): *Pediatric and Adolescent Sports Medicine*. Boston: Little Brown and Co., 1984, pp. 167-178.

19. Roberton MA, Halverson LE: *Developing Children: Their Changing Movements: A Guide for Teachers*. Philadelphia: Lea and Febiger, 1984.

20. Gallahue DL, Ozmun JC: *Understanding Motor Development: Infants, Children, Adolescents, Adults*. Boston: McGraw-Hill, 1998, p. 210.

21. Gabbard CP: *Lifelong Motor Development*, (2nd ed). Dubuque, IA: Brown and Benchmark, 1996, p. 6.

22. Keogh J, Sugden D: *Movement Skill Development*. New York: Macmillan, 1985.

23. Schmidt RA, Lee TD: *Motor Learning and Control: A Behavioral Emphasis*. Champaign, IL: Human Kinetics Publishers, Inc., 1999.

24. Singer RN: Motor skills and learning strategies. *In:* O'Neil HF (ed): *Learning Strategies*. New York: Academic Press, 1978.

25. Weiss MR, Klint KA: "Show and tell" in the gymnasium: An investigation of developmental differences in modeling and verbal rehearsal of motor skills. Research Quarterly for Exercise and Sport 58(2):234-241, 1987.

26. Rose DJ: *A Multilevel Approach to the Study of Motor Control and Learning*. Boston: Allyn and Bacon, 1997, p. 104.

27. Lazlo JI, Bairstow PJ: *Perceptual-Motor Behavior: Developmental Assessment and Therapy*. New York: Praeger, 1985.

28. Kimmerle M: Lateral bias in dance teaching. Journal of Health, Physical Education, Recreation and Dance 72(5):34-37, 2001.

29. Piaget J: *The Origin and Intelligence of Children*. New York: International Universities Press, 1952.

30. Côté-Laurence P: Development of rhythm literacy for dancers. *In:* Young Overby L, Côte-Laurence P (eds): *Dance Education: A Lifetime of Experiences*: Proceedings of the Focus on Dance Education Conference. Reston, VA: The National Dance Association, 1996.

31. Campbell PS, Scott-Kassner C: *Music in Childhood*. New York: Schirmer Books, 1995.

32. Wolff PH, Gunnoe CE, Cohen C: Associated movements as a measure of developmental age. Developmental Medicine and Child Neurology 25:417-239, 1983.

Josie Hazen

What is an Experienced Dancer?

The Role of Practice

   Physical Abilities

   Repertoire of Dance Skills

   Learning Abilities – Information Processing Abilities

What is an Expert Dancer?

   Knowledge Base

   Body Structure

   Information Processing Abilities

   Practice

Chapter 7

The Experienced Dancer

Having looked at the capabilities and limitations of the novice adult and the child learner in the two previous chapters, we now turn to the third category of learners, the experienced dancer. The experienced dancer has accumulated many years of training and performing, and has reached a high level of skill proficiency. An experienced learner differs from a beginner, not only in physical, but in mental abilities as well. Some teachers prefer to work with advanced students, while others excel with beginners. Regardless of their teaching preferences, teachers who have experienced working with both groups can describe ways in which beginners differ from experienced students. In this chapter, we examine the characteristics of an experienced dancer, the role of extensive practice on learning and performance, and finally, the development of expertise in dance.

What is an Experienced Dancer?

In advanced classes, most students have danced for a number of years. They have taken technique classes in one, two, or sometimes three dance forms, and have performed in concerts. They have superior physical capabilities, are fast learners, and solid performers. They are what we may call ideal students. You notice however that other students are not quite at that level, yet they seem to have the same amount of experience. How do we explain that? Let us first differentiate between skill, skilled action, and a skilled or skillful performer. In this text, a skill is a learned motor action. A skilled action or performance is one produced with maximum proficiency and ease. It may be a jazz pirouette executed with a clear and stable beginning and ending, the body pivoting around its perfectly vertical axis, or a grand jeté executed with vertical and horizontal flight, and fully extended legs at the peak of the jump. A skilled or skillful dancer is someone who is very good or particularly adept at performing dance skills.

Only when the dancer has reached a certain level of mastery can his actions be referred to as skilled. According to motor learning theory, a skilled dancer is someone who has acquired consistency in performance, self-monitoring capabilities, and adaptability.[1,2] These characteristics are the result of highly refined physical and mental capabilities which, in turn, produce superior performance.

> An experienced dancer demonstrates consistency in performance, self-monitoring capabilities, and adaptability.

A skilled dancer is one who can perform a skill over and over again at will and in exactly the same fashion. Recall that one of the characteristics of the attempt stage is inconsistency in performance. Experienced dancers show more consistency than beginners. When a dance skill is performed the same way, its temporal and spatial features remain relatively stable from one execution to the next.[1] Consistency in performance is attained as an individual gains mastery over the skill, meaning that he now has in memory a refined image and plan of action for that skill. His movements appear smoother, and his performance almost effortless. An experienced dancer has developed a high level of motor control, and is therefore reliable and predictable on stage.

The second characteristic of an experienced dancer is his ability to detect and correct errors. The skilled learner is able to monitor his performance internally, thus no longer requiring extrinsic feedback from the instructor or the mirror. He has developed the ability to recognize problems in the skill. For example, familiarity with the skill and a keen kinesthetic sense tell the dancer that his arms were lifted too high or his feet were not together during the jump. The ability to detect and correct errors is closely linked to the kinesthetic sense. The skilled dancer senses his body movements and positions very precisely. He has, for example, developed an accurate mental image of the technically correct jump, and this image includes the sensory information associated with that jump.

> Through a refined kinesthetic sense, the experienced dancer can detect and correct movement errors accurately and rapidly.

The third characteristic of an experienced dancer is adaptability, his ability to adapt to changes in the environment. You all know students who manage to perform beautifully regardless of environmental changes such as smaller stage space, deficient sound system, or personal motivation. These students have learned to adapt their performance to fit the present condition. Because they can do so remarkably well, the audience is often unaware of the difficulty. As described in Chapter 5, performance in dance is fairly predictable. Most dance skills are closed, and are generally learned and rehearsed the way they will be performed on stage. Nonetheless, skills are rarely performed exactly the same way twice. Each performance brings its own context. An experienced dancer is able to perceive environmental changes and to adjust quickly. Skilled performers are capable of modifying their action, even as it is being performed.[1] A dancer's capability to adapt to changes increases with his progress in learning a skill, which is a function of extensive practice.[2] Dancers who possess this extraordinary ability have acquired high motor proficiency and are, therefore, dependable performers.

The Role of Practice

How does one become skilled in a particular area? How does a dance student progress along the skill-learning continuum? Practice is required for any motor skill to be mastered. Consider the daily routine of world-renowned professional dancers who religiously practice each day to maintain their performance level and take classes to expand their skill vocabulary. The question is: Does practice alone guarantee attainment of high skill level? Motor learning theory questions the old adage "practice makes perfect." Rather, it argues that skill development and mastery only come with meaningful and guided practice[3] (perfect practice makes perfect). Practice represents the essence of the learning process described in Chapter 4.

Empirical evidence argues that an individual can improve a specific skill by practicing that skill, not variations of it.[3] This makes perfect sense for dance skills which are closed and serial in nature. For example, students will learn a stylized locomotor step by practicing it until it is performed well. Practicing a variation of the step would not help learn the targeted stylized step. Likewise, an allegro combination can only be perfected by practicing it repeatedly. Because the experienced dancer knows all the individual steps, his main challenge is to link each step and its coordinated arm and head movements into a fluid dance phrase, and perform it to a musical phrase. The dancer will perfect the combination by repeating it as many times as necessary. However, when skills are being learned in class, the element of motivation must be considered. Students may be bored by practicing a skill the same way over and over. Even experienced dancers can get bored when not challenged. Bringing variation to a learning task helps keep students focused and motivated. For example, if the technical point of linking elements together is one of the goals of the course, the teacher would want students to have as many different experiences as possible rather than practicing the same sequence over and over again. Exactly what does practice do? Practice influences the dancer's physical abilities, repertoire of dance skills, and learning abilities.

Physical Abilities

High physical capabilities come about as a result of a fine-tuned body control system, a system composed of neuromuscular mechanisms that underlie the production of movement. With extensive practice, the expe-

Marliese Kimmerle

Figure 7.1
Over years of practice, advanced dancers have acquired a high level of motor control.

rienced dancer has refined his basic motor abilities and skills. Physically, the skilled dancer has greater body control than the inexperienced dancer. He has better balance, coordination, agility, a correct body alignment, and greater stamina. The experienced dancer has accumulated thousands of mental images and motor plans for all categories of motor skills and is consequently able to perform a wide variety of skills and learn new combinations of these skills with relative ease. The skilled dancer is knowledgeable about his body and can move efficiently in a variety of dance contexts.

Repertoire of Dance Skills

Advanced dancers have acquired a high level of motor control as a result of years of practice. Consequently, they are able to perform complex dance skills with remarkable ease and manipulate the skills to adapt to new situations. They are able to perform all six categories of body actions, with numerous variations in components, and within a large variety of contexts. Skilled dancers have mastered the repertoire of one, and sometimes two or more dance forms. An experienced dancer has acquired a solid control of center, one of the foundations for all dance technique training and performance. This allows him to correctly perform dance skills involving changes in base of support, gestures, rotation, elevation, and locomotion. A keen sense of balance is another category of body action mastered by an experienced dancer. As a result, he can consistently demonstrate solid arabesques or attitudes specific to a dance form. Years of training in rotation and elevation provide the dancer with the ability to perform complex locomotor patterns that often combine most if not all categories of dance actions.

In addition to greater control of body actions, experienced dancers can manipulate at will components that color a body action and make it a dance skill. A skilled dancer can perform any number of body actions with a specific time, space, and force quality. You probably have examples of advanced students who can demonstrate a sequence of skills originally learned with a 3/4 meter, transform it to fit a 4/4 meter, or perform it at a faster tempo. These students are able to make all sorts of spatial adjustments regarding directions or levels, or vary muscular tension to produce different aesthetic images.

> Experienced dancers are able to perform all six categories of body actions, with numerous variations in components, and within a large variety of contexts.

The third aspect affected by practice is the context, or the situation in which the dance skill is performed. As they have reached the autonomous learning stage, experienced dancers are better able to focus on the context of the dance skills. Skilled dancers differ greatly from beginners in their ability to perform with other dancers, their ability to synchronize their actions to music, and their ability to combine long phrases of actions that have specific pathways. Advanced students have danced to a variety of accompaniments, from percussion, lyrical music, sounds, voice, to contemporary abstract and non-metric music. The great advantage they have over beginners is the experience of moving with different textures of sounds. These in turn stimulate contrasting qualities and aesthetics in movement. Additionally, skilled dancers are able to pay attention to other dancers around them while performing, a skill with which less experienced dancers would have difficulty.

In summary, skilled dancers have acquired a tremendous vocabulary of dance skills. Dance skills are second nature to them. In fact, it is not uncommon to see advanced students who are strong in more than one form of dance. The third factor influenced by practice is the dancer's learning abilities.

Learning Abilities – Information Processing Abilities

What makes a skilled dancer able to learn more quickly than a beginner, memorize longer sequences, pay attention to relevant cues and ignore the others, or capture the essence of a phrase seen for the first time? Skilled dancers can do everything better and faster than novices. Why? As they have accumulated an impressive record of dance experiences, these dancers have also acquired special learning abilities that are based on their superior capability to process information. These include perceptual, attention, memory, and error detection and correction abilities.

Perceptual Abilities

Through extensive practice, experienced dancers have developed keen visual, kinesthetic, and auditory perceptual skills. They have mastered ways to rapidly detect, identify, and recognize the specifics of a demonstrated movement. This means that, for these dancers, in contrast with beginners, one demonstration is usually sufficient to give them a sense of the new movement. You see them immediately repeat the movement quite accurately, unless of course it is from a totally new style and repertoire. It is easy for experienced dancers to pick up all relevant cues, form a mental image of the movement, retrieve or construct a motor plan, and finally execute the movement. Their refined kinesthetic sense provides an additional source of information as they watch the demonstration. They know how the movement feels. For these learners, the attempt stage is relatively short and simplistic.

> Unlike beginners, experienced learners are able to see, feel, and hear important cues simultaneously when watching a demonstration.

Another characteristic of skilled learners is their ability to perceive information coming from more than one modality at once. Experienced dancers have a high capacity to detect the movements of many body parts at the same time, as well as their respective spatial, force, and temporal features. In addition to a refined kinesthetic awareness, skilled dancers typically have a greater sense of rhythm than beginners. Considering that counts are important in dance skill learning, advanced dancers truly have an advantage over beginners. With practice, they have improved their ability to identify complex elements of rhythm, and discriminate between durations, meters, and patterns. Experienced dancers, some more than others, have refined rhythmic abilities specific to dance.

Experienced learners have gained an impressive knowledge base in dance, and therefore know how to learn, what to look for, what to ignore, and what aspects of the movements are more important for efficient performance. One of the challenges faced by teachers of advanced students is to keep them motivated to learn. This may best be accomplished by selecting material that is complex enough to warrant their attention and stimulate their interest. Research indicates that advanced students may pay less attention to dance material that is too easy, and may be less motivated to learn it.[4] To a certain extent, perceptual abilities are not easily dissociated from a learner's attention capacity, especially when considering skilled learners.

Attention Capacity

Attention is a limited, serial, and selective capacity. With practice however, this capacity can be stretched to meet the demands of the task. In contrast to beginners, skilled dancers do not need help in detecting important cues when watching the demonstration of a new skill sequence. Experience tells them what to look at, what is important and what is not. For example, they can notice how the sequence begins, which body parts are most active, which part of the sequence requires the most muscular force, whether there is repetition or not, and how the sequence ends. Experienced dancers have developed attention capacity that allows them to process great amounts of visual, auditory, and kinesthetic informa-

Josie Hazen

Figure 7.2
Experienced dancers can
produce aesthetically
pleasing positions. They
have mastered a keen sense
of proper body alignment.

tion. They learn a skill faster, therefore can handle more content during a lesson than can beginners. Additionally, they are not easily distracted by outside information that is irrelevant to the skill. For the most part, advanced students are focused and relatively independent learners.

Memory Capacity

Practice and experience play a critical role in the development of short-term memory capacity. A learning strategy most important in dance is the ability to memorize large amounts of information. This strategy is especially crucial when dealing with serial skills such as those found in dance. The effect of practice can be clearly seen on the memory capacity of skilled dancers. In contrast to beginners, skilled dancers have learned to chunk information efficiently, therefore leaving enough memory space for other information. Experimental evidence with dancers supports this view.[4] It was demonstrated that advanced dancers used different strategies for learning and remembering jazz sequences than novice dancers. Subjects viewed the dance sequences via a videotaped demonstration by a professional dancer. After given fifteen minutes to learn each sequence, participants were asked to perform it. Although both groups used counting to facilitate recall of the steps, the advanced subjects differed from the novices in two ways. First, they used more aspects of the music to facilitate retention than novices. In addition to the beat, they used pitch changes, specific instruments, and rhythmic groupings. A second difference was their ability to chunk steps into larger items than novices. Novices encoded each individual step as one item, whereas advanced dancers grouped steps according to a dance skill. For example, a "step-together-step" would be three separate items for a novice while it would be a "chassé" for an experienced dancer. Advanced dancers also grouped the steps according to musical phrases, something the novices could not do.

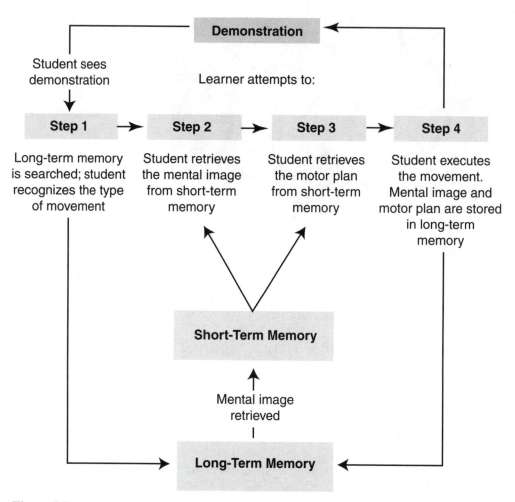

Figure 7.3
The role of short-term and long-term memory during the experienced dancer's attempt stage.

Since advanced dancers have so much information stored in long-term memory, it is easy for them to retrieve a skill they need and adapt it to the new context. Figure 7.3 illustrates this point. Recall that beginner adults do not have dance experiences in long-term memory (*see* Fig. 5.6). In contrast, skilled dancers rarely start from scratch. We all have memories of students performing successfully in several choreographies during the end of term recital. We can also appreciate the incredible background of professional dancers who have learned a large number of dances over the course of their career.

Finally, another benefit of a well-furnished long-term memory is the potential for transfer. Transfer of learning may be defined as the gain (or loss) in the capability for performance on one skill as a result of experience on some other skill.[5] Transfer may be from one skill to another skill, or from a skill learned on one side of the body to the other side, the latter being termed bilateral transfer. Although empirical evidence indicates that transfer is generally minimal, and only between similar skills, it is common belief among dance teachers that students who have mastered basic skills tend to transfer their proficiency in those skills to new skills. There are countless examples of students who are proficient in one dance form, and who tend to transfer their knowledge and motor capabilities into learning another dance form. It would seem that students who have a great deal of experience in dance certainly approach a new dance skill with a totally different frame of mind than a novice student. With experience comes confidence and a host of other factors that, indirectly perhaps, influence learning. Consequently, advanced dancers are better able to face new skills than beginners.

One of the few studies looking at transfer in dance suggests that bilateral transfer does occur in dance, but not necessarily in the direction typically used in traditional dance teaching.[6] Under four treatment conditions of practice (one demonstration, one practice; one demonstration, several practices), and direction of transfer (preferred to non-preferred side; non-preferred to preferred side), novice and experienced dance students watched one demonstration of a complex eight-movement dance sequence. They were asked to either practice it once or several times, and then to perform the sequence on the opposite side. The significant finding was the unexpected direction of transfer from the non-preferred to the preferred side. Basically, this means that learning a sequence on the non-preferred side first will facilitate learning on the preferred side to a greater extent than learning the sequence on the preferred side first. Of course, findings from only one experiment are not sufficient to make a definite statement about how dance should be taught. There is not doubt that transfer of learning in dance must be further investigated.

Error Detection and Correction Capacity

The last mental process affected by practice is the ability to monitor ongoing performance. The skilled dancer has developed over the years a keen sense of kinesthesis in addition to an "eye" and "ear" for dance. These perceptual abilities, in addition to a great attention and memory capacity, provide the necessary tools for the learner to monitor his own performance. It is always rewarding for a teacher to watch an advanced student practice a complex dance skill and know exactly which parts need work and which do not. That student is able to compare the skill just executed with his memory of the correct skill, and make proper adjustments for the next try. What did the teacher do to produce such an independent learner? It is suggested that, as learners become more skilled, they rely more on intrinsic feedback (feedback produced by their movements) than they do on the extrinsic feedback of their teacher.[7] Efficient teachers know that, and therefore train their students to pay more and more attention to what their body tells them.

Although he may not have performed the new skill before, the advanced dancer has likely executed components and variations of it. Mental

Table 7.1   Characteristics of Experienced Dancers Throughout the Learning Process

Stages	Characteristics
Attempt	**The experienced dancer understands the new skill presented visually and verbally**
	Has keen visual, kinesthetic, and auditory perceptual abilities
	Can perceive the entire skill at once
	Can detect all relevant visual and auditory cues and ignore irrelevant ones
	Can analyze all components of the skill accurately and rapidly
	Can recall all components of a skill or all skills of a sequence in the proper order
	The experienced dancer has acquired a large number of dance images in long-term memory
	Can retrieve the proper mental image of the skill from long-term memory and bring it to short-term memory
	Can retrieve or construct an accurate motor plan for the new skill
	Can execute the new dance skill successfully
Correct	**The experienced dancer has stored in long-term memory sensory images of how the correct movement "feels"**
	Can monitor his own performance by attending to internal feedback provided by the movement itself; does not rely on external feedback from the instructor
	Can anticipate the next or a specific beat; can synchronize accurately
	Can identify elements of rhythm accurately
	Can detect and correct movement errors accurately and rapidly
Perfect	**The experienced dancer has developed a highly refined control of his body**
	Can perform complex dance skills successfully and consistently
	Can adapt to a change, modify a movement, and perform successfully on stage

images and kinesthetic sensations of these variations are brought back from long-term to short-term memory for evaluation of the new skill. A new plan of action is prepared and a skilled action is then produced. These students are constantly refining one aspect of the skill or another. They are self-sufficient and always seem to be practicing to improve their performance.

In summary, skilled dancers have developed a capacity to learn and perform dance skills at a level significantly greater than novice dancers. They have gained a knowledge base in dance that allows them to be highly efficient performers onstage. Table 7.1 is a summary of the characteristics of skilled dancers that represent all stages of the learning process. A careful review of the components is helpful in understanding how experienced dancers differ from novices.

There are different categories of skilled athletes and performers. Highly skilled athletes perform at the professional level while highly skilled dancers perform in professional dance companies in international and world events. Do all experienced or skilled dancers reach the highest level of skill mastery? As you well know, years of training in dance or sport alone do not always lead to superior performance. All novices do not become experts. It is not uncommon to see students who, after having reached a certain level of motor competency, fail to reach mastery. There are many skilled dancers, but how many reach national and international recognition in dance?

What is an Expert Dancer?

The topic of expertise has been intensely debated in the movement sciences over the last decade or so.[8-10] According to studies conducted with athletes, dancers, and musicians, there are clear differences between novices and experts. The first differentiating characteristic of expert performers is that they know a lot about their activity. The knowledge base they have acquired over years of practice provides them with the tools to make decisions and solve motor problems faster and more accurately than non-experts. Consequently, experts, whether dancers, musicians, or athletes, are exceptional performers. They also display superior mental capabilities. The question is: How does one become an expert? Some scientists argue that expertise is determined by innate attributes while others maintain that practice is the determining factor. It has been proposed that a more encompassing view of expertise, one that integrates biological and environmental factors may be a more sensible theory.[10]

Knowledge Base

In certain disciplines, experts are often known as super brains. These individuals have been endowed with gifted mental capabilities specific to their field. Expertise is related to the knowledge one has in a particular area. Two kinds of knowledge have been proposed by cognitive psychologists, declarative knowledge and procedural knowledge. Declarative knowledge or "knowing that," is conscious and explicit knowledge that can be expressed verbally. Procedural knowledge, or "knowing how," is implicit knowledge that is unconscious, and not easily explained verbally.[11] These two kinds of knowledge are associated with performance differences between experts and novice athletes, and experts display high procedural knowledge.[12] Over time and with experience, an expert dancer has gained a superior procedural knowledge base that allows him to successfully perform highly complex dance sequences, and adapt to new situations rapidly and correctly. In dance, declarative knowledge refers to knowing about the skills and steps learned in technique training, whereas procedural knowledge is being able to perform highly

> Expert dancers have a superior procedural knowledge base that allows them to successfully perform highly complex dance sequences, and adapt to unplanned situations rapidly and efficiently.

complex dance skills and sequences successfully in a variety of settings.

The concept of expertise may be linked to the theory of multiple intelligences proposed in the early 1980s.[13] The theory postulates that there are seven intelligences: linguistic, musical, spatial, mathematical, body-kinesthetic, intrapersonal, and interpersonal. A dance expert is someone who has achieved superior bodily-kinesthetic intelligence coupled with several other intelligences such as musical intelligence. This view is supported by a dance researcher who states that, in order to perform at a high level, a dancer must possess the majority if not all of the other intelligences.[14] In dance, not only do we have experts in each dance form, but we also go a level deeper and label these experts according to the method they promote: experts of the Cecchetti method, Graham or Limon experts, and so on. What these experts have in common is mastery of a specific technique of movement. Within the field of dance, therefore, one becomes an expert performer in a specific form.

> According to the theory of multiple intelligences, dance experts have achieved the highest level of bodily-kinesthetic intelligence, coupled with other intelligences such as musical intelligence.

One's knowledge base is developed through experience in a specific area. Renowned choreographers, critics, performers, teachers, historians, and therapists represent but a few specific domains in the various fields of study in dance. These experts have developed a superior knowledge base that distinguishes them from experienced peers. One becomes good at what one does by doing it over time. For example, a dancer improves her performance by practicing over an extended period of time. What else can he do well besides perform? Can a knowledge base transfer over other areas of expertise? Can knowledgeable performers critique dance or create meaningful dance sequences? Empirical evidence on these questions is scarce.

In two related studies, questions concerning differences between expert and naive dancers were addressed. The first study compared experienced dancers' creative abilities with those of naive dancers.[15] The second examined the preferences of expert performers and experienced teachers in assessing videotaped dance sequences.[16] Participants in the first study (eight individuals ranging from novice to 25 years of experience) were individually administered a creativity test. In a limited time period, they were asked to create and present three distinct dance sequences, each made up of seven basic body actions organized in a specific order. The analyses were based on body actions, space configuration, movement quality, and transitions. The videotaped sequences clearly showed differences between experts and novices, not only in the number of different movement ideas, but in their contextual relevance and overall aesthetic quality as well. The naive participants' sequences included basic body actions, with linear floor patterns, and minimal dynamic changes and transitions. The most experienced dancer, on the other hand, created complex sequences of dance skills organized in diverse spatial and dynamic configurations, and with smooth transitions.

In the second experiment, two experienced Laban-based creative dance teachers working at the university level, and two professional modern dancers, were asked to analyze videotapes of three short sequences created and performed by one naive and one expert dancer (each of whom had participated in the first study). The four criteria used in the first study were also used to analyze the sequences. Teacher judges and professional dancer judges' analyses differed in three aspects, terminology, quantity of information, and movement preferences. However, all judges agreed that the expert's sequences were aesthetically pleasing, while the aesthetic context was absent in the naive subject's sequences.

Although limited in sample size, these studies provide some insight into the knowledge base of experts and novices, and suggest that dance practice may be the leading factor in the development of knowledge in dance expertise.

From our experience teaching individuals of all skill levels, and watching professional dancers perform in a number of dance forms, we know that outstanding students and dancers, in addition to a superior body of knowledge in dance, are gifted with special innate physical attributes. According to the literature, several genetic predispositions have been identified as possible predictors of expertise: personality traits, intelligence, physical characteristics, and information processing abilities.[17]

Body Structure

Is there such a thing as a perfect body for dance? Could we say that a mesomorphic body type is most suitable for modern dance?[18] It has been argued that, "because sport and dance are associated with ideal physical requirements (e.g., body dimensions, a body free from injury and ill health, and a body conditioned to yield superior performance), domains that emphasize movement mastery are somewhat different from many other domains."[19,20] We know that tall and large dancers are at a disadvantage in ballet for obvious reasons. Balanchine was known for his preference for a particular female body type in his ballets.

Although physical traits such as skeletal frame size, bone width and length, and percent body fat can be altered by other factors during the growing years, they are mostly genetically determined. Students who have a large skeletal frame may be faced with difficulties in most ballet classes because their body does not allow them to be highly flexible. Likewise, students with problematic hip joints, back, or feet may encounter limitations in their technique. In this regard, there may be little that can be done. These students will reach a certain level of competency with practice, but are unlikely to become experts. An ideal body struc-

Panagiota Klentrou

Figure 7.4
An expert dancer can perform with superior technical skills, with feeling, sensitivity, musicality, and artistry.

ture for dance, whatever that may be, might be what distinguishes experts from skilled dancers. Jazz, in contrast to ballet, may require a more muscular body whereas dance forms such as folk and creative dance may accept a greater range of body structures.

An expert can perform with great technical skills, with feeling, aesthetic awareness, grace, sensitivity, musicality, and great artistry. Much more than a strong technician, an expert dancer is able to deliver a personalized interpretation of the message the choreographer wishes to give the audience. In addition to a gifted body structure, an expert differs from a skilled dancer in his ability to comprehend and assimilate information rapidly and accurately. Consequently, he is able to execute a complex and long dance sequence immediately after seeing it the first time. This cognitive ability is due to a superior body of knowledge acquired over the years. Although an individual's mental capacity is genetically determined, environmental conditions can enhance that capacity. Experts have mastered the ability to accurately and rapidly process information from their body and the environment.

> Physical factors, although mostly genetically defined, can be modified through intensive training during the growing years.

Information Processing Abilities

Successful motor performance is often linked with the performer's ability to detect, perceive, and use appropriate sensory information to plan a motor response.[2] The learning abilities associated with experienced dancers are even more refined in experts. Expert athletes have acquired greater mental capabilities and domain-specific knowledge than novice athletes.[8,19,21] They have superior perceptual and attention abilities, therefore are faster at recognizing visual patterns and organizing information in meaningful units. They display unusual recall and error detection and correction abilities, therefore can memorize larger amounts of information than experienced dancers and are self-sufficient learners. These abilities represent the "know how" or implicit procedural knowledge in dance.

Empirical studies on expertise in dance are few. The research reported here is concerned mostly with memory and retention. One well-known research effort compared young experts' ability to recall structured and unstructured ballet sequences with that of young novice dancers.[21] The young experts were students at the National Ballet School of Canada, and the novice group consisted of young students who attended local ballet schools. Subjects were asked to view a videotaped sequence of eight ballet steps presented twice, and to immediately attempt to recall it either by naming the steps or performing them. There were two types of sequences, sequences choreographed by dance experts, and sequences composed of randomly selected steps. Results indicate that both groups recalled the ballet sequences better than the random sequences, and that the young experts displayed higher recall than the novices. However, as expected according to the relation between skill level and game structured information,[22] no differences were found in the recall of the unstructured sequences between experts and novices, indicating that expertise is domain specific, and that young experts have already acquired superior memory abilities. Similar results were found in modern dance.[23]

The study[21] examined another variable most pertinent in dance learning, that is, the effect of music on the recall of dance steps. Young experts watched the eight step sequences with music and were then asked to perform them with or without music. Interestingly, the rate of recall was greater when the experts performed them with the music than without. This may indicate that the young experts had encoded both visual and auditory information from the demonstration and that music facilitated recall of the steps.

A recent experiment with advanced and novice jazz dancers examined differences in learning and retention strategies between both groups.[4] Subjects were given 15 minutes to learn a videotaped jazz sequence and were then asked to perform it after a brief rest interval. They were free to view the videotape as many times as they wanted during the learning period. Participants were filmed during the entire study. The findings indicated differences in learning strategies between both groups. Contrary to novice dancers, expert dancers relied on music, chunked information differently, and used verbalization during rehearsal. In addition to paying attention to the demonstration, advanced students were able to selectively attend to several aspect of the music and to use them to facilitate retention, whereas novice students tried to ignore the music, as it interfered with learning the steps. The differences found in the chunking strategies were another interesting finding. Advanced students organized the dance sequences into fewer but larger segments of movements while novices tended to encode each step or movement as a separate item. For example, an advanced dancer would encode a "chassé" as one item, but it would be four items for a novice student: "step, together, step, pause." Finally, advanced dancers incorporated small hand and foot gestures and verbalization as a way to rehearse the steps prior to performing them, while the novices did not.

Expert dancers showed different learning strategies than novices. They processed music as part of dance skills, encoded information into larger items, and used verbalization and hand/foot gestures to help memorization.

Studies on expertise in artistic sports may contribute to understanding the mental processes of dance experts. For example, when compared to novice gymnasts, expert gymnasts were more successful at identifying which body parts provided the most useful information about the performance of a skill.[24] These results indicate that experts have learned to recognize key features in a movement and to ignore unimportant features. In other words, they are able to selectively attend to meaningful visual information. Such findings may be applied to dance skills, as both dance and gymnastics are comprised of closed and serial, static and dynamic skills. Research is needed in this area to understand the mental capabilities of dance experts. Knowing how dance experts process information as they learn and perform would certainly shed light into how instructors should teach students to become good dancers.

In summary, dance experts have been genetically endowed with gifted innate physical and cognitive abilities. It is clear that these alone are not sufficient to produce talent. This is when practice and training come into play.

Practice

There are two theories on the development of expertise. The first theory proposes that expertise is genetically transmitted.[9] According to this view, talent is a consequence of innate gifts. Balanchine, the great choreographer, shared this view, as he stated that:

> One is born to be a great dancer. No teacher can work miracles, nor will years of training make a good dancer of an untalented pupil. One may be able to acquire a certain technique facility, but no one can ever "acquire an exceptional talent." I have never prided myself on having an unusually gifted pupil. A Pavlova is no one's pupil but God's.[25]

This theory meets opposition in the field of research on expertise, because it seems to be an obvious conclusion that if innate talent is not nurtured then it is unlikely to grow to its full potential.

The second theory argues that expertise is determined solely by deliberate practice,[8] negating the contribution of genetic factors. The proponents of deliberate practice argue that it takes a minimum of ten years or 10,000 hours of practice to develop expertise. The main point of the theory is that practice is the key element in the development of talent, and that a minimum of ten years of intensive full-time preparation is required to achieve international status in sports, dance, and music. Although the deliberate practice concept has been under scrutiny for the last two decades by those promoting the role of genetics in the development of expertise, it is clear that practice will continue to play a major role in explaining expertise.

In dance, we all know that outstanding dancers have started dancing at a very early age. In fact, the ten-year rule finds anecdotal support from Martha Graham's claim that it takes ten years to make a mature dancer.[26] By practice we mean, of course, a serious commitment and dedication to dance, a commitment so strong that these individuals are able to maintain the motivation to train the body under the most strenuous conditions.

In an attempt to bring the discussion further, other researchers have presented a more conservative position that expertise may be influenced by both genetics and practice.[10] This view argues that expertise is a product of genetic capabilities and practice. It is clear that the "nature-nurture" dichotomy will continue to be debated by proponents of each theory for a long time. Nonetheless, it would seem that a prudent and reasonable view would be to consider that it is the integration of both nature (genetics) and nurture (practice) that constitutes the expert performer.

Summary

Experienced and expert dancers are a very special category of learners. They stand out in the crowd, in the dance class, and on stage. As with novice adults and children, experienced and expert dancers have their own capabilities and characteristics. They have acquired a capacity to learn and perform dance skills at a level significantly greater than novices. Instructors must be prepared to teach students of all levels. They must be able and willing to modify lesson material and teaching methods to suit the needs of all students. A quote from Graham is most appropriate as a conclusion:

> I can never forget the evening I was staying late at the school, and the phone rang. I was the only one there and I picked it up to hear a mother ask about classes for her child. "She is a genius. Intuitive. Unique. It must be nurtured now." "Really," I answered. "And how old is she?" Her mother replied, "Two years old." I told her that we only accept children at nine (today much earlier, thanks to vitamins and computers and home training). "Nine!" she cried. "But by nine she will have lost all of her genius." I said, "Madam, if she must lose it, it is best she lose it young."[27]

References

1. Rose DJ: *A Multilevel Approach to the Study of Motor Control and Learning*. Boston: Allyn and Bacon, 1997.
2. Magill RA: *Motor Learning: Concepts and Applications*, (6th ed). Boston: McGraw-Hill, 2001.
3. Schmidt RD, Wrisberg CA: *Motor Learning and Performance: A Problem-Solving Approach*, (2nd ed). Champaign, IL: Human Kinetics Publishers, Inc., 2000.
4. Poon PPL, Rodgers WM: Learning and remembering strategies of novice and advanced jazz dancers for skill level appropriate dance routines. Research Quarterly for Exercise and Sport 71(2):135-144, 2000.
5. Schmidt RA, Lee TD: *Motor Learning and Control: A Behavioral Emphasis*, (3rd ed). Champaign, IL: Human Kinetics Publishers, Inc., 1999.
6. Puretz S: Bilateral transfer: The effects of practice on the transfer of complex dance movement patterns. Research Quarterly for Exercise and Sport 54(1):48-54, 1983.
7. Knudson DV, Morrison CS: Qualitative Analysis of Human Movement. Champaign, IL: Human Kinetics Publishers, Inc., 1997.
8. Ericsson KA, Charness N: Expert performance: Its structure and acquisition. American Psychologist 49(8):725-47, 1994.
9. Howe MJA, Davidson JW, Sloboda JA: Innate talents: Reality or myth? Behavioral and Brain Sciences 21:399-442, 1998.
10. Singer RN, Janelle CM: Determining sport expertise: From genes to supremes. International Journal of Sport Psychology 30:117-150, 1999.
11. Anderson JR: *Cognitive Psychology and its Implications*. New York: W. H. Freeman, 1980.
12. Annett J: On knowing how to do things: A theory of motor imagery. Cognitive Brain Research 3:65-69, 1996.
13. Gardner H: Frames of Mind: The Theory of Multiple Intelligences. New York: Basic Books, 1983.
14. Maletic V: Toward a multidimensional dance education. *In:* Côté-Laurence P, Wilson VJ (eds): *Proceedings of the International Conference on Movement Education for a New Age*. St. Catharines, Ontario: Brock University Press, 1989, pp. 29-38.
15. Côté-Laurence P: Beginners and expert dancers: Do their creative abilities differ? Presented at the Joint North American Society for Psychology of Sport and Physical Activity / Canadian Society for Psychomotor Learning and Sport Psychology Conference, Muskoka, Ontario, Canada, June 1996.
16. Côté-Laurence P: Defining dance expertise: Knowledge base of experienced teachers and professional dancers. Presented at the Canadian Society for Psychomotor Learning and Sport Psychology Conference, Niagara Falls, Ontario, Canada, October 1997.
17. Allard F, Burnette N: Skill in sport. Canadian Journal of Psychology 39(2):294-312, 1985.
18. Sheldon WG, Dupertuis CW, McDermott E: *Atlas of Men: A Guide for Somatotyping the Adult Male of all Ages*. New York: Harper, 1954.
19. Singer RN, Janelle CM: Determining sport expertise: From genes to supremes. International Journal of Sport Psychology 30:117-150, 1999.

20. Starkes JL, Deakin JM, Allard F, Hodes NJ, Hayes A: *Deliberate practice in sports: What is it anyway? In:* Ericsson KA (ed): *The Road to Excellence: The Acquisition of Expert Performance in the Arts and Sciences, Sports, and Games.* Mahwah, NJ: Lawrence Erl, 1996, pp. 81-106.

21. Starkes JL, Deakin JM, Lindley S, Crisp F: Motor versus verbal recall of ballet sequences by young expert dancers. Journal of Sport Psychology 9:222-230, 1987.

22. Chase WG, Simon HA: Perception in chess. Cognitive Psychology 4:55-81, 1973.

23. Starkes JL, Caicco M, Boutilier C, Sevek B: Motor recall of experts for structured and unstructured sequences in creative modern dance. Journal of Sport and Exercise Psychology 12:317-321, 1990.

24. Vickers JN: Knowledge structure of expert-novice gymnasts. Human Movement Science 7:47-72, 1988.

25. Ellfeldt L: *Dance, from Magic to Art.* Dubuque, IA: Wm. Brown Publishers, 1976, p. 211.

26. Graham M: I am a dancer. *In:* Carter A (ed): *The Routledge Dance Studies Reader.* London: Routledge, 1998, pp. 66-71.

27. Graham M: I am a dancer. *In:* Carter A (ed): *The Routledge Dance Studies Reader.* London: Routledge, 1998, p. 71.

Part Two

Applying the Foundations to Dance Teaching

Josie Hazen

The Dance Teacher's Role

   Preparing for the Dance Lesson: Evaluation and Selection

   Observing During the Dance Lesson: Adaptation

Approaches to Observation

Learning Outcomes

Chapter 8

Effective Dance Teaching

Determining what makes an individual a good dance teacher is very difficult, if not impossible.[1] There are many variables involved in shaping the learning environment, from the teacher's contribution to the lesson (knowledge and comfort level in the subject area, communication skills, rapport with students), the students' disposition (comfort level in dance and with the teacher, and motivation to learn), to other internal and external factors. However, we can make an attempt to define what is good teaching. Research in pedagogy has shown that the main ingredients that characterize effective teaching in the classroom are:

- A high percentage of time devoted to academic content,
- High rates of on-task behavior exhibited by students,
- Appropriate matching of content to student abilities,
- A warm and positive classroom climate, and
- A class structure that contributes to high rates of on-task behavior.[1]

There is a growing awareness in the dance community that dance teachers need to evaluate how they teach.[2,3] Dance researchers and educators have made attempts to describe competencies for effective dance teaching[4-8] and so have professional organizations.[9] Some of the characteristics that have been identified include: competent performance skills, pedagogical skills, knowledge of the students, curriculum development, assessment skills, technology skills, and advocacy.[8] What is becoming increasingly clear is that the technical knowledge acquired as a dancer, by itself, is insufficient for quality teaching.[4] Knowledge of the body and a movement vocabulary, what is referred to as subject

matter knowledge, is not enough and must be combined with pedagogical knowledge, to create pedagogical content knowledge.[4] To this knowledge base we must add knowledge of the student. In a national document for teacher competency in dance,[9] of the five core ideals, student
learning is the first. Observation and knowledge of student's abilities
and fostering their development is a key requirement. This basis should
ensure that the appropriate matching of dance content to student abilities
takes place. The final component is an understanding of the skill acquisition process and how the teacher may influence that process, which
takes us into the fields of motor learning and development.[10] Teachers
need a solid knowledge base; "To achieve respect and leadership in the
field today, dance educators require knowledge about knowledge ... em-
ploying information science analogies and cognitive science explanations to all aspects of the dance teaching and learning process."[11] The
ultimate test that shows how well this knowledge is applied in teaching
is in students' behavior. Effective teaching results in successful, meaningful learning experiences for the students.[2]

The Dance Teacher's Role

In Part One we covered the knowledge base required for effective dance
teaching. This has included an analysis of the nature and difficulty of the
dance material, an understanding of the learning process and the learner's
capabilities. In this section we focus on the application of that knowledge and the role of the teacher in facilitating learning. With the knowledge base, the teacher is able to evaluate the needs and capabilities of the
students, and the difficulty of the dance material. She is then able to plan
an effective dance lesson and unit by selecting and organizing appropriate dance material and choosing appropriate teaching methods for instruction, demonstration, and correction in order to create a positive learn-

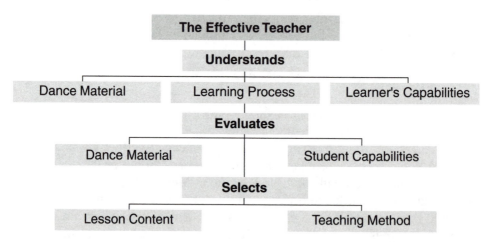

Figure 8.1
Making choices prior to the dance lesson.

ing environment. The essential premise is that the teacher who understands the material of dance, the learning process, and the learners' capabilities, is more likely to select appropriate teaching material and methods than the one who does not fully appreciate these three components. This brings us back to the model of effective teaching first introduced in Chapter 1 and presented in Figure 8.1.

The second level of effective teaching focuses on the role of the teacher during the lesson. This level entails the teacher's ability to observe what goes on in the classroom, and to make changes, if necessary, to facilitate student learning. Each of these steps is reviewed here and will be examined in more detail in the subsequent chapters.

Preparing for the Dance Lesson: Evaluation and Selection

Teaching dance involves making choices. Consider the different types of choices a teacher would make as she tries to identify the needs of her dance students. In one case, this might be a second grade classroom of typical boys and girls in their first folk dance class. In another case, this might be a group of 16-year-old females in their fifth year of ballet training in a dance studio. What does the teacher bring to these situations?

The teacher starts with a clear understanding of the dance material, in this case, the nature and difficulty of the dance skills that make up the available material in folk dance or ballet. She also understands what learning difficulties these skills present, and how the learning capabilities differ between a seven year old and a 16 year old.

From this foundation, the teacher can now evaluate the students' readiness for dance skill learning, as well as examine the material in the syllabus or the instructions of the folk dance, and make a decision as to whether these are appropriate. As a result the teacher selects a number of ballet skills or choses one folk dance over another. At the same time, the teacher decides which steps will require careful and repeated demonstration, what aspects of the skill will likely create some difficulty and require a lot of feedback, and how much new material can be incorporated in a lesson.

> An effective teacher evaluates the difficulty of the material and the readiness of the student.

The choice of content and instructional methods must be carefully balanced in order to facilitate learning. It is likely that, for the beginning young students, simple dance material would be chosen, and a lot of assistance provided in order to aid learning. The older, more experienced dancers, on the other hand, can manage more complex dance skills and will need little assistance. Figure 8.2 illustrates that balance.

An experienced teacher has acquired a large repertoire of material based on years of experience with a variety of instructional methods and with different groups of students to assist her with making those choices. In contrast, an inexperienced teacher often resorts to a prepared curriculum

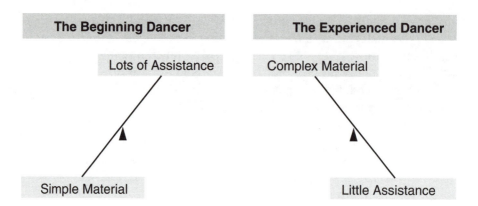

Figure 8.2
Balancing choices to suit the learner.

and uses familiar instructional methods. She may do this without evaluating whether they are appropriate to her students. In this book we provide the tools that teachers can use to be more effective.

Observing During the Dance Lesson: Adaptation

The second level of effective teaching focuses on what the teacher does during the lesson. She will present the skills, monitor the students' responses, provide them with corrections, and evaluate the learning process. She will make choices during the class itself. This process is outlined in Figure 8.3. These on-the-spot decisions made while teaching include: the type and amount of correction, the necessity to re-demonstrate, the number of repetitions, and how quickly to proceed to the next skill. The process of evaluation and selection is ongoing throughout the dance

> Ongoing observation of the class is critical for adapting both content and instructional methods.

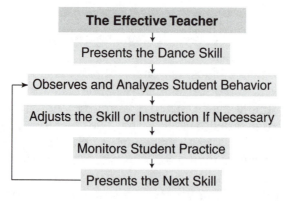

Figure 8.3
The role of the effective teacher during the dance lesson.

Figure 8.4
During the lesson, observation is critical to making corrections and selections of skills for the students.

lesson. It is the teacher's observational skills that will guide her in the process of making appropriate adaptations in content and instructional methods, resulting in effective teaching and successful learning. Ongoing observation of the class is a critical factor in this process. The student also must observe and is very much an active participant in the learning process.

Some general comments on the process of observation are presented in the following section. The specific role that class observation plays in adapting content is explored more fully in Chapter 9. The function of observation in decision-making regarding feedback is discussed in Chapter 11.

Approaches to Observation

There are different approaches to observation in the dance class based on individual differences between teachers and the demands of the dance form. There is no one ideal approach to observation that suits all teachers. Individuals may have different levels of observation skills and use them differently in the dance form they teach. The following scenarios serve as an illustration.

Scenario 1:

The talented jazz dance teacher, fresh from the latest dance workshop, is enthusiastically demonstrating a new skill he has just learned. It involves a complicated sequence of shoulder and hip isolations and the high school class is fascinated. He stands in front of the class and dances with them, to ensure that they copy this unique move, and also so that they can pick up on the dynamics. He watches the class behind him in the mirror, to see if they are picking up the skills.

Scenario 2:

An experienced elementary school teacher is watching her class from the sidelines. The students are reviewing a folk dance she taught yesterday. She carefully looks around the room at each of the children, then stops the class and gives some further instruction.

Which of the two appears to be a better teacher? Both teachers are observing, but the amount and type of observation varies with the dance form, the skill being performed, the experience of the students, and the experience of the teacher. The first teacher uses observation only to verify if the class understood the body actions and he can stop demonstrating. The second teacher may be evaluating how much the students have remembered and what aspects of the dance needs to be reviewed or corrected.

There is no ideal answer for the balance between the need for demonstration and for observation across different skills and dance forms. Some dance skills, such as simple locomotor patterns, do not need a demonstration. Other skills belong to the standard vocabulary of that dance form and will be familiar to the students, such as the standard ballet barre exercises they have done every day. Although students may not yet be able to perform the skills perfectly, they have a clear understanding of what the criteria are and need corrections, not demonstrations. However, other dance skills are not standardized and are unfamiliar to the students, such as many jazz or modern dance skills. It is essential that the teacher demonstrate the skill for them. The extent to which observation is needed for the teacher or the student, therefore, varies. Despite personal preferences and differences due to dance form, we can identify some common issues and guidelines for observations that apply in all contexts.

> The key components of systematic observation have been identified as analysis, planning, and position.

Observation is a critical teaching skills. Convincing arguments have been made that observation must be systematic and that teachers must be trained to use it effectively.[12-14] Not all teachers are naturally good observers. Nor does being a skilled performer guarantee that the teacher has good observation or movement analysis skills.[13,14] Observational skills can however be learned. What different observational systems share is the need for advance preparation. The key components of systematic observation have been identified as analysis, planning, and position.[13] Analysis includes thorough familiarity with the skills in order to identify components critical to the skills to be presented.

A variety of observation models have been developed in the disciplines of pedagogy and kinesiology.[14] These models differ in what aspect of motor behavior is observed and in the level of analysis. Observations can be made of specific body parts in a skill such as the position of the hip or shoulder, or knee extension. One can also look more globally at the total body configuration, what has been called the "gestalt" of the

Table 8.1 Observations of the Leap

Focus	Observation
Joint action	How much does the hip rotate in the back leg?
Force application	How is the foot planted at take-off?
Total body	Is there too much vertical and not enough horizontal flight?
Sequence	Can the child perform four continuous leaps?
Timing	Is the leap synchronized with the music?

movement,[14] for example, the overall picture one has of the leap through space. Did the dancer achieve a full extension of both legs in the split position? To further illustrate the choices of different observational criteria, several examples of possible observations of a leap are provided in Table 8.1. The selection of criteria is dependent on both the age and skill level of the student.

An illustration of both a global and a detailed approach can be seen in the developmental literature where two methods of analyzing fundamental motor skills are presented.[15] One is a whole body approach where the teacher examines the total skill and identifies one of several developmental levels. The other is a component approach with separate assessment of foot, trunk, and arm actions.

While much of the discussion of analysis is concerned with the technical or mechanical aspect of a skill, a more global approach to analysis is to look at the skill itself, the context of the class, and the students who are attempting to learn the skill. The dance analysis model presented in Chapter 2 has given the reader the tools to prepare for the observation by analyzing the skill difficulty ahead of time. The exploration of the learning process presented in Chapter 4 should prepare the teacher to recognize potential learning difficulties. Subsequent chapters have identified how learner characteristics may affect the learning process. As a result, the teacher should be able to identify the focus of the observation during the skill acquisition process.

Following the analysis, the teacher must be able to plan how, where, when, and how much observation will be carried out. Positioning for observation is an important component of this planning. One could also add decisions about the number and extent of the observations over time, as well as plans to control the teaching situation with a view to facilitating observation.[14]

Carrying out the actual observation while teaching is a not an easy task in the practical world of coping with 20 to 30 students in a class. The amount of observation must be balanced with the need for demonstration. Then, there is the choice of observing the whole class or focussing only on those individuals having difficulty. One suggestion is to alternate scanning the room with more focused observation.[16] Another way to simplify this process is to focus on only a few key criteria. Advance planning should allow the instructor to anticipate what aspect of the skill will cause difficulty. Will there be errors in the motion or position of a specific body part, or the timing, or partner synchronization? The teacher might select different aspects to observe on subsequent days.

Finally, the purpose of carrying out the observations is to evaluate, diagnose, and intervene.[14] Having identified the student's learning problems the teacher must formulate appropriate feedback and plan subsequent learning experiences. These practical issues will be examined in more detail in Chapters 9 and 11.

Learning Outcomes

The ultimate goal of effective teaching is to ensure that students learn.[3] We expect teachers to have behavioral objectives when they teach, that is, they expect students to achieve set goals. These may range from skill proficiency, to passing an exam, to participating in an enjoyable recreational experience where the students acquire social skills. Achievement goals may be legislated by educational or professional administrative bodies that set specific criteria or standards for proficiency.[17] These standards may represent broad skill categories such as the criteria from the National Dance Education Standards for kindergarten to grade four: "accurately demonstrate eight basic locomotor movement (such as walk, run, hop, jump, leap, gallop, leap, slid and skip), traveling forward, backward, sideward, diagonally, and turning."[18] The criteria may also be quite specific, for example naming a specific ballet skill to be achieved to pass a Royal Academy of Dance exam.[19]

Since we are concerned with the physical skills relevant to dance (and not improvisation, choreography, aesthetics, or dance history) the acquisition of proficient dance skills is one of the expected learning outcomes. In the current educational climate, there are growing expectations that students achieve competency in all areas of education. Therefore specific skill criteria for dance have been developed for each level of education. In some jurisdictions these criteria are national,[17] in others, they are regional.[20] In the private sector, performance outcomes may be that a certain percentage of students pass their ballet exams. If proficiency is a desired outcome, the goals set for the students should be meaningful, attainable, set according to individual differences, and focus on performing the skills well as opposed to competing with others.[10,21] A number of dance educators, however, have put out a call that dance teachers should aim for more than technical improvement.[3,7]

While the acquisition of technical skill is a dominant learning outcome, there are other possible goals for participating in a dance class. Some goals are short-term outcomes for a lesson or for a dance course. Others are long-term goals that may affect the learner's future learning experiences in dance and in other learning situations. Which goals are emphasized is based on what is valued in the educational systems and what is of personal value to the teacher or students. In addition to increasing one's skill level in existing skills, other goals may be: increasing one's vocabulary of dance skills; becoming adaptable in using old skills in new contexts; achieving a sense of competency, satisfaction, and enjoyment in dancing skillfully;

becoming an independent dance learner; and finally, transferring learning strategies to other learning situations.

The goals of increasing skill level and vocabulary would probably be considered the minimum outcome of competent teaching. The other goals may or may not be attainable by each student in all classes. Some students are not exposed to sufficient variations in movement components or context to develop adaptable skills. They may be competent in specific skills in a specific context but are not flexible. For example, they can only turn to the right side or take-off from the left foot. They have great control moving in a slow, sustained fashion, but loose control and confidence when asked to speed up. They may have learned skills in a ballet class, but cannot adapt the style to feel comfortable in a jazz class.

Having students enjoy skill learning during the dance class and achieving a sense of competency as a result, is certainly much more likely if both the material and the instructional methods are suited to the age and skill level of the student as opposed to setting some arbitrary collection of skills that must be mastered. This goal should be achievable with the application of the material in the next three chapters.

If the teacher fully understands the learning process, then one of the outcomes should be to develop independent learners, that is, students who understand the learning process and can be in charge of their own dance learning. The dance classroom should be a place where a student is challenged to think and make decisions regarding her own skill development. A result of effective teaching is that eventually the student does not need the teacher to guide her learning process. An experienced dance learner has acquired many of the learning strategies outlined in Chapter 7. By the time the student reaches the perfect stage, she should be able to use a variety of learning strategies independently to practice and perform skilled movements.

> One of the outcomes of effective teaching should be the development of independent learners.

If we take this last goal beyond the dance class, then a final aim that a serious and dedicated teacher should have is to produce not only good dancers, but students who are also good learners. Her students' dance learning experiences can facilitate learning in other contexts. While there is a potential for transfer of learning, transfer is not automatic; it must be made explicit.[6] For example, the teacher may provide cue words as a memory aid for a sequence of complicated steps and encourage students to mentally rehearse these words as they wait to cross the floor. This rehearsal strategy will be equally helpful before starting a dive or gymnastic skill. Similarly, providing an effective image to help students find the correct head alignment can introduce the students to the use of visualization.

Good teachers, as they are instructing, demonstrating and giving feedback can also pass on to the students some learning strategies, that is, techniques that they can use to enhance learning and improve performance in other physical activities. There are expectations that the students share in this responsibility; that they are highly motivated and observant and are actively involved in achieving their own learning goals.[3,10]

In sport pedagogy, a challenge has been issued to sport skill instructors: "Although it would be ideal for learners to be able to manage their own learning, a major role of instructors is to assist learners in developing appropriate behaviors and strategies"[22] and "The most productive instructional or training programs would appear to be those in which learners are prepared for subsequent learning situations, once formal guidance has been completed."[23] This philosophy of the role of the teacher is equally applicable to dance teachers as it is to physical education teachers or sport coaches.

Summary

Effective teaching requires competence in two roles: evaluating and selecting learner-appropriate material before the lesson and adapting content and teaching methods based on obervation of learning as the lesson progresses. The knowledge base needed to analyze key components and critical learning difficulties inherent in dance skills was presented in Part One. This provides the basis for the selection process outlined in Chapter 9. It can also guide the teacher's class observation to identify what component of a skill is creating a learning difficulty. Adaptation of the teaching methods requires familiarity with the available choices for demonstration, instruction, and feedback, which are presented in Chapters 10 and 11.

The effective teacher must also consider learning outcomes. A premise outlined in this chapter is that the goals of effective dance teaching go beyond the acquisition of proficient dance skills to the development of effective learning strategies that are transferable to future skill acquisition in other contexts. If we accept this perspective on the purpose of teaching, then not only do we as teachers need to understand what the learning process consists of, but so do the students. One of our responsibilities is to make students aware of the cognitive processes that go on as they move and learn so that students can play an active role in controlling and facilitating their own learning. The remaining chapters of the book provide the material for making wise choices that will result in effective teaching and positive learning outcomes.

References

1. Siedentop D: *Developing Teaching Skills in Physical Education* (2nd ed). Palo Alto, CA: Mayfield, 1983.
2. Lord M, Chayer C, Girard L: Increasing awareness of your strategies for teaching dance technique. Impulse 3:172-182, 1995.
3. Schlaich J, Dupont B: *The Art of Teaching Dance Technique Activities*. Reston, VA: American Alliance for Health, Physical Education, Recreation and Dance, 1993.

4. Fortin S: The knowledge base for competent dance teaching. Journal of Physical Education, Recreation and Dance 64(9):34-38, 1993.
5. Gray J: Dance, 1990 and beyond: Future trends. Journal of Physical Education, Recreation and Dance 61(5):50-53, 1990.
6. Hanna JL: *Partnering Dance and Education: Intelligent Moves for Changing Times*. Champaign, IL: Human Kinetics Publishers, Inc., 1999.
7. Lord M: Reflections on the preparation of effective dance teachers. Journal of Physical Education, Recreation and Dance 64(9):49-41, 1993.
8. Stinson SW: Realities, myths, and priorities: Teacher competencies in dance. Journal of Physical Education, Recreation and Dance 64(9):45-48, 1993.
9. National Board for Professional Teaching Standards: *What Teachers Should Know and be Able to Do*. Washington DC: National Board for Professional Teaching Standards, 1994.
10. Overby L: Motor learning knowledge in the dance curriculum. Journal of Physical Education, Recreation and Dance 64(9):42-48, 1993.
11. Gray J: Dance, 1990 and beyond: Future trends. Journal of Physical Education, Recreation and Dance 61(5):50, 1990.
12. Barrett KR: Observation for teaching and coaching: Principles to guide improvement. Journal of Physical Education and Recreation 50(1):23-25, 1979.
13. Barrett KR: Observation of movement for teachers: A synthesis and implications. Motor Skills: Theory into Practice 3(2):67-76, 1979.
14. Knudson DV, Morrison CS: *Qualitative Analysis of Human Movement*. Champaign, IL: Human Kinetics Publishers, Inc., 1997.
15. Gabbard CP: *Lifelong Motor Development*, (2nd ed). Dubuque IA: Brown and Benchmark, 1996.
16. Wall J, Murray N: *Children and Movement: Physical Education in the Elementary School*, (2nd ed). Madison WI: Brown and Benchmark, 1994.
17. Consortium of National Arts Education Associations: *National Standards for Arts Education: Dance, Music, Theatre, Visual Arts: What Every Young American Should Know and be Able to Do in the Arts*. Reston, VA: Music Educators National Conference, 1994.
18. Consortium of National Arts Education Associations: *National Standards for Arts Education: Dance, Music, Theatre, Visual Arts: What Every Young American Should Know and be Able to Do in the Arts*. Reston, VA: Music Educators National Conference, 1994, p. 23.
19. Royal Academy of Dance: *Children's Examination Syllabus for Girls and Boys*. London, UK: Royal Academy of Dance, 1984.
20. Ministry of Education and Training. *The Ontario Curriculum Grades 9 and 10: The Arts*. Toronto: Ministry of Education and Training, 1999.
21. Magill RA: *Motor Learning: Concepts and Applications*, (4th ed). Madison, WI: Brown and Benchmark, 1993.
22. Singer RN: Motor skills and learning strategies. *In:* O'Neil HF (ed): *Learning Strategies*. New York: Academic Press, 1978, p. 98.
23. Singer RN, Suwanthada S: The generalizability effectiveness of a learning strategy on achievement in related closed motor skills. Research Quarterly for Exercise and Sport 57(3):205, 1986.

Josie Hazen

Evaluating the Dance Material

   Evaluating a Dance Skill

   Evaluating a Combination/Dance

   Evaluating a Lesson/ Unit

Evaluating the Needs of the Learner

   Physical Abilities

   Repertoire of Fundamental Motor Skills

   Repertoire of Dance Skills

   Learning Abilities

   Characteristics of the Learner

Selecting Appropriate Material

   Selecting Material for the Novice Versus the Experienced Dancer

   Selecting Material for the Child Dancer

Chapter 9

Selecting Dance Skills for the Learner

This chapter focuses on the teacher's role in planning content by applying the foundation knowledge from the first section of the book to the realities of the teaching situation. Both the dance material and the learner's capabilities must be evaluated in order to select appropriate material for the dance lesson or unit and make adjustments during the actual lesson.

It is the beginning of a new term with a new group of students. All teachers, experienced or not, must make choices regarding the content of the dance material for the unit and for each class. There are a lot of questions to be answered. What do I teach to whom? When? Why? Whether to simply follow this curriculum guide, this sample lesson plan? How to adapt the dance lesson to this age group, to this skill level? Should different skills be selected to teach a studio class and a general high school class? Is this class ready to handle triplets (square dancing, double pirouettes)?

An experienced teacher will have a large repertoire of dance material from which to choose, and years of teaching a variety of students to assist with making those choices. A beginning teacher has the choice of relying on ready-made packaged curricula and lesson plans and trying to implement them with the hope that they fit. Alternatively, he can evaluate the wealth of teaching material that is available and select skill and age appropriate material based on an understanding of the students' capabilities. We would argue strongly for the latter, that the teacher must make intelligent choices, rather than arbitrarily selecting the day's or the term's skill content for the dance class or blindly following a prepared guide. It is certainly possible to follow someone else's curriculum, but if this is done without some evaluation of the

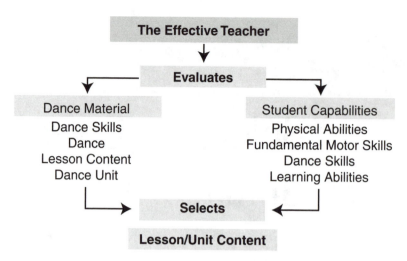

Figure 9.1
The teacher's role in planning the lesson

material and the students' capabilities, it is a hit and miss exercise as to whether or not the class will be successful. The choice of content must be based on observation and evaluation of the student's capabilities and an awareness of the demands of the dance material.

> Both the dance material and the needs of the dance student must be evaluated to ensure successful learning experiences.

Depending on the teacher's philosophy, the context in which he is teaching, the dance form taught, and the curriculum requirements, the selection process can begin with the dance material or the needs of the students. The crucial point is that ultimately both must be examined in order to make wise choices and ensure successful learning experiences. Figure 9.1 shows the factors that must be taken into consideration in each area.

Evaluating the Dance Material

The teacher who starts this process from the dance material, may find himself in one of several situations. He may have available a comprehensive curriculum that includes the skills to be covered in a specific progression for a typical class and/or for a whole unit. This is the case in some ballet, modern, or jazz classes, where there is a structured body of technique readily available. It is often already organized as beginner, intermediate, and advanced material. The teacher in this instance is left with little choice of content, with the exception perhaps of the combinations at the end of the class.

Sample lessons geared to particular grade levels may also be available in many elementary school textbooks. A creative dance lesson for first grade for example, may focus on time, with sudden and sustained actions performed solo. By the third grade, the theme has progressed to using sudden and sustained actions in small groups incorporating words.[1] The teacher in this context can choose the actual tasks to develop the theme.

Folk dance material is often grouped in difficulty categories, such as easy, moderate, or advanced, rather than by grade level. This may be based on the locomotor skills or the dance formation or pattern[2] to provide some guidance for the inexperienced teacher.

Alternatively there may be general skill categories and achievement guidelines prescribed that are adjusted for grade or skill level.[3,4] The teacher is expected to choose the actual dance tasks. The National Standards, for example, suggest that kindergarten to fourth grade children should demonstrate the eight basic locomotor skills, while fifth to eight graders should demonstrate basic dance steps from two different styles.[5]

Finally, the teacher may have an open choice to select from available resources or his own dance background. What differs in these scenarios is the amount of guidance regarding the difficulty level that is provided and the amount of choice left to the individual. In any of these situations, it is the teacher's responsibility to evaluate the material and not simply teach it without question. It is not enough to know that this material is easy or difficult and has been identified as appropriate for a particular grade or skill level, but also to understand why this is so. The dance analysis material in Chapters 2 and 3 provided the tools for this evaluation. Combined with a knowledge of the capabilities and/or limitations of his class, the teacher can then not only select those skills that will suit the class, but also anticipate any learning difficulties and make adaptations during the class. For example, a particular center combination of one-footed balances may be appropriate for the class, but they are not yet ready to handle the skills on demi pointe. A folk dance may be successful with a younger-than-recommended age group if instead of skipping or doing a polka step, they can simply walk. If the rapid direction changes can be eliminated in a dance like the "Teton Mountain Stomp," one is left with only walking and stomping. A jazz combination may be successful for beginners if performed in half time.

> Evaluation of the dance material must take place for specific dance skills, for the culminating activity, for the lesson and for the unit.

In all of the above situations, the evaluation of dance material with the learner in mind must take place for specific dance skills and for a culminating activity. In addition, the teacher must decide what skills and how many to include in a lesson and unit.

The analysis of dance material presented in Chapter 2 and the organizational guidelines in Chapter 3 provide the basis for this evaluation. In this section, the focus is on applying the theory using the checklists, questions, and illustration provided as tools for the teacher to carry out his own evaluation.

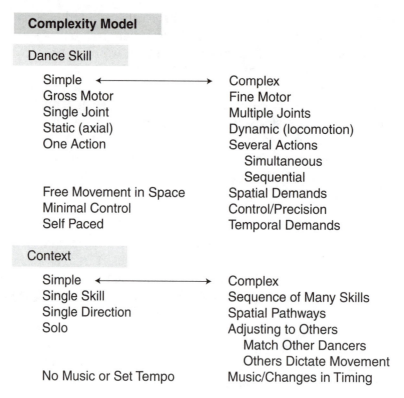

Figure 9.2
The Complexity Model.

Evaluating a Dance Skill

Any dance skill can be evaluated in terms of its inherent difficulty by examining the body action, the components, and the context. Initially, the skill is categorized as one of the six body actions: control of center, changing base, arm and leg gestures, rotation, elevation, or locomotion. Then the time, space, and force components are identified. The context in which the skill has to be performed may be an integral part of the skill or it may be open to adaptation. Once these three levels are identified one can then proceed to evaluate the difficulty of the skill in question. Figure 9.2 is included here as a review of the complexity model to assist in this evaluation.

Let us examine two types of traveling turns that a teacher may consider including in a class for adults – a three step turn and a chaîné turn. Both are dynamic skills that require a specific pathway through space and involve a rotation using alternate steps. Each has a specific timing. If we compare the two, however, we find that the chaîné has more difficulty elements. It typically consists of a series of turns, not just one, and therefore requires the maintenance of precise body control and momentum in order to stay on a straight path. It is performed on half toe with arms coordinated and controlled and the head turned with precise timing. These requirements are difficult for beginners. The three step turn, on the other hand, is usually performed only once or only repeated to the other side, with a complete weight shift and a hold on the last step to assist with the direction change. The turn can be accomplished with no assistance from arms or a head turn, so the whole body can move as a unit. Apart from starting with only two turns and not a long series, there are no other elements that can be removed from the chainé turn. The difficulties are inherent in the skill itself. We can however add arm positions, a head snap and half toe to the original three step turn to make it more challenging. This process can be carried out with any skill, with the purpose of identifying what difficulty elements, if any, can be removed or added to a skill.

Evaluating a Combination/Dance

A similar process can be carried out in order to evaluate a culminating activity, such as a center or a locomotor combination, that the teacher has in his repertoire or a dance with instruction found in a manual. Table 9.1 provides a checklist as the basis for asking a series of questions about any culminating activity. One would start by evaluating the individual skills included and determine if these have already been performed competently by the class. The Israeli folk dance "Cherkassiya" is used as an illustration here. It is classified as advanced for the elementary school level.[2] It requires rapidly switching to three different dance steps while changing directions, reversing the foot pattern, and holding hands in a circle to a fairly fast tempo. While there are no complex partner actions and the tempo does not change, sufficient difficulties are identified to suggest it be limited to older children or teenagers with dance experience.

The reverse process can of course be applied if the teacher wishes to make up a combination. A combination can be built up with one element

Table 9.1   Analyzing the Difficulty in a Dance or Combination

Simple	Complex
Repeating the same steps	Doing many different steps
	Changing rapidly from one to the other
Simple locomotor skills	Complex dance steps
	Arm actions added
	Stylistic characteristics
Side by side, unison partnering/group	Partners opposite each other
	Leading/following
	Doing different patterns
	Changing partners
Going in one direction	Rapidly changing directions, often
	Complex spatial pattern to the dance
	Many turns
Simple, even beat	Varying rhythm
Long phrases	Short phrases, unequal length
Same music	Music changes frequently, tempo changes
Slow or medium tempo	Fast tempo

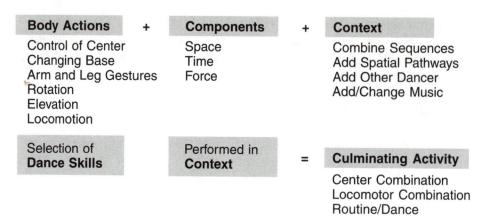

Figure 9.3
Content of a typical lesson.

at a time: a sequence of skills, a spatial pathway, new music, and partner or group patterns. All the elements can be added at once. A simple step-hop can be turned into a complex sequence of forward, sideward, backward, with the addition of a trunk lean, coordinating one's movements with a partner who starts on the opposite foot.

Evaluating a Lesson or Unit

If the lesson format or the skills to be covered in a unit are available in resource material it is still worthwhile to examine this content. Figure 9.3 first introduced in Chapter 3, reviews the content of a typical lesson and unit. It summarized the components that all learners, even beginners, must cover. Some question to ask include the following:

- Have I covered all six categories of body actions?
- Could I substitute an easier or more difficult body action for the one illustrated if it does not match the student's skill level?
- Am I spending too much time on static work and not enough time on dynamic skills?
- Can I vary the space, time and force characteristics of the skill to avoid boredom?
- Do they know the individual skills well enough that I can introduce skill sequences?
- Have I taught all the individuals skills that are needed in the culminating activity?
- What is the balance of time spent on learning individual skills and learning combination or dances?

Evaluating the Needs of the Learner

Some teachers prefer to start with the students and evaluate the number and quality of skills they can perform, as well as their learning abilities, and then select dance activities that can expand their repertoire, improve their skill level, and avoid frustration. For example, a teacher in a creative dance class might identify that overall, the children are poor jumpers, and select an open-ended jumping task that allows each child to experiment with different types of jumps. A folk dance teacher has determined that the grade three students can all skip, so he goes through a list of folk dances to find one that includes skipping and direction changes or partnering. A modern dance teacher during the first class realizes that the students have poor use of their feet and selects weight bearing and weight shifting skills in the next few lessons in order to avoid injury.

> How do I know that the class is ready for the material?

The key question the teacher has to ask is: How do I know that the class is ready for the material? It is critical that the teacher understand the capabilities and limitations of his students in order to adapt the ready-made teaching material or plan content to expand their skill vocabulary. The students' readiness for dance class depends on their physical abilities, repertoire of fundamental motor skills, repertoire of dance skills and their learning abilities (*see* Chapters 5, 6 and 7).

Observation skills are crucial here, particularly on the first day of class. In elementary school classes the teacher will have some idea of readiness based on the developmental age of the students. Teenagers or adults, on the other hand, presumably have already done some self-selection of a class level to suit their own perceptions of competency. However, neither age nor personal opinion are a foolproof method of evaluation. The teacher would be well advised to plan a general screening lesson for both children and adults to evaluate their status (Table 9.2).

Physical Abilities

This text focuses on cognitive aspects of learning and not physiological aspects of training and conditioning, that is, the functioning of the brain and not the body. However, the state of the body that the student brings to the class affects what he can learn. A child whose body proportions are top heavy, an adolescent whose body proportions have recently changed dramatically or an adult whose muscles have atrophied from years of inactivity and whose range of motion is severely restricted, bring different states of readiness and different learning problems to a class. There are also large individual differences between one student and another (for example, joint flexibility, muscular strength, muscular and cardiovascular endurance) that will affect the individual's capability to perform specific skills. The ability to perform the splits, do repetitive jumps without tiring, or to achieve a high extension for example, is a question of physical limitation and not a learning problem. There are some skills that clearly will not be achieved no matter how often the student practices or how carefully he is instructed.

Table 9.2   Example of Screening Lessons for Fundamental Skills and for Dance
Skills

Categories	Fundamental Motor Skills (Age 6 and up)	Dance Skills (Older child or novice adult)
Body actions		
Control of Center	Curl and stretch	Curl, uncurl the spine, forward and side
Changing Base	Lunge and return forward and side	Plié and relevé in parallel and turnout
Arm & Leg Gestures	Balance on one leg	Tendu and développé front, side, back
Rotation	Push turn on the spot	Three step traveling turn
Elevation	2 foot vertical jump	Run leap
Locomotion	Run and stop	Triplets
Components		
Time	Slow down/speed up	Pattern combining slow and fast beats
Space	Follow the leader in a straight line	Combine forward, side and back
Force		Change dynamics, hold position release
Context		
	Solo	Synchronize with partner
	In own space	Travel forward, backward and sideways across floor

Repertoire of Fundamental Motor Skills

We take for granted that most students past the age of six or seven,
and certainly all adults, will have reached a mature level of fundamental motor skills, that is, they can run, hop, jump, leap, and have
static and dynamic balance. Therefore we should be able to begin by
teaching specialized dance skills. The competency of fundamental
motor skills is not simply a question of maturation however, it is also
one of practice.[6,7] It may be necessary to go back and actually teach
the difference in take-off and landing between a hop, a jump, and a
leap before teaching a pas de chat. Standing still on one leg is not an
activity of daily life, and may not have been practiced since kindergarten. Adding a leg gesture of a brush or a leg extension may well
present a serious balance problem that requires a quick refresher
course on static balance compensation. A sample list of skills to be
considered when "screening" for fundamental motor skills for a
learner aged 6 or older is presented in Table 9.2.

Repertoire of Dance Skills

The presence of specialized dance skills distinguishes the experienced
from the inexperienced dance students. However, years of experience
alone, may not be enough. Two years experience in dance classes does
not guarantee that students have covered the basic actions required. They

may have good flexibility, be competent in performing pliés in the five basic positions, have good balance and extension in leg work, and yet be weak in jumps, turns, and locomotor work depending on which skill categories the previous teacher has emphasized.

Mere exposure to dance skills does not guarantee a high level of skill. A students may comment, "I've already taken a beginner class and I'd like to enroll in the intermediate level." The student may in fact be familiar with the standard skills and class routine, but has poor alignment, cannot use the feet properly, and has no sense of space or awareness of timing when traveling. A screening lesson of dance skills would include skills that cover the six basic body actions, introduce some variations in space, time, and force and experiment with increasing the difficulty of the skill context (*see* Table 9.2).

Learning Abilities

This area is more difficult to evaluate until the teacher has taught the class. It may take several lessons before a teacher has a good sense of the overall class level and of individual difficulties. Learning dance skills involves the ability to observe and remember body positions and steps, the ability to make corrections when given feedback, to monitor one's own performance for errors, and to challenge oneself to improve to some level of skill achievement. There is a great deal of individual variation in these capabilities, and certainly some developmental limitations on the readiness to learn. As seen in Chapter 5, a series of questions can guide the teachers' observation, such as:

- Do the students have the general idea of the skill or are they missing many key elements?
- Can they identify what they are supposed to do even though they cannot perform the skill correctly?
- Can they remember the order of the steps even though they cannot connect them very well?
- What happens when I stop demonstrating?
- Do they appear to recognize their mistakes and make attempts to change their performance?
- Can they make any of the corrections I have given them?
- Are they performing the steps correctly, but do not know where they are going in space?
- Are they ahead of the music?
- Are they not able to coordinate the skill with a partner?

These four basic components — physical abilities, fundamental skills, dance skills, and learning abilities — determine an individual's readiness to learn in dance. Table 9.3 highlights the differences in abilities between learners that will be explored in more detail. These differences determine where one starts with dance content and what the students may be able to achieve.

Table 9.3   Four Components that Indicate Readiness to Learn

	Novice	**Experienced**	**Young Child**
Physical Abilities	Range of conditions	Are strong, flexible	Body proportions differ Have flexibility May lack strength
Fundamental Skills	Mature	Mature	Immature form
Dance Skills	Few Low skill level	Many High skill level	Few or none
Learning Abilities	Normal	High	Poor

Characteristics of the Learner

In the previous three chapters, three groups of learners were identified: the novice dancer, the experienced dancer, and the young child. To emphasize the contrast between the child and adult learner, we have focused on the young child. As the child matures to 10 to 12 years of age, he will approach the adult level. For most perceptual and cognitive skills, a child of 10 to 12 is considered mature.[6,7] We have separated teenagers from this group. There are obvious physical differences between a 12 and an 18 year old in terms of body size, strength, flexibility, and body composition that may affect the ability to perform specific skills such as full splits, back bends, or jumps. Also there are six additional years of opportunities to learn motor skills, and to store them in memory. However, in terms of ability to learn novel dance skills, there are more similarities between a 12-year-old and an 18-year-old novice dancer than there are differences. The older child may in fact also be an experienced dancer. The 12 year old who has been in ballet class since age six would be classified as an experienced learner and would be quite out of place with a group of 18 year old beginners. Tables 9.4, 9.5, and 9.6 summarize the key learner characteristics presented in Chapters 5, 6 and 7. They can serve as a guide for the selection of material.

Selecting Appropriate Material

The readiness to learn dance skills represents a combination of physical and mental maturation and motor experience. The concept of readiness also includes the student's motivation to learn and the teacher's role in modifying the learning environment and the task at hand to promote mastery.[7-9]

The goal of selecting appropriate material that will promote mastery can be met by asking the following questions:

- What are the students ready to learn?
- What do they need to learn in terms of the weaknesses or gaps in their skills?
- How do I keep them interested and motivated to learn?

A final goal would be to ensure that the material is adaptable enough to suit the individual differences in the class.

Table 9.4   Characteristics of the Novice Adult

Capabilities	Limitations
Physical Abilities	
Has completed growth spurt	Large range of individual difference
If physically active, should show	May be overweight, not flexible,
normal strength, range of motion	lack strength in specific muscle groups
and endurance	May have chronic postural misalignments
	May have past injuries
	If recently post-puberty, may still be
	adjusting to new body proportions
Fundamental Skills	
Should have mature form of locomotor,	Depending on past practice, may still
static balance, body management skills,	be in immature stage
If physically active may have high skill	If largely sedentary, may lack
level	Body control and balance
	Arm/leg coordination
Repertoire of Dance Skills	
Some exposure to rhythmic activities,	Most dance skills will be novel
folk dance, social dance forms, aerobics	
Familiarity with a few common dance steps	
Learning Abilities	
Some stored memory of skills	
Attention capabilities are good	Overload with a lot of new information
Can retain/recall information for single skills	Inexperience with sequence learning
Capable of metacognition	Poor body awareness during movement
Has acquired some learning strategies	

Gabrielle Laurence

Figure 9.4
Selecting material for the
novice adult.

To achieve these goals we return to the analysis of dance material first introduced in Chapter 2 and reviewed here in Figure 9.3. In order to select a dance task or activity, the teacher chooses the difficulty of the body actions, the variations in movement components, and the difficulty

Table 9.5   Characteristics of the Young Child

Capabilities	Limitations
Physical Abilities	
Will likely have good flexibility	May lack strength
	May not be able to isolate and control appropriate body parts or muscles
	Large age range of physical maturation
Repertoire of Fundamental Motor Skills	
Should be in mature stage of walking, running, jumping	At youngest age will still have difficulty with hop, skip and one leg balance
	Competency is highly dependent on practice
Repertoire of Dance Skills	
Few, beyond simple locomotor patterns	Almost all dance skills will be novel
Learning Abilities	
Large shift between 5 and 10 years	Poor attention capabilities
Beyond 10, similar to novice adults	Difficulty retaining skill in short-term memory and recalling in long term memory
	May have difficulty understanding the task demands in terms of space, time or force
	Can't plan or remember sequences
	Poor kinesthetic skills
	Inability to detect errors or correct
	Can't coordinate with others or music
	Has few or no learning strategies

Marliese Kimmerle

Figure 9.5
Selecting material for the child learner.

of the context. The teacher thus has a range of choices in any dance activity to meet all of these goals.

These choices are made as part of advance planning to select the initial content of the class. During the lesson, the teacher continues to make choices by adding variations and progressions if students learn quickly, or removing a difficulty element as he identifies some learning problems for all or some of the students. To illustrate these choices, we will ex-

Table 9.6 Characteristics of the Experienced Dancer

Capabilities	Limitations
Physical Abilities Strength Good range of motion Sound body alignment	Generally few (individual differences, such as body type) May have injuries
Repertoire of Fundamental Motor Skills Competent in body management and locomotor skills	Due to focus on dance, may not have developed throwing, kicking, catching skills
Repertoire of Dance Skills Dance skills are mostly automatic Has large skill repertoire Can easily and consistently perform complex skills	When faced with novel sequences may need to develop new motor plans New components/context may be challenging
Learning Abilities Large repertoire of dance skills readily retrieved from memory Superior attention capacity Easily retains and recalls long sequences Has a refined kinesthetic sense High capacity for error detection and correction	May have to adapt to new instructor Injury may force new way of learning May face learning interference when switching dance styles (e.g., from ballet to modern dance)

Marliese Kimmerle

Figure 9.6
Selecting material for the
experienced dancer.

plore the differences in selecting for the novice versus the experienced dancer, and for the adaptations needed for the child learner.

Selecting Material for the Novice Versus the Experienced Dancer

The starting point for selecting material is the Complexity Model (Figure 9.2) with its continuum of skills from simple to complex and the recognition that elements can be added or deleted to suit the students. This allows the teacher to meet the goals of matching readiness, selecting areas of weakness for extra work, and adapting to individuals with higher or lower skill levels. The elements on the left generally result in a simple skill for the novice, and those on the right produce elements of difficulty that are cumulative. Table 9.7 provides an example of a simple and complex version of the same skill, a leap.

Note that "simple" and "complex" are relative terms. Although the actions on the left are simpler than those on the right, even a basic run, run, run, leap contains some elements of difficulty as a result of the necessity to perform the actions in sequence. In a typical modern, ballet, or jazz class, the expected class structure involves working within a specific musical framework and the class organization usually involves linear patterns across the floor with others. In a creative dance with children, one might have a simpler level, with leaps being done at the child's own pace, with any number of steps, anywhere around the room.

No master list of simple and complex skills is attempted here. This would be an impossible task across the different dance forms. The example of the analysis of the leap can be applied to any skill. Dance texts in each dance form make some attempt to organize the material from easy to difficult, as do most syllabi and school curricula. However these books do not always include the rationale or analysis necessary to provide a new teacher with the basis for making his own decisions. It is logical, for example, to find that dances that include basic locomotor patterns of walking, jumping, or skipping (such as "7 Jumps") are considered easy and those with dance steps may be medium or advanced (such as "Cherkassiya").[2] On the other hand, the category of "formation" was less helpful since many non-partner dances are advanced and many couple dances listed as easy. Clearly, a more detailed analysis by the teacher is needed. The complexity

Table 9.7   Simple and Complex Versions of the Leap

Simple	Complex
Body Action	
Run, run, run, leap	Stag leap (or split leap, or other leg variation)
No arms action required	Oppositional arms, or held arms
Components	
Accent on 4	Place leap and accent on 1, 2 or 3
Straight line	In a circle, or on alternating diagonals
Low to ground, cover distance	Emphasize height
Context	
One skill, same leg	2 runs, leap done on alternating legs
Repeat same skill	Combined with other jumps and turns
Solo	Synchronized with chorus, or with partner
Even 4/4 timing	Difficult musical timing

model provides the basis for the analysis of difficulty presented in Table 9.1. These can function as a guide to work through any dance resource material. It can also be used to organize the teacher's own collection of material learned from classes and workshops.

Similarly, the model can be used to plan variations and progressions. Both novice and experienced dancers may become bored with repetition of the same material. Making the

> The complexity model can be used as a tool to evaluate the difficulty of any dance activity.

tasks more difficult or simply different will ensure that students stay motivated. This is also one goal of good planning. An example of the

Figure 9.7
A simple plié can be made more interesting and difficult by adding trunk and arm variations.

Table 9.8   Plié Progressions in a Modern Dance Class

Body Action
Plié, learning to control center, bear weight on two feet

Add other Body Actions
Do in parallel, 1st, 2nd, and 4th
Breathing of the arms
Forward curve/extension of spine
Arm swing, center and out, or forward and backward
Lateral trunk bend
Trunk circle, right, center, left and up
Arm circle sideward combining right and left arms

Add Components
Sustained actions 4 counts for plié 4 to extend
Change to 2 counts, to one count
Change to accent plié on 1st count, extend on 2, 3, 4

Add Context
Add other skills: relevè, developpè
Do sequence once with right arm leading, once with left
Add musical accompaniment; change type of music used
Do 1st facing front of room, turn to right for 2nd position back of room for 4th on right, left of room for 4th on left
Have partners face each other, do mirror body sides in sequence

plié, a skill that students have to practice in every technique class, is given to illustrate how one can add progressions as the class becomes more skilled or to provide more challenges for the experienced dancer (Figure 9.7 and Table 9.8).

Finally, this analysis can be used as self-evaluation after a class to help plan a more successful lesson. Think of a class you taught that went badly, or a class you took that frustrated you. If you can remember the class content, try to answer the following questions:

- Was the skill itself difficult? Why?
- Is there anything about the skill itself that could have been changed?
- Did you recognize any of your own limitations in learning the skill, or those of the students?
- Was the context in which you had to do the skill(s) the problem? If so, which aspects?
- Could any of these have been simplified?

You can of course reverse these questions if instead of being frustrating the class was too easy and therefore boring.

Selecting Material for the Child Dancer

The need to select simple material appropriate for the young child is obvious. However, based on the concepts presented in Chapter 6, additional questions beyond simplicity must be asked. Table 9.9 pre-

Table 9.9   Questions to Determine Readiness of the Child to Perform a Dance Skill or Dance

Body Action
   Is the child able to perform the physical action?
   • Does the child have the fundamental motor skills required as the basis for this skill (e.g., leap, skip, balance)?
   • Can he isolate and control the muscles/body parts in the skill?
   • Can he attend to feedback from the appropriate body parts?

Components
   Does the child understand the spatial, temporal and force demands of the task?
   • Can he identify the dynamics of the skills and is he aware of his own dynamic range?
   • Can he cope with skills that require laterality and directionality?

Context
   Does he have the capabilities to deal with the complexity of the task context?
   • Does he understand the spatial patterns?
   • Can he identify and reproduce the rhythm pattern and the music phrasing?
   • Can he plan the total sequence of the movement?
   • Can he plan his movements to coordinate with other?

sents a set of questions about material for a young child. As the child matures from five to ten he will make improvements and these limitations will no longer apply.

This set of questions can be used to evaluate some sample dance tasks. If we return to the achievement standards for kindergarten to fourth grade – traveling in various directions using the basic locomotor patterns[5] – we can construct different tasks for two age groups. Kindergarten students could be asked to walk or run anywhere in the space while avoiding others and stop when the music stops. They will have less success with this activity if they are asked to skip. They may be able to stay with the clear beat on a drum, with some ability to slow down and speed up the tempo. There would be no expectation of starting on a particular foot, using arms correctly, or perfect timing. By the fourth grade, children should be able to cope with a partner skipping dance in a circle that requires forward, backward, and sideward traveling and a clapping pattern with their partner.

Similar to selecting material for the novice adult, one can add or remove elements of difficulty to make the material appropriate for the child. A difficult dance step can be replaced with walking. Holding hands with a partner or confusing direction changes can be eliminated.

A final point in selecting material for children is performance expectations. Novice adults likely have expectations that they will master the dance skills and they will strive to improve. The young child may simply be enjoying the experience of dancing. Rather than challenging the child to learn material that is more complex than he is ready to learn, we might also select simple, easy material for the pure fun of dancing.

Summary

Selecting lesson or unit content may start with the dance material in a teaching situation where the curriculum is prescribed. If this is the case, adaptations can still be made from general skill categories to specific skills. Based on an evaluation of the students' capabilities, the difficulty may be altered by adjusting the time, space, and force components and through the selection of the context of skill combinations, pathways, people, and music. An alternative approach is to initially evaluate the four areas of readiness of the students and then select dance material that improves their skill level, expands their skill repertoire, is appropriate for their learning abilities, and can be adjusted to suit the individual differences found within the class.

A review of the characteristics of child learners and novice and experienced adults was provided to assist with the selection process. Sample skill analyses were included to illustrate how the complexity model can be used to evaluate and simplify skills and plan variations or progressions to challenge the experienced dancer.

References

1. Boorman J: *Creative Dance in the First Three Grades*. Toronto, ON: Longmans of Canada, Ltd., 1969, p. 16-19.
2. Canadian Association for Health, Physical Education and Recreation: *Folk Dance in the Elementary School: Basic Skills Series*. Ottawa: Canadian Association for Health, Physical Education and Recreation, 1980.
3. Consortium of National Arts Education Associations: *National Standards for Arts Education: Dance, Music, Theatre, Visual Arts: What Every Young American Should Know and be Able to Do in the Arts*. Reston, VA: Music Educators National Conference, 1994, p. 23.
4. Ministry of Education and Training: *The Ontario Curriculum Grades 9 and 10: The Arts*. Toronto: Publications Ontario, 1999.
5. Consortium of National Arts Education Associations: *National Standards for Arts Education: Dance, Music, Theatre, Visual Arts: What Every Young American Should Know and be Able to Do in the Arts*. Reston, VA: Music Educators National Conference, 1994, pp. 23, 39.
6. Gabbard CP: *Lifelong Motor Development*, (3rd ed). Boston: Allyn and Bacon, 2001.
7. Gallahue DL, Ozmun JC: *Understanding Motor Development: Infants, Children, Adolescents, Adults*. Boston: McGraw-Hill, 1998.
8. Magill RA, Anderson DI: Critical periods as optimal readiness for learning sport skills. *In:* Smoll FL, Smith RE (eds): *Children and Youth in Sport: A Biopsychosocial Perspective*. Dubuque, IA: Brown and Benchmark, 1996, pp. 57-72.

9. Seefeldt V: The concept of readiness applied to the acquisition of motor skills. *In:* Smoll FL, Smith RE (eds): *Children and Youth in Sport: A Biopsychosocial Perspective*. Dubuque, IA: Brown and Benchmark, 1996, pp. 49-56.

Jose Hagen

Verbal Instructions

   Clarity of Instructions

   Use of Imagery

   Quantity of Instructions

   Repetition of Instructions

Demonstration

   The Role of Demonstration in the Dance Class

   What Elements Can be Demonstrated

   Frequency of Demonstration

   The Model: Teacher or Student?

   Location of the Model

   Learning Strategies

Assessing the Effectiveness of Instructional Methods

Chapter 10

How to Select Instructional Methods

Y ou enter a dance studio and observe a colleague's class in action. What might you see? Perhaps students are moving and the instructor is watching. Maybe they are listening to the instructor. They could be watching her demonstrate the skill. The purpose of a technique class should be twofold: students learning dance skills and students learning to dance. Experienced teachers propose that a technique class should help students develop instruments capable of doing any dance movements, as well as an underlying sense of performance.[1,2] Regardless of the dance form, the learning process in a technique class consists of verbal instructions describing the skill, a demonstration, practice time, corrections, and more practice time. This chapter is concerned with verbal instructions and demonstration, while Chapter 11 focuses on corrections. The "practice" component is indirectly addressed in several chapters; it is through practice that learners develop motor and cognitive skills. As proposed in Chapter 8, the role of the teacher, after having selected the lesson material, is to determine the instructional methods most suitable for that particular lesson and group of students, and to teach the dance material to the class. This chapter addresses how a teacher could accomplish these roles efficiently.

Experienced teachers will agree that there is no perfect method for teaching dance. However, there are certain rules that may increase teaching efficiency. We have seen in the previous chapter that one of the characteristics of effective teaching is evidenced by an instructor who devotes the majority of class time to learning and practicing skills.[3] Good instructional methods, therefore, are those which maximize the time students actually spend practicing the skills and dancing. Inappropriate teaching methods may cause students to spend a great amount of the class time listening to the teacher or trying to decipher a dance skill that has been poorly presented. All dance teachers should be concerned with the effectiveness of their teaching strategies in assisting students to achieve the goals of a technique class: to learn dance skills and to learn to dance.[4]

A dance skill may be presented verbally, visually, kinesthetically, or via any combination of these modalities. The two modes commonly used to provide technique-related information in a dance class are verbal instructions and demonstrations. It has been suggest that efficient teaching methods are those that use verbal, visual, and kinesthetic instruction.[5] The material presented in this chapter, although part of the intuitive background of outstanding teachers, is not typically passed on to new teachers. This chapter highlights key elements related to verbal instructions and demonstration. The focus is largely on the attempt stage. It is hoped that questions such as "How does a teacher present a new skill to a beginner?" "When and why should demonstration be used?" or "How can the teacher help students grasp a difficult skill?" will be answered.

Verbal Instructions

Verbal instructions are typically used for two purposes: to initiate a learning sequence and to provide corrections to students. The former is addressed in this chapter, while Chapter 11 examines the latter. The type of verbal instructions may vary depending on the dance form. In a modern, jazz, or ballet lesson, the two main objectives are learning the skills and learning to dance. Therefore, the teacher's verbal instructions are focused on executing individual skills and then on performing sequences of skills. Although quality of movement and motor skill proficiency are also stressed in a creative dance class, learning tasks often call for exploration and experimentation of movement concepts. In this dance form, verbal instructions tend to describe the problem to be solved rather than a dance skill or sequence of skills. Similarly, a folk dance instructor formulates her instructions differently than a jazz instructor. Her lesson objective may be for students to learn one, possibly two dances; therefore, verbal instructions may be more global and less frequent, as more time is spent practicing and performing the entire dance rather than specific dance steps.

> The key function of verbal instructions is to direct the learners' attention to a particular aspect of the skill.

The most important function of verbal instructions in a dance class is to direct the learner's attention to a particular aspect of the skill. An efficient teacher would want to ensure that her verbal instructions are clear, complete, concise, and manageable. Information on what to do in the classroom in order to achieve this goal is presented in the next section.

Clarity of Instructions

The clarity of instructions is one of the most crucial qualities of a talented technique teacher.[1] In the attempt stage, students are trying to figure out what they are supposed to do. Therefore, verbal instructions must be brief and to the point. The teacher's role is to help students identify which cues are relevant and which are not. Clear instructions leave no ambiguity as to what to do: the leg is either bent or straight, the head facing forward or to the right, or the counts are either in a 3/4 meter or a 4/4 meter. If it is more important to pay attention to the action of the feet at the beginning, then it must be pointed out. Renowned artist Dan Wagoner suggests that "to help a student learn technique, one must be as clear as possible in presenting the material and try to help students know exactly what is expected of them." [6]

> The clarity of instructions is one of the most crucial qualities of a talented technique teacher.

Clarity of instruction cannot be overemphasized. As suggested in Chapter 8, with advance planning efficient teachers are able to translate the critical characteristics of a skill into teaching cues. These critical features include the preparation, body parts involved, alignment, weight shift, spatial configurations, timing, muscular tension, and other aspects of the skill. For example, a good preparation cue for a turn to the right may be "shift your weight to your left foot." An assumption is made here that the instructor can only give clear instructions if she fully knows the material at hand (e.g., the new skill consists of three body actions, the most important being the action of the feet). The knowledgeable teacher is also aware of common mistakes and tendencies, and keeps those in mind when formulating the initial instructions.

One potentially confusing component that adds to the complexity of dance skills is its timing. In ballet, more than in any other dance form, the verbal description of a skill typically includes precise counts. [7] The teacher must be clear on the counts the first time around, and be consistent. If, for example, a shift of weight from both feet to the left foot is to take place on the first count, then it must be clear that the preparation, the plié on both legs à la seconde, takes place on the "and" preceding that count. The instructor may want students to arrive at a balance position on count two, and hold it on counts three and four. These instructions are clear; students know exactly what to do and at what time. Those of you who have witnessed the embarrassing situation of an instructor trying to figure out the counts of a sequence in the middle of a class know only too well that this is not the way to teach.

In addition to providing precise timing for an exercise, the teacher must also give clear and accurate preparation counts. Preparation counts can be either "ready-and-one," or counting a preparation bar. The "ready" is the warning signal for students to ready themselves to move, or to prepare the motor plan, and the "and" is the signal to activate the motor plan to move into the first position so it coincides with the "one." [8] Preparation counts vary with the length and tempo of the skill. The tempo of the preparation counts must match the tempo for the execution of the skill.

If the sequence is on four counts, then the preparation counts should also be four counts. For a movement with a fast 3/4 tempo, you would want to give at least three fast counts for preparation. If the tempo is slow, then perhaps "three and" would be sufficient. The role of preparation counts is to help students prepare; these counts should therefore reflect the incoming sequence.

> **Preparation counts must match the length and tempo of the exercise.**

Verbal instructions can be more meaningful to students if the instructor can relate the instructions to skills they have already learned.

By pointing out similarities and differences between skills, the instructor can also promote transfer of learning, another educational goal stressed in Chapter 8. The instructor would point out, for example, that the arm position for the new skill or new folk dance is the same as that of a skill or a folk dance they know. This will direct learners to information they have in long-term memory, thus decrease the amount of new information they must process.

A final point on clarity of instruction addresses the use of short verbal cues to help memorization. After the initial instructions have been given, the teacher may continue to provide verbal instructions, but in simplified terms to help students memorize the sequence of actions. For example, the terms "right-left-right-together" would represent a sequence of four steps, or "toe-heel-toe-close," a battement tendu exercise. Students can also use these cues to internalize and memorize the skill. Very often, such short terms are given with a certain intonation to stress a beginning or an accent; they may also include the count. If students have difficulty understanding the teacher's instructions, perhaps it is because they are

Table 10.1   Examples of Clear and Unclear Verbal Instructions

Clear Instructions	Unclear Instructions
Bend your supporting leg	Bend your leg
Shift your weight to your left foot (to prepare for a turn to the right on the right foot)	Pay attention to the preparation phase of your turn
Complete your leg extension on count 2 and hold the position on counts 3 and 4	Move your leg and hold it
Bring your arms down to shoulder level	Your arms are too high
Make sure that you are in the air on "and" and that you land on "one"	Execute one jump per beat
Extend both legs during the jump	Reach with your legs
I want your arm to reach the vertical on count 3, not before	Move your arm slowly
Eliminate the stops between the landing, the turn, and the ending position	Move with more fluidity

not clear. One way to test this is to ask students to repeat the instructions: if they are clear, students can repeat them. Examples of clear and unclear instructions are given in Table 10.1.

To summarize, it is crucial that teachers provide clear verbal instructions in the attempt stage for two reasons, to dictate to students what they should do and provide a basis for corrections. The criteria that the teacher uses to describe the skill will also be used for corrections later on. Therefore, clear verbal instructions should enhance the quality of the learning process for both teacher and students. Another method for providing clear verbal instructions is through imagery. In the following section, some general concepts on dance imagery are presented.

Use of Imagery

The terms imagery, mental practice, mental imagery, and metaphor are commonly used in the literature on motor skill learning and performance.[9,10] Imagery is described as a form of mental practice, where the individual visualizes herself actually performing the skill. Imagery may be used for various purposes, the most important of which for teaching dance skills is to aid skill acquisition.

Dance imagery generally refers to mentally seeing a body position or the performance of a dance skill, with the goal of improving it. The most common images used in dance are visual images (images that provide a sense of what the movement looks like) and kinesthetic images (those that give a sense of what the movement feels like). Dance imagery is used for different purposes, depending on the dance form, type of class, and age groups. In a technique class, imagery is often part of the language used to describe a position, a skill, or the dynamics and style of performing that skill correctly. For example, imagery may be used to help students develop proper alignment[11,12] or learn to move correctly.[13-15] In a creative dance lesson, an image may be used to portray a skill, a creative idea, or an imaginary environment for the dance.[16]

Research indicates that imagery can facilitate communication between teacher and students, thus enhance learning and performance.[11,15] Using an image or metaphor to clarify a vague concept is part of the language of most dance teachers. Although imagery appears to be an integral part of verbal instructions, its use is nonetheless a teacher's personal choice. Some teachers may prefer anatomical instructions while others may favor imagery instructions. Studies on teachers' practices show a variety of preferences in imagery use across dance forms and student levels.[17,18] From a developmental perspective, it may be logical to suggest that children often need images of known objects or events to comprehend a skill or performance concept, for example, the muscular sensations from a correct action. With young children, the image of Goldilocks and the Three Bears could be used to portray large, medium, and small steps. It may be argued that, regardless of age, beginners require assistance in getting

Table 10.2   Examples of Imagery Used in Dance

Alignment

Imagine your pelvis as a bucket full of water, connecting the dancer from the floor to the top of the head[34]

Feel as though your body is growing in height[19]

Seeing the body in profile with the segments placed one on top of the other; seeing a straight line from behind the ear through the shoulder, hip, in front of the ankle, and through the foot[19]

Action of the rib cage

When you inhale, the rib cage lifts and widens like an accordion[34]

Développé

Imagine a light source deep in your hip socket, sending a thin laser beam through and beyond your développé leg[11]

Battement

Imagine a strong gust of wind brushing down your back, blowing your battement up and out in front of you[11]

Fall to the floor

As you fall to the floor, imagine that a fluffy cushion of air breaks your fall[13]

Travel

Imagine running over a hot surface[13]

Arms during travel

Imagine that your arms are a sash or silk cloth that floats as you travel through the air[13]

Fall/Rebound

Think of the space as a spring that compresses as you fall and that propels you back in the rebound[13]

Exploration of body shape and floor pathways

Imagine how spaghetti looks and feels before and after it is cooked[16]

the idea of the skill; imagery may be more beneficial to beginners than more experienced dancers. A variety of images for different tasks found in the literature are presented in Table 10.2.

Good dance images are those understood by students. Like any other instructional aid, a particular dance image may not work for all students in the class. Teachers must always be prepared for alternative images or techniques. The effectiveness of images for specific dance forms, age groups, and skill levels, has yet to be fully explored. Since imagery helps enhance communication, teachers should be encouraged to use it as one component of their instructional methods.[15,18,19]

Quantity of Instructions

Picture for a moment an instructor you had who talked forever to describe a skill. Disturbing empirical data on the time spent by students listening to instructions show that students spent an enormous amount the time listening to verbal instructions.[3] Such findings should convince dance instructors to rethink their methods of teaching, and to seriously reexamine how dance skills are learned. Motor skills, including dance skills, are learned through physical practice, lots of practice. Therefore, the greatest proportion of time in a dance class should be spent on physical practice, not listening.

Good teachers know that students cannot learn everything at once. As seen in Chapter 5, beginners are limited as to how much information they can retain. Lengthy descriptions do not help students who are attempting to identify important cues. Why describe five or six elements in the initial presentation of the new skill, when beginners do not have the capability to remember all of them? Beginners have difficulty paying attention to more than one or two instructions. When the teacher asks students to pay attention to one aspect of the skill, it is unlikely that they can also attend to another aspect. Therefore, the teacher should begin with the most important aspect first. As presented in Chapter 7, experienced dancers, however, have acquired the capability to attend to more than one element at a time.

> Good teachers do not emphasize many cues at once, do not describe long sequences, and do not talk excessively when presenting a new skill.

The number of actions a beginner can remember is another point of consideration. A sequence of eight actions, for example, should be taught in sections to make learning and retention more manageable for beginners. The instructor should teach the first two or three actions; when students can perform those, then she would add the next two actions, and so on. Experienced students are likely to retain and repeat all eight actions after one presentation, but this is not the case with beginners. With practice, students develop strategies to memorize more information at once.

Repetition of Instructions

As a typical dance class consists of students with a wide range of skills and skill levels, it is likely that, no matter how clear verbal instructions are, they will likely need to be repeated during the attempt stage. There is no rule as to how many times instructions must be given other than to say that it is a function of the complexity of the skill and the capabilities of the learners. What is important, however, is to keep verbal instructions consistent throughout the learning cycle for that particular skill. When verbal instructions are repeated, the teacher must repeat them exactly the same way, and reiterate what she wants students to pay attention to. For example, the emphasis may be on the weight shift and timing in a Lindy step. The signal to indicate that students have understood what to do is a correct execution of the step. When most students can perform the skill relatively well, they are ready to move on to the next skill.

Verbal instructions in a technique class are typically accompanied by a demonstration. A demonstration allows learners to directly observe a skill. This is especially critical when teaching novice dancers, as they have little familiarity with this type of motor skills.

Demonstration

The terms "demonstration," "modeling," and "observational learning" are used interchangeably in discussions of motor learning and development. Most of what is known about the role of the demonstration in the learning process for motor skills has been guided by social cognitive theory.[20] This theory views observational learning as an information processing activity. Essentially, when a student observes a model, she translates the movement information into a symbolic memory code that forms the basis of a mental image stored in memory. This mental image is used for two purposes: as motor plan to produce the action and as reference point for error detection.[9]

A demonstration is one of the most effective ways to convey information to learners in the early stages of learning a motor skill.[21] A demonstration is often referred to as the teaching tool that gives the most amount of information in the least amount of time. A demonstration can fulfill different functions depending on the skill, the learners' capabilities, and the learning stage. During the attempt stage, a demonstration helps the learner perceive the important features of the new skill, whereas in the next two stages, it serves to solidify the mental image used to self-monitor the performance of the skill.[21]

Demonstrations are particularly important for beginners. Beginners have a limited vocabulary of movements stored in memory and little familiarity with dance skills; they rely heavily on visual information during the attempt stage of learning. Children are good at imitating, but have difficulty formulating a visual image based on verbal descriptions. It is suggested that a combination of verbal instructions and demonstration provides the most efficient way to teach motor skills to children.[22] The role of the teacher working with beginners is to provide a demonstration whenever possible to complement verbal instructions.

Gabrielle Laurence

Figure 10.1
A teachers's verbal cues during the demonstration help students focus on key points.

The Role of Demonstration in the Dance Class

Picture yourself describing a polka step to your class. You probably demonstrate the weight shift as you talk to them. Demonstrating a dance skill is second nature to many experienced dance teachers. In dance, a demonstration is probably the best means of communicating information about the global physical action and its components. The saying, "a picture is worth a thousand words," is certainly true when teaching dance, even more so to beginners. Evidence suggests that individuals who observed a model in a complex sport skill developed coordinated movement patterns earlier than those who received verbal instructions only.[23] As mentioned in Chapter 2, most dance skills are complex in nature, therefore, it is important that learners see a model perform the new skill before attempting to imitate it. The demonstration in a dance class serves two purposes: to provide an accurate image of the body action and to clarify the skill's space-time-force components.

> The role of the demonstration is to provide an accurate image of the body action, and to clarify the skill's space-time-force components.

The role of the demonstration may vary from one dance form to another. Training in modern dance, jazz, ballet, and folk dance to a certain degree, seems to use the demonstration in a relatively similar fashion, to show how the skill is performed. The major difference between these dance forms and creative dance is that, in creative dance, in addition to highlighting a correct skill, the demonstration is often used to show a novel way of turning, jumping, or combining skills with variations in space-time-force components in order to stimulate or generate other novel movement ideas.

In summary, the intent of the demonstration in a typical technique class is to illustrate a specific skill, or a particular aspect of a skill. With experience, teachers learn to recognize the intricacies of a good demonstration. Experienced artists and teachers are an excellent source of knowledge on teaching dance. For insightful comments and suggestions on the topic, we recommend *The Art of Teaching Dance Technique*[1]; it includes the testimonies of several outstanding modern dance teachers.

What Elements Can be Demonstrated

The basic premise is that the demonstration must match the verbal instructions. A demonstration may emphasize either the body action or its components. Most demonstrations in dance serve to represent the physical action of the body. The typical progression in a technique class is: the first demonstration shows the mechanics of the body action, then the demonstration emphasizes specific dynamics. Finally, the model performs the skill in a realistic dance context. The example of a side fall illustrates this progression. It is always a good idea to demonstrate the skill in full at the beginning to give students a sense of what the skill looks like at normal speed. The side fall would then be demonstrated slowly, and in parts. The body action would probably be taught starting from a kneeling position rather than standing position. The instructor might want to explain the weight shifting and the arm action separately. She might encourage students to try the fall on both sides to determine which is their preferred side for that particular skill. After having analyzed and studied each of these parts, students should then be ready to try the side fall from a standing position.

> It is suggested to first demonstrate the skill in full and at normal speed to give students a global sense of how it should be performed.

If the element to be demonstrated is the timing of the skill, which is often the case in dance, the teacher should clap the rhythm separately. It is important that students hear the precise rhythm or count of a skill, especially if it is complex. The rhythm of a skill or sequence of skills is not always evident to students. For example, the syncopated rhythm of a jazz sequence is not easily internalized by watching a model perform the phrase. A study

Figure 10.2
In certain dance forms, the instructor commonly performs the skill with the students in order to provide an ongoing reference point.

on synchronization of steps with a beat showed that students who had heard the rhythm of a sequence, in addition to a visual demonstration, performed better than those who had only received visual modeling.[24] Clearly, the importance of rhythm in the acquisition of dance skills varies between dance forms. In ballet, precision is an integral part of skill acquisition.[7] In that case, the instructor must bring the students' attention to the counts of the exercise. What is important to remember is that teachers must emphasize key aspects of the skill, in whatever form is best to make the message as clear as possible to students.

A novel dance skill should be first demonstrated in its entirety, at the normal speed, in order to give students a global sense of how it should be executed. For beginners, however, the skill will probably be taught in sections, and perhaps at a slower speed, if needed. The first demonstration is often what stays in the learner's memory, and, as such, is critical. Once the skill is familiar to the students, the teacher does not need to

Table 10.3   Examples of Elements that can be Demonstrated in a Dance Class

Body Action
  Weight shift before a turn
  Action of the gesturing leg
  Position of legs and arms during a jump
  Action of one body part in relation to another part
  Fall to the floor
  Line of the body during a balance position

Timing - Rhythm
  Timing of whole action or of separate sections
  Action that falls on the accented beat
  The preparation or action before the first beat
  A change from a 4/4 to a 3/4 meter
  A change from a slow to a fast tempo
  On which count one dancer begins, in relation to another dancer

Space
  Size of gesture
  Distance covered during a movement
  Orientation of the body at the start and end of a movement
  A change of direction in a traveling sequence
  Location of one dancer in relation to other dancers
  Floor pattern of the dance sequence
  Eye focus

Quality - Energy
  Lightness of steps
  Sustained quality of gestures
  A change in muscular tension during a movement
  Energy required in a jump
  Smoothness of landing

Dance Sequence
  Smooth transitions between actions
  Flow of the dance sequence

fully demonstrate it. The demonstration could simply be a reminder or a review of the skill; in this case, the teacher will "mark" the skill with shorthand or abbreviated movements, often of the hand or foot, with smaller amplitude and faster tempo. This type of demonstration, often used in the perfect stages, is more a memory aid than a complete illustration of the skill. In the last part of the chapter, "marking" is suggested as one of the learning strategies recommended to students. Table 10.3 provides examples of what can be demonstrated in a dance class.

Frequency of Demonstration

In a typical technique class, the instructor rarely lets students learn by trial and error; it is best to provide a model as early as possible to help students develop a mental image of the skill. Empirical evidence strongly suggests that a demonstration is necessary at the onset of learning, when the new skill is presented.[9] There is, however, no rule as to how many times to demonstrate a skill. Depending on the length and difficulty of the skill, beginners may need several demonstrations until they reach the correct stage. If the skill is a sequence of actions, more demonstrations are likely to be required than if the skill is a single body action. There is always the danger of giving too many demonstrations, which may result in learners becoming dependent on visual modeling. How does one know what is appropriate practice?

> A demonstration is critical at the onset of learning; depending on the complexity of the skill and experience of the learners, several demonstrations may be required until students reach the correct stage.

Renowned artist and educator Martha Wittman argues that demonstrations should be kept to a minimum to ensure that students do not become "over-reliant on a teacher or assistant, but become engaged with the class and whatever is going on as directly as possible."[25] Another renowned artist and educator, Jeff Slayton, explains that he will show the movement three times to beginners, and if it is still not clear, he will show it again but will make sure they pay attention.[26]

The Model: Teacher or Student?

As a general rule, the dance instructor usually demonstrates the skill. Motor learning literature indicates that, whether the demonstrator is the teacher or a peer is of little importance, as long as the model is able to accurately perform the critical features of the skill.[9,27] There are several positions on this issue. There is support for using a skilled model when a complex movement is introduced. An unskilled model may be beneficial for beginners, as they participate actively in the problem-solving activities of the model attempting to do the skill. These positions are reviewed extensively in motor learning texts[9,27] and are summarized in Table 10.4.

Table 10.4   Who Should Demonstrate Dance Skills: Summary of Findings[9,10,31]

The common practice is to use a skilled model to demonstrate the action.

The single most important characteristic of a model is her ability to perform the skill correctly.

Accurate demonstration leads to better learning; watching a skilled model leads to correct imitation of an efficient movement.

There is conflicting evidence about the positive influence of a skilled model and an unskilled (or peer) model.

Learning can be facilitated by having beginners observe other beginners before attempting the skill.

The advantage of watching an unskilled model repeatedly practice the skill to be learned is that the observer is actively and cognitively involved in solving the problem, along with the model.

A skilled models offers very little error information that learners can use to develop their own error-detection mechanism.

It may be best to use a skilled model for complex skills; a peer model can be efficient for movements that are a variation of familiar movement patterns.

There is no overwhelming consensus as to who should demonstrate a skill. This indicates the very complexity of teaching and learning motor skills. Teachers use different models for different reasons, and develop preferences based on successful experiences and resources available to them. Successful experiences in the classroom may come with diversity of methods rather than using only one type of demonstration.

Although a technique class generally includes live demonstration, there may be instances where the instructor chooses to use other visual aids such as videotapes or photographs. Consider the impact of watching an outstanding artist perform a dance sequence. Not only does viewing a performance show a technical aspect performed brilliantly, it may also act as a stimulant and motivator. Sometimes this may be what students need more than anything else. It is therefore crucial for teachers to know their students and be able to detect the mood of the class; this can aid in timing when to expose them to effective demonstration tools.

Regardless of whether the demonstration is live or filmed, it must always be supplemented by verbal cues. It is important to remember that verbal cues help students focus on specific aspects of the skill. The instructor could point out the action of the free leg before and during the demonstration, for example. In essence, verbal cues direct the learners' attention to that body part only, and help them consciously ignore, for the time being, what the rest of the body does.

Location of the Model

All dance teachers will agree that the model should be positioned so that all students have a clear view of the demonstration. The best place is generally at the front of the class. However, experienced teachers are familiar with the tendency for their students to have a favorite spot when they arrange themselves for class: some students prefer to be on the front row, while others always opt for the back. In the absence of a personality profile of each student, a generalization is that territorial preferences are often related to students' skill and confidence level. The teacher might want to vary the classroom configuration periodically to allow students in the back row to be at the front, and vice versa. A change in the class organization may be another way to show impartiality toward students and ensure that all are able to clearly see the demonstration.

The model may choose to face students or demonstrate with her back to them. Which location is better? The answer depends on a number of factors. Complex spatial patterns with the feet may best be shown with the demonstrator's back to the students, while a simple arm gesture could be demonstrated facing them. A lateral flexion would best be demonstrated facing students, whereas an abdominal contraction may be best portrayed in a profile orientation. A recent study indicated that students showed a preference for spatially compatible mapping (e.g., students and model facing the same direction when learning a dance skill).[28] This spatial orientation, most common in many dance classes, certainly facilitates copying movements.

It is always a good idea to demonstrate a skill in more than one orientation. Certain skills must be seen at different angles in order for students to see their three-dimensional shape. The location of the model also varies depending on the part of the lesson. In the introduction phase, with experienced students, the instructor or model often faces them. Later on, when new skills are introduced, the model and students will face the same direction. What is important to remember is that, when planning a lesson, the teacher must think in terms of the learners, what aspect of the skill is demonstrated, and which position and angle give the best view. Table 10.5 summarizes recommendations on the location of the model.

A final aspect pertaining the model's orientation is the direction of the demonstration and transfer of learning. On which side should the demonstration be first given, the right or the left side? Can students transfer a skill from one side to the other? Traditionally, the teacher introduces and demonstrates a skill or sequence of skills to the students' right, and asks them to transfer it to the left side. It has been suggested that teachers evaluate the extent to which they are laterally biased in their demonstrations.[29] A demonstration should be given on both sides to encourage students to gain proficiency of motor control on both sides, and avoid asymmetries. Why not introduce a skill to the left or non-preferred side sometimes? Additionally, time must be allocated during the lesson to allow students to practice a skill on their non-preferred side as well as their preferred side.

Bilateral transfer is described as an individual's ability to learn a skill more easily on one side after it has been learned on the opposite side.[9]

Table 10. 5 Where Should the Model be in Relation to the Class

For new skills, imitation is easier when facing the same direction as the students

For known skills, facing students is fine

For simple skills, facing students is fine

For complex skills, imitation is easier when facing the same direction as the students

For complex skills, demonstrate in more than one angle to help students see the three-dimensional shape

For footwork involving directional changes, face the same direction as the students

For arm gestures, facing students is fine

If students are in a circle formation, it may be best to be in the center, and demonstrate at different angles

Vary the "front" of the class; ask students to turn 90 or 180 degrees, to vary placement of students vis-à-vis the model

Should a skill be first taught on the preferred or non-preferred side? There are conflicting but limited results on this issue. Two studies using dance sequences examined this question. The first study showed greater transfer of learning from the non-preferred to the preferred side than from the other most commonly used direction.[30] The second study showed no difference in bilateral transfer.[31] Such limited findings do not warrant inferences to larger populations. Nonetheless, demonstrations and practice time on both sides are recommended to develop skilled and versatile dancers.

> A skill should always be demonstrated and practiced on both sides to ensure greater versatility in performance.

This issue becomes even more important when teaching children. As presented in Chapter 6, young learners have developmental limitations that must be considered in the dance class. They are in the process of consciously becoming aware of a preferred side. It is important to give them every opportunity to experience motor skills on both sides.[32]

Learning Strategies

We have seen in Chapters 5 and 7 that novice and experienced dancers behave differently in the dance class. A recent study with novice and advanced dancers showed that both groups behaved differently while watching a dance sequence being demonstrated.[28] Students were asked to watch a demonstration and repeat the sequence. The experienced students verbalized what they saw during the demonstration, and also moved along with the model. In contrast, the novice students just stood and watched. As expected, the advanced dancers retained more dance steps and performed them with greater accuracy than the novices. These findings support an earlier study that showed that young ballet expert dancers used descriptive words to recall dance movements.[33]

Figure 10.3
To clarify a point the instructor might direct students to move with her while listening to her cues.

Such findings suggest that teachers should encourage beginners to encode visual information through more than one modality. Students should be encouraged to "mark" (partial, abbreviated movements that correspond to what is being demonstrated) the sequence, and also verbalize (short words that correspond to what is being demonstrated) in some way what they see. These strategies can also help students group skills in such a way as to memorize the sequence more rapidly. Observation strategies such as marking and verbalizing can then be used as memory aids. The benefit of learning strategies can be seen immediately after a demonstration, as students attempt to replicate the skill.

Along with these strategies, the teacher must verify a basic step in learning: ensure that students understand what the skill is. The simplest method for this is to ask questions prior to the first attempts. Students should always be encouraged to ask questions, no matter how much material must be covered during the lesson. Understanding the skill at hand is not only a prerequisite for learning, it may also create a more reassuring and enriching climate for learning and dancing.

Students who adopted learning strategies give a clear message that they are responsible for their own learning. Responsible learners are consciously aware of and participate in every aspect of the lesson, that is, the physical activities of moving and dancing, and the cognitive activities of comprehending, perceiving, detecting, correcting, and planning their dance skills. Responsible learners are also independent learners. As suggested in Chapter 8, good teachers produce not only good dancers, but independent learners as well.

Assessing the Effectiveness of Instructional Methods

Is there one single teaching method that produces the greatest results in learning and performing dance? Of course not. No single method will guarantee success for all students. There are many factors that influence the learning process in a dance classroom. Some factors cannot be changed by the instructor, whereas others are under her direct control. Factors that cannot be changed pertain to students' background and capabilities, as well as dance skills. What the teacher can change is the way these skills are presented to them. Teaching methods can indeed alter students' cognitive and motor capabilities.

One of the greatest rewards a teacher can ever receive is a student telling her that she was always afraid to do a particular movement, or could never do it before, and now, she succeeded for the first time. The potential was there, but somehow, previous teachers were unable to transform this potential into a successful action. Any caring teacher should be concerned with improving her effectiveness in the classroom. Table 10-6 contains a series of questions that may help teachers reflect on their teaching practices, habits, or style. Such reflective exercise can be done individually or with a colleague. A teacher may also ask a colleague to observe her teaching and offer feedback. Observation and feedback shared in a spirit of collegiality can greatly enhance teacher effectiveness.

Table 10. 6   Questions to Ask When Reflecting on Verbal Instructions and Demonstrations Used in the Dance Class

Verbal instructions

Do you…
Provide clear and unambiguous instructions?
Point out similarities between the new skill and skills they know?
Select the most important aspects of the skill first?
Include all the important aspects at once?
Use visual or kinesthetic images to help them get a clear idea of the skill?
Get impatient when a students asks you to repeat the instructions?
Repeat the exact same instructions the second time around?
Remember exactly what you asked them to do in the first place?
Ensure that they pay complete attention to what you say?
Vary the amount of instructions depending on the students' level?
Ask some students to repeat the instructions to verify whether they understood?
Leave enough time for them to practice a few times before you interrupt them?

Demonstration

Do you…
Demonstrate all movements?
Demonstrate the entire skill or parts only?
Ask students to demonstrate the skill?
Demonstrate the skill in its normal tempo?
Slow down the speed of the action first?
Explain the key elements of the skill before the demonstration is given?
Demonstrate with your preferred side first?
Repeat a demonstration?
Demonstrate common errors?
Verbalize key elements as you demonstrate?
Always demonstrate facing students?
Vary the angle of demonstration for certain actions?

Summary

Considering the complexity of dance skills and the learning process, and the diversity of students' background and capabilities, it is extremely difficult to make a global judgment on which method is the best for teaching dance. However, there are certain ways of presenting a dance skill to a particular group of students that may be more conducive to learning than others. Further research on the effectiveness of verbal instruction and demonstration in teaching dance will shed more light on these issues. Thus far, discussions have appeared primarily in the literature directly related to motor learning and development. These studies have provided invaluable knowledge about teaching. The next step is to bring these findings to a more specific level by using dance tasks and dance students.

References

1. Schlaich J, DuPont B: *The Art of Teaching Dance Technique*. Reston, VA: National Dance Association, 1993.
2. Welsh T, Fitt S, Thompson W: A comparison of forward and backward chaining: Strategies for teaching dance movement sequences. Impulse 2:262-274, 1994.
3. Siedentop D: *Developing Teaching Skills in Physical Education* (3rd ed). Mountain View, CA: Mayfield, 1991.
4. Lord M, Chayer M, Girard L: Increasing awareness of your strategies for teaching dance technique. Impulse 3:172-182, 1995.
5. Skrinar M, Moses NH: Whos's teaching the dance class? *In:* Clarkson PM, Skrinar M (eds): *Science of Dance Training*. Champaign, IL: Human Kinetics Publishers, Inc. 1988, pp. 289-297.
6. Schlaich J, DuPont B: *The Art of Teaching Dance Technique*. Reston, VA: National Dance Association, 1993, p. 3.
7. Côté-Laurence P: The role of rhythm in ballet training. Research in Dance Education 1(2):173-191, 2000.
8. Penrod J, Plastino JG: *The Dancer Prepares: Modern Dance for Beginners,* (4th ed). Mountain View, CA: Mayfield, 1998.
9. Magill RA: *Motor Learning: Concepts and Applications,* (6th ed). New York: McGraw Hill, 2001.
10. Schmidt RA, Wrisberg CA: *Motor Learning and Performance. A Problem-Based Learning Approach*, (2nd ed). Champaign, IL: Human Kinetics Publishers, Inc., 2000.
11. Hanrahan C, Salmela JH: Dance images: Do they really work or are we just imagining things? Journal of Physical Education, Recreation and Dance 61(2):18-21, 1990.
12. Minton S: Exploring the mind/body connection with imagery. Kinesiology and Medicine for Dance 14(1):29-32, 1991/92.
13. Franklin E: *Dance Imagery for Technique and Performance*. Champaign, IL: Human Kinetics Publishers, Inc., 1996.
14. Franklin E: *Dynamic Alignment Through Imagery*. Champaign, IL: Human Kinetics Publishers, Inc., 1996.
15. Hanrahan C: In search of a good dance image. Impulse 2(2):131-144, 1994.

16. Purcell TM: The use of imagery in children's dance: Making it work. Journal of Physical Education, Recreation and Dance 61(2):22-23, 1990.
17. Minton S: Assessment of the use of imagery in the dance classroom. Impulse 4:276-292, 1996.
18. Overby LY: The use of imagery by dance teachers: Development and implementation of two research instruments. Journal of Physical Education, Recreation and Dance 61(2):23-27, 1990.
19. Minton S: Enhancement of alignment through imagery. Journal of Physical Education, Recreation and Dance 61(2):28-19, 1990.
20. Bandura A: Social foundations of though and action: A social cognitive theory. Englewood Cliffs, NJ: Prentice Hall, 1986.
21. Knudson DV, Morrison CS: *Qualitative Analysis of Human Movement.* Champaign, IL: Human Kinetics Publishers, Inc., 1997.
22. Weiss MR, Klint K: "Show and Tell" in the gymnasium: An investigation of developmental differences in modeling and verbal rehearsal of motor skills. Research Quarterly for Exercise and Sport 58(2):234-241, 1987.
23. Magill RA, Schoenfelder-Zohdi B: A visual model and feedback of performance as sources of information for learning a rhythmic gymnastics skill. International Journal of Sport Psychology 27:7-22, 1996.
24. Wuyts IJ, Buekers MJ: The effects of visual and auditory models on the learning of a rhythmical synchronization dance skill. Research Quarterly for Exercise and Sport 66(2):105-115, 1995.
25. Schlaich J, DuPont B: *The Art of Teaching Dance Technique.* Reston, VA: National Dance Association, 1993, p. 43.
26. Schlaich J, DuPont B: *The Art of Teaching Dance Technique.* Reston, VA: National Dance Association, 1993, p. 41.
27. Rose DJ: *A Multilevel Approach to the Study of Motor Control and Learning.* Boston: Allyn and Bacon, 1997.
28. Poon PL, Rogers WM: Learning and remembering strategies of novice and advanced jazz dancers for skill level appropriate dance routines. Research Quarterly for Exercise and Sport 71(2):135-144, 2000.
29. Kimmerle M: Lateral bias in dance teaching. Presented at the International Association for Dance Medicine and Science conference, Alcala de Henares, Spain, November 2001.
30. Puretz SL: Bilateral transfer: The effect of practice on the transfer of complex dance movement patterns. Research Quarterly for Exercise and Sport 54(1):48-54, 1983.
31. Makowicki SZ: The effect of left-side instruction of complex dance patterns on transfer time in adolescent dance students. Masters Dissertation Abstracts 33(1):3, 1994.
33. Starkes J, Deakin JM, Lindley S, Crisp F: Motor versus verbal recall of ballet sequences by young expert dancers. Journal of Sport Psychology 9:222-230, 1987.
32. Kimmerle M, Bowes Sewell K: Dance students' perception of lateral bias in the dance class. Presented at the International Association for Dance Medicine and Science conference, Alcala de Henares, Spain, November 2001.
34. LaPointe-Crump JD: *In Balance. The Fundamentals of Ballet.* Dubuque, IA: Wm. C. Brown Publishers, 1985, p. 38.

Marliese Kimmerle

The Role of Feedback in the Dance Class

Types of Feedback Appropriate in the Dance Class

   Extrinsic Feedback

   Intrinsic Feedback

   Timing of Feedback

   Frequency of Feedback

The Role of Observation in the Dance Class

   What Should the Teacher Observe?

   When is Observation Important?

Evaluating Instructional Practices

Chapter 11

How to Provide Feedback

Y ou have introduced a new skill to your class of beginners. The students have seen a demonstration, have tried the skill a few times, and have received your corrections. They are now attempting to correct their performance of the skill. You notice that some students continue to move haphazardly, seemingly ignoring your corrections. Why? Do they believe that these corrections do not apply to them? Or perhaps they think that they have made the corrections? How do they know their learning is progressing well and how they are performing? In addition to selecting appropriate dance materials and instructional methods, the effective teacher must also provide meaningful feedback to learners to assist them with the acquisition of new skills. In order to effectively provide feedback, the teacher must observe students, determine where the problems are, and decide how to communicate these to the students.

The main challenge facing students during the correct stage is to learn to detect and correct their own performance errors. Beginners can only do so with the help of the teacher. In order to improve, learners need to know what parts of the skill they are doing correctly and what parts need to be changed. This chapter examines the role of feedback in dance skill learning. In the previous chapter, verbal instructions were used to introduce a skill. In this chapter, verbal information refers solely to corrections made by the instructor after a skill has been executed. Although a few references are made to folk and creative dance, we will focus mainly on the typical technique class found in modern, jazz, and ballet. Lastly, the chapter addresses mostly the adult learner, as very little is known about feedback for children.

Again, the theoretical framework for understanding feedback is grounded in motor learning theory. First, issues related to the use of feedback in dance are presented, followed by a section on observational skills for teachers. The final section offers teachers some practical guidelines on feedback and observation.

The Role of Feedback in the Dance Class

It has been well documented that feedback is one of the most critical factors in motor skill learning.[1-3] Feedback is generally defined as information on the performance of a skill that allows an individual to improve the skill. In dance, feedback is an integral part of instruction. Experienced dance educators argue that giving corrections to students is a basic ingredient to a technique class.[4-6] Without some form of feedback, the student has no way of knowing how he is doing, or how close he is from the targeted skill. It is through feedback that students learn dance skills and improve their performance level. However, not all dance classes aim for skill acquisition and achievement. People often enroll in recreational dance classes for the sheer enjoyment of dancing. Feedback, as examined in this chapter, applies to students interested in developing their skills in certain dance forms.

As seen in Chapter 4, feedback is most crucial in the correct stage of learning. It is during that stage that the mental image and motor plan of a skill continue to be developed. The beginner is highly dependent on the teacher's corrections because he is unable to self detect the correctness of the skill being executed. For example, a student may not sense that his leg is not fully extended or that the arms are not at shoulder height. There are many reasons for his inability to do so: poor kinesthetic sense, not paying attention, or lack of experience. Without feedback from the instructor, the learner would have great difficulty progressing to the third stage of learning. Picture yourself trying to learn to read music and play the piano on your own. How far would you go without an instructor?

> Feedback is most crucial in the correct stage, where the mental image and motor plan of the skill are being developed.

An intervention in teaching motor skills, feedback plays three major roles: correction of movement errors, reinforcement of correct technique, and motivation to practice.[7] Although good teaching in dance includes all these functions, this chapter examines the first role of feedback, mainly to assist learners on how to perform the dance skill better on subsequent practice. Regardless of dance form, most feedback given in a technique class is used primarily to correct errors and generate a new response that is closer to the targeted skill than the previous response. The types of feedback most appropriate in dance is knowledge of performance, and includes extrinsic and intrinsic feedback.

Types of Feedback Appropriate in the Dance Class

In the motor learning literature, knowledge of performance is information on the movement form or quality. In contrast to sport skills, where the goal of the skill is to achieve an environment outcome (e.g., the throw was successful), the goal in dance is to perfect the form of the skill (e.g., the legs were fully extended during the jump). Therefore, knowledge of performance is the most appropriate feedback for dance.[8] Corrections such as "keep your turnout symmetrical," "fully arch your foot," "maintain your trunk vertical," or "focus directly in front of you," are examples of feedback called "knowledge of performance"; they inform the dancer about the mechanics and form of the skill. Feedback discussed in this chapter refers to knowledge of performance. The terms feedback, knowledge of performance, and correction, are used interchangeably the discussion that follows. In a technique class, knowledge of performance is either extrinsic or intrinsic.

> The type of feedback most appropriate in dance is knowledge of performance, which is information about the mechanics and form of a skill.

Extrinsic Feedback

Extrinsic feedback, often called augmented feedback, is information provided to the learner by an external source such as the instructor, while intrinsic feedback comes mainly from the learner's sensory receptors (e.g., what he sees, hears, or feels).[1,2] The type of correction typically used early in the learning process is extrinsic feedback. There are three forms of extrinsic feedback commonly used in dance: feedback from the instructor, the mirror, and videotape. For the most part, the instructor provides either verbal or tactile corrections during a technique class.

Verbal Corrections

Verbal correction, the predominant mode of intervention in teaching dance skills, essentially provides information on how to perform the skill on the next trial. The correction must be based on what the instructor pointed out in his initial verbal instructions. Similar to verbal instruc-

Gabrielle Laurence

Figure 11.1
Effective corrections involve feedback on one aspect of the skill at a time.

tions, verbal corrections can be provided for any aspect of the skill. Experienced teachers have been observed to make verbal corrections on four aspects of dance skills: the mechanics of the body action, ways to improve the performance, the timing or counts, and the aesthetics of the movement.[6] In essence, these represent the aspects of dance skills promoted in Chapter 2: the body actions, the components, and the context. In order to be effective, the teacher's verbal corrections must be on one aspect at a time, must be specific, must be understood by students, and must be constructive.

The first guideline for appropriate feedback is to limit the number of corrections provided at one time. As presented in Chapter 5, learners, especially inexperienced dancers, have a limited cognitive capacity to process and retain large amounts of information. In order to be effective, feedback should be provided on only one aspect of the skill at a time, and students must be given sufficient time to practice between corrections. For example, the instructor sees three problems: the arms, the gesturing leg, and the hips. To point out to the students all three errors at once would delay the learning process. The first correction should be on the most important aspect of the skill. Once the instructor is satisfied that the correction has been made, then the second most important aspect of the skill can be corrected, and so on. In a creative dance lesson for example, if students are asked to experiment with symmetrical and asymmetrical body shapes, feedback must be on the clarity of these shapes and not on the locomotor patterns that link them. Remember, verbal instructions and corrections must be consistent with one another.

> Effective corrections stress only one aspect at a time, are specific, understood by students, and worded in a constructive manner.

The second guideline is the specificity of feedback. In order to guide students, feedback should be as specific as possible.[7] Clear verbal corrections assist students in modifying a precise aspect of the skill. A beginner may not know or feel that his back leg is not fully extended during a jump. A precise correction will tell him what to change. A general feedback such as "your jump is not correct, do it again" provides no specific help to the learner. Remember, learners rely heavily on the instructor's feedback when they are in the process of developing a mental image of the correct skill. Vague and general corrections serve to confuse students. Remember also that good corrections are brief and concise. The instructor should use as few words as possible to give the information to the student. Lengthy feedback is not necessary. However, there are times when general comments such as "good work" or "that was better," are necessary; they provide positive feedback and serve to encourage and motivate students.

Verbal corrections are only as effective as the student's comprehension of the message. The third guideline is to ensure that students understand the verbal corrections.[6,7] Corrections are meaningful and useful only if students understand what the problem is. One of the difficulties in providing meaningful guidance is the selection of language that is appropriate for a particular group of students, and for a particular skill. Verbal corrections given to young students on alignment would likely be formulated differently than those given to adult beginners. For proper arm position, for example, the teacher may remind young children to put their arms around a big balloon, whereas he would ask adults to think of the curved line in their arms.

The instructor should periodically verify that everyone understood the corrections provided. It is preferable to repeat and explain a correction early on, and maintain a positive climate.

> Effective verbal corrections are those understood by students. Unclear feedback leads to unchanged performance.

Unclear corrections might lead to frustration for the students and the teacher. A correction that is not understood is likely to be ignored by the students, and thus produce no change in their performance. If the entire class executes the skill incorrectly, it is likely that the instructions were unclear.

The fourth guideline is that the feedback should be delivered in the proper tone. There are many ways to tell a student that he did the movement incorrectly. Verbal corrections must be worded in such a way that the learner appreciates what he must do, and is not discouraged. Experienced teachers know that negative feedback can have a devastating and long-lasting effect.[7] Extensive research on coaching behaviors indicates that young athletes responded most favorably to supportive feedback and behaviors than to punitive feedback.[9] Although negative feedback may work with some more experienced students, and in some circumstances, it is best to avoid using that type of feedback, especially with beginners. Formulated in a constructive way, a correction gives the student the message that he can accomplish the task. Beginners may interpret the correction as directed to them as persons. More experienced and confident students learn to take the correction for what it is: a comment on their execution of a skill. Consider the two statements, "let's concentrate on this" and "your turn is still wrong." For the recipient, there may indeed be a large psychological difference between these statements.

Verbal corrections can be given to individuals or to the class. A typical technique class includes both types of feedback. Group corrections, after the skill has been tried a few times, are always appropriate of course, provided that they apply to more than one or two students. Although some recommend that more corrections should be given to the entire class rather than to individual students in a class of beginners,[4,5] individual corrections are often necessary. Individual corrections are required throughout the learning cycle, although they are more important at the

Table 11.1   Characteristics of Effective Verbal Corrections

Effective verbal corrections are:
  Clear and concise information on what aspect to change in the movement
  Specific to one aspect of the skill at a time
  Worded in a constructive manner
  Worded in a language familiar to the learner
  Provided as soon after the movement as possible
  Individualized as often as possible
  Repeated when necessary
  Accompanied by tactile feedback when necessary
  Directed to the class when they apply to most students

onset of learning. In contrast, general corrections are often directed to the class.

Verbal feedback by the instructor is the most common type of feedback used in a technique class. The instructor can also provide tactile feedback. Table 11.1 summarizes characteristics of effective verbal corrections in the technique class.

Tactile Corrections

Tactile corrections seem to be a favorite among experienced dance teachers.[6] It has been reported that tactile forms of correction work best in making students feel the proper motion; in the motor learning literature, this form of correction is termed "physical guidance."[2,3] This type of individual feedback is common in the dance technique class because, in addition to being highly specific, it can be provided to several students while the class is moving. For example, by touching the student's knee joint, the instructor directs his attention immediately to that joint, and the student gains a better sense of what to do to correct the problem. This type of feedback is quite effective in bringing students' attention to a problematic part of the body, thus helping them develop their kinesthetic sense.

> Tactile corrections help beginners develop their kinesthetic sense for properly executed dance skills.

The success of tactile correction depends directly on the learner's level of kinesthetic awareness. As part of technique training, a dancer must be able to know exactly where his limbs are in space and how much effort is required to produce a particular action or maintain a certain position. Students acquire kinesthetic acuity through practice accompanied by various types of feedback. In some situations, the teacher may physically move a student through an action, for example, move a joint or body part to make him feel the action. The teacher may also hold a student in a specific position to give him the kinesthetic sense of the action or position.[7]

Figure 11.2
Tactile corrections should
suggest a motion without
forcing movement.

A word of caution is necessary here. Ensure that your students agree about being touched by the teacher.[6] It is suggested that the teacher inform students that he will correct them by touching. Some students may object for a number of personal reasons. When used, tactile corrections must be gentle, suggesting, and must never force a change in a joint or limb.[6] The teacher can either remind the students that their trunk is not at the vertical, gently move the trunk back, ask that they look at themselves in the mirror, or the teacher can videotape students so that they can watch their actions themselves. Characteristics of effective tactile feedback are presented in Table 11.2.

In summary, the most common types of extrinsic feedback in a technique class are provided by the instructor' verbal and tactile corrections. Students can also receive corrections via two other external sources: the mirror and video.

Table 11.2   Characteristics of Effective Tactile Corrections

Effective tactile corrections:
   Are physical guidance to correct a movement
   Are specific to a body part
   Reinforce verbal corrections
   Gently suggest, never force a motion
   Are provided after the student is informed and consents
   Assist the student in feeling the correct motion
   Can be felt by the student on the teacher's body
   Contribute to the development of the kinesthetic sense

The Mirror

Most jazz, modern dance, and ballet studios are equipped with mirrors. Students taking technique classes in these forms have learned to dance while looking in a mirror. Folk dance and creative dance classes rarely use mirrors. Regardless of students and teachers' preferences in the dance class, a dance performance takes place on a stage where there are no mirrors. Considering that the ultimate goal of a teacher is to teach students how to dance, it is logical that the learning environment should resemble the real performance setting. This line of thought leads to some logical questions: What do we know about the effectiveness of the mirror as source of visual feedback? Does it work? When? For whom? Research on the effectiveness of the mirror in dance learning is scarce.

> The mirror provides instant visual feedback on the correctness of a body position and/or bodyline.

The advantage of the mirror is that it provides instant visual feedback on the correctness of a position and body line. For example, the student sees whether the arms are at the proper height, whether the hips are at the same level, or whether the trunk is truly vertical. Basically, the mirror is useful for basic body alignment, to see the spatial difference between tense and relaxed shoulders, or a hip that is higher than the other when it should not be. Periodic use of the mirror is most useful for actions that take place on the spot.

Students can learn to feel the correct position by seeing it in the mirror. In this regard, the mirror can help a student develop his kinesthetic sense. However, for sequences involving locomotion across the floor, with head and direction changes, the mirror is of little use. In fact, teachers know how disruptive the mirror can be when students are more preoccupied with looking in the mirror as they execute leaps and turns across the floor than they are on performing the sequence correctly. A teaching strategy to encourage students to not always rely on the mirror is to vary the front of the class so that students are not always facing it. The teacher could have the class sideways in relation to the mirror. In this orientation, students do not look at themselves, yet they can verify a position in profile periodically.

Mirrors can be great learning tools when used judiciously. When overused, however, the mirror can become a crutch. Experienced teachers wisely advise caution regarding the overuse of the mirror when teaching beginners in a ballet class.[4] Students should not always rely on the mirror. Instead, they should be encouraged to rely on their internal sensory receptors for information about the position of their joints and body parts. You must have witnessed students who cannot dance in the room unless they are facing the mirror. These students are never fully concentrating on what they are doing as they are busy focusing on the direction of the mirror. They have not learned the spatial orientation of the movements.

Figure 11.3
Students must learn to be aware of the position of their joints and limbs and to discern them without having to rely on extrinsic feedback.

Teacher must train dancers to become independent of extrinsic feedback. They must teach their dancers to be aware of the position of their joints and limbs, and to discern them without having to always rely on visual aids. The mirror offers assistance early in technique training. However, it must not prevent students from developing their kinesthetic awareness. Table 11.3 summarizes the effective use of the mirror in the technique class. Remember that dancers cannot carry a mirror on stage with them, but they can always carry their kinesthetic acuity with them, regardless of where they dance.

A final point about the mirror: As much as it is a positive source of feedback for talented and confident students, the mirror may be intimidating for less confident students. That may explain why some students tend to stay at the back of the class, away from the mirror. You may deal with this problem in a neutral, non-judgmental way by periodically rotating students during class; this would allow everyone to be near the mirror, at least for one part of the lesson.

Table 11.3   Effective Use of the Mirror in the Technique Class

The mirror can be used to:
  Show stationary movements and positions
  Illustrate a correct and incorrect position
  Emphasize a body alignment aspect
  Clarify a spatial aspect (height of limb or relationship between two body parts)
  Specify the starting and ending position of a movement
  Show symmetrical and asymmetrical shapes
  Observe students while performing the movements with them
  Observe students while demonstrating
  Monitor students from different vantage points in the room
  Detect a student who needs attention
  Show students how to verify the proper alignment of critical body parts

Video

The video replay of a student's performance or skill execution can be an effective source of visual feedback. In fact, a student watching himself perform a skill may provide the most revealing form of feedback because it leaves little room for interpretation. Can all learners benefit from watching themselves on video? Should we assume that a beginner's focus is directed to the appropriate aspect of the action?

Skilled performers tend to benefit more from unguided video feedback than novice performers, unless video feedback is supplemented with verbal cues.[2] This is not surprising. Experienced learners have a clear mental image of the skill, know the important technical aspects, and know how to detect and correct their errors. Therefore, they have the tools that allow them to analyze their actions on the monitor.

> Video feedback is most effective when supplemented with the instructor's verbal cues.

Conversely, beginners require assistance in understanding what they see, and what they should see. To the novice dancer, the video replay may contain too much information. The instructor must watch the video with the students and provide attention-focusing cues in order to optimize the effect of this form of extrinsic feedback on learning. It is also suggested that students be allowed enough time to view the video, in order to better familiarize themselves with this form of feedback.[2]

There is no doubt that video can be an effective means of providing accurate feedback to students about how they execute specific dance skills. It is also an excellent tool to help students gain an awareness of their body capabilities and style of movement. When used periodically, students may actually be able to see progress in their technical performance. Characteristics of effective use of the video in the technique class are presented in Table 11.4.

Table 11.4   Effective Use of the Video in the Technique Class

Video of a skilled model
  To demonstrate the technically correct performance of a complex skill
  To give students a sense of the entire dance
  To show the skill in a dance context
  To compare a skill performed in two different dance forms
Video of the student
  To analyze the student performance
  To show the student how to identify correct and incorrect aspects of the skill
  To emphasize correct aspects of a performance
  To compare different levels of skill proficiency
  To show progress in performance from the beginning to the end of the semester
  To motivate students
  To appreciate aesthetics of correct technique in dance perfomance

Intrinsic Feedback

In addition to feedback from the instructor, the mirror, and video, students learn to detect valuable information about movement from their own body. The learner's ability to shift from extrinsic to intrinsic feedback takes place during the transition from the correct to the perfect stage of learning. Intrinsic feedback is described as the sensory information one receives when producing a movement. For example, when he moves, the learner feels the muscular tension in his joints and body parts, hears the sound of his feet, and sees his arms or legs in the surrounding space. With proper guidance and practice, the dancer gains a keen sense of his body in motion. In dance, there is no doubt that the most important sources of intrinsic feedback comes from the dancer's kinesthetic sense.

> Intrinsic feedback is sensory information a dancer receives when performing a skill.

Kinesthetic acuity develops through proper guidance from the teacher, and through practice. One of the major differences between novice and experienced dancers is their ability to detect the exact position of their body and body parts in space. Beginners need extrinsic feedback, whereas advanced dancers are known to rely entirely on intrinsic feedback. They need to learn to sense whether or not the knees are bent, or whether the arms are too high or too low. Furthermore, the ability to detect and correct movement errors is directly related to the refinement of the dancer's

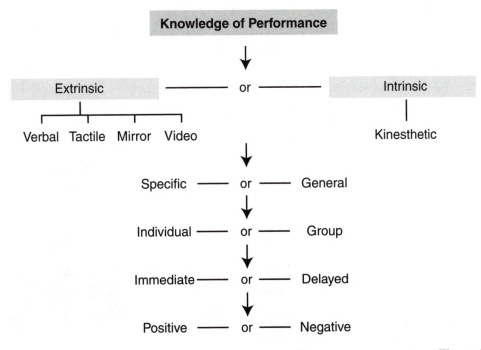

Figure 11.4
Categories of feedback appropriate in the dance class.

kinesthetic sense, a key factor in the learner's reliance on extrinsic feedback. The categories of feedback appropriate in the technique class are listed in Figure 11.4.

As we have seen, there is a variety of tools available for providing feedback to students. With this information in hand, the next step is to determine when feedback is appropriate and how often it should be given.

Timing of Feedback

Should a correction be given during or after the action? Evidence suggests that corrections should be provided immediately after the performance so that they can be used to plan the next action.[7] Ideally, individual corrections are provided to students who need them. An immediate correction allows the learner to modify the incorrect plan of action and prepare for the next attempt. A typical way the teacher can provide individual tactile corrections is by circulating throughout the class while students are doing the exercise and touching students to remind them of a problem that needs attention. Short verbal cues such as "look up," or "your hip," could also be used as a reminder, to help students direct their attention to a particular aspect of the skill while they are doing the exercise.

However, it is not always possible to give immediate individual corrections when teaching a group of 20 students. The key is to observe students and determine who needs help, what help is needed, and to give them corrections as soon as possible through a combination of group and individual feedback. Regardless of class size, at one time or another, a good teacher will manage to give individual feedback to every student in the class. Many instructors are tempted to pay more attention to the skilled students. However, every effort must be made to give each stu-

Figure 11.5
For slow actions there is sufficient time to provide corrections while students are moving.

dent performance enhancing feedback. Giving feedback to a student is, for better or for worse, a form of individual recognition, and, as such, may have significant psychological implications for a healthy and long-lasting self-image.

Group corrections, typically used after a skill has been performed, can be quite effective early in learning, provided that they apply to the majority of the students. This is often the case with beginners during the very first attempts at the skill. For example, if the class has the timing wrong, it is important to stop students immediately, repeat an explanation of the rhythm, and then have them try the skill again. There is nothing to be gained by letting students finish the exercise before pointing out the incorrect timing. Another instance where immediate feedback is crucial is when there is risk of injury. If, for example, you see a student landing poorly after a powerful jump, you want to correct him immediately.

> Group corrections immediately after the performance can be quite effective provided that they apply to most students.

Although immediate feedback is a generally accepted rule in teaching, teachers are encouraged to let students practice before correcting them. Practice provides each student with time to analyze his own performance, detect errors, and make changes to the motor plan for a better execution of the skill. For some students, immediate feedback may be more frustrating than helpful, as they simply need more time to figure out the skill. Whether a correction can be given during or after the action depends on the skill and the skill level of the learners. For slow actions, such as an adagio sequence, there is time to provide corrections while students are moving. When the exercise is short or quick, the correction is possible only after the movement. Suppose triplets (a series of steps repeated several times across the floor) are being taught, then the instructor could perform the steps alongside the student to help him.

Experienced dancers are able to concurrently execute the action and listen to the teacher who is giving verbal corrections. They can also make use of delayed feedback, as they have well developed error detection and correction mechanisms. In contrast, beginners have a short attention span and limited memory capacity, therefore, corrections must be provided immediately after the movement. They would have difficulty paying attention to corrections while moving.

Frequency of Feedback

Another question frequently asked is: How often should corrections be given? Although there are conflicting results on the effect of frequent feedback on learning, there appears to be no advantage to giving feedback after each execution. This may, in fact, cause the learner to become dependent on the instructor's feedback, as in the case of overuse of the mirror. Students must always be encouraged to analyze their own skills so that, when there is no feedback coming from the instructor, they can still closely monitor their own progress. As a general rule, however, more feedback is required early in the correct stage, to help students develop a sense of the correct executions. The frequency of feedback should be decreased as students become more comfortable with the new skill. By then, they are better able to detect and correct their own errors. How the instructor selects which feedback to use is a function of many aspects of the lesson: the content to be taught, the dance form, and of course the instructor's preferred style of instruction. Effective dance teachers know each of their students and selects the type of feedback that works best for them.

The type of feedback provided in a technique class may differ depending on the dance form. There is little interpretation as to how students are to perform skills in ballet, some modern dance forms, jazz, and folk dance. In contrast, individual interpretation is allowed in other modern dance forms, and is strongly encouraged in creative dance. Feedback, therefore, varies in that respect. One of the major differences between dance forms is the strictness of the skills performed to a specific count. Jazz, modern, ballet, and folk dance possess this characteristic, ballet being probably the most rigid. Feedback in a ballet class, therefore, often includes the precise count of the skill.[10] Not only must the leg arrive at prescribed position in space, but it must reach that position at a precise count. In a modern dance or jazz class, feedback may be focused more on the dynamics of the skill, for example, when the release of flow in a sequence is not smooth.

> In a technique class, feedback on the timing of a skill is common to most dance forms.

Unlike in ballet, jazz, modern, or folk dance, a creative dance class focuses not only on technique, but also on making and appreciating dance. Typical feedback may therefore be on a technique, composition, or assessment aspect. Feedback on a technical aspect, similar to the other dance forms, may center on a body action, components, or on elements of context. For example, students might be encouraged to fully extend the free leg to produce the longest line or to illustrate extension in space. In a modern dance class, however, the leg would need to be fully extended because that is what the step or technique requires. Feedback on a component may be on the speed or muscular tension of the gesture, whereas feedback on an element of context may be on the space between two partners, or the dynamics of a group of dancers.

The Role of Observation in the Dance Class

What observational skills are required to enable the teacher to provide meaningful feedback to students? People observe for different reasons. In a dance class, the teacher observes students and students observe the teacher for different reasons. In this section the focus is on the teacher observing students. The observational skills introduced in Chapter 8 serve two main purposes: to assess students' capabilities in order to plan the content of the lesson and select instructional methods, and to assess their performance in order to provide feedback. Interestingly, the criteria for observation in these two instances are often similar. In this section, observation is viewed as the basis for providing appropriate corrections to students.

A dancer is having difficulty learning a new jump. The instructor's role is to help him improve the jump. Essential to this improvement is the instructor's ability to analyze the jump qualitatively. He must diagnose the dancer's strengths and weaknesses and then provide intervention that will help him improve. Student progress depends on appropriate feedback. All experienced teachers know that verbal instructions and demonstration alone are not sufficient to trigger learning of dance skills. Feedback and practice will do it. But feedback on what? Practice of what?

> Teachers use their observational skills to assess their students' learning, and offer an intervention that will improve their performance.

The capacity to make effective corrections during a lesson is directly linked to the teacher's ability to see what the problem is and to know how to fix it. It is argued that one of the qualities of an outstanding technique teacher is a "good eye," the ability to give meaningful corrections.[6] The importance of observational skills in teacher training has been acknowledged by dance scholars as competencies for dance education.[11-13] Good observational skills require the integration of knowledge about dance skills, the learning process, and the learners' capabilities. Qualitative analysis includes two parts: observation and intervention. The latter, intervention or feedback, was presented in the first part of the chapter. The former is now discussed.

Although observational skills are critical in many aspects of the learning environment, they are certainly instrumental for making corrections during the correct stage. If there is a positive change in the way the skill is performed, then the instructor can infer that the student is learning. Similar to the development of preferences for instructional methods, a teacher often identifies preferred observation techniques, more or less on a trial and error basis. There are, however, certain basic rules concerning what and when to observe.

What Should the Teacher Observe?

What does the teacher observe? As a general rule, the teacher observes what he asked students to do in the first place. The main points given in the verbal instructions and demonstration are therefore the main points observed. Assuming that this rule is followed, a dance skill can be analyzed in a number of ways. Keep in mind that dance skills are closed skills, therefore they are mostly performed the same way in an unchanging environment. A simple yet basic observation approach is to view the skill on a time continuum, that is, the preparation, the action itself, and the follow through.[7] For each part, the skill may be further dissected in terms of body parts: What does the supporting leg do? Where should the opposite arm be? What about the trunk action? Finally, the spatial, timing, or dynamic components of the skill may be analyzed. As experienced teachers might suggest, in the end, effective teaching is common sense. If the teacher is not sure what the problem is, he could simply ask the student to execute the skill again. A second observation would likely help diagnose the problem.

> A skill can be analyzed according to three phases: the preparation, the action itself, and the follow through.

The key in effective observation is the teacher's thorough knowledge of the skill. This means that he knows what a correct execution of the skill looks and sounds like. For example, an unusual rhythm in the dancer's performance may catch a teacher's attention. He could then turn his attention to watching the movement to detect what the error might be. The ability to detect what is wrong in the movement is, of course, going to determine the appropriateness of the intervention.

When is Observation Important?

When is observation most important in the learning process? Observation is critical throughout the learning cycle for a particular skill, but is critical during the first several attempts, as part of the correct stage. Students' first attempts usually tell a lot about their skill and comprehension level. The instructor sees whether they understood what to do and how well they can do it. They then can plan their intervention to assist students in reaching the perfect stage of learning for that particular skill. In the correct stage, students are very much dependent on the teacher's corrections in order to reach a higher level of motor proficiency. No two students are the same, therefore, the teacher's role is to actively observe and assess their performance and provide individual guidance as much as possible.

The teacher's vantage point for observation is also an integral component of the process. It has been suggested that the critical feature of the skill should determine where the observer should stand, and that "the best vantage point for observing a particular movement or critical feature is at right angles to the plane of motion."[14] As most dance skills are three-dimensional, the teacher would want to watch the skill from more than one vantage point. Some teachers prefer to observe while stationary, others while moving around/through class; some watch a student from far, others may prefer to stand right next to the student; some stand in front of the class, others observe students from behind; some prefer to watch from the mirror.

Gabrielle Laurence

Figure 11.6
The critical feature of the skill should determine where the observer is located.

Observational skills are learned through training, experience, and reflective practices. Is it possible not to see a student who continues to make the same mistake time and time again? Yes, if the teacher does not pay attention to what the students are doing. This can happen if the teacher is too busy looking at himself in the mirror, planning the next exercise, or talking to a visitor instead of watching the students. As a general principle of good teaching, remember that a teacher is there to manage learning, and that this requires undivided attention.

A teacher's observational preferences develop over time. In order to be effective and successful in a particular dance form and for a particular age group, a teacher's observation strategies must include a variety of criteria, styles, and techniques. Good teachers are not always predictable in what they say, how they say it, how they correct, or whom they correct. They are, however, predictable in what they observe and what they correct: they observe and correct what they wanted students to do in the first place, because they are focused on the learning task from the beginning until the learning goal has been achieved.

Evaluating Instructional Practices

The following is an exercise to stimulate discussion and reflection on the practices of feedback and observation. Readers are encouraged to refer to their own teaching and learning experiences and, when appropriate, provide examples to illustrate their positions.

Part A. Discuss advantages and disadvantages, or the appropriateness, of the following situations, specifying a particular dance form and a particular group of students.

> The teacher executes the skill incorrectly, and asks students to make corrections.
> The teacher stops the class, and has students listen to a correction given to one student.
> The use of tactile feedback.
> Minimizing verbal corrections.

Repeating a correction only once.

Providing a detailed analysis of the skill when students cannot perform the skill after several attempts.

Encouraging students to ask questions about the skill any time during the learning process.

Using the mirror excessively during the correct stage of learning.

Encouraging students to work on a problem on their own outside class time.

Verifying that students have understood the corrections.

Teaching students to rely more and more on their kinesthetic sense of the correct movement.

Filming students during a technique class.

Not giving enough practice time between corrections and/or skills.

Providing frequent feedback during the correct stage.

Asking students to correct one another after a specific correction.

Keeping verbal feedback informational and constructive.

Circulating among students while observing rather than staying in one place.

Getting angry with students when they do not make the correction.

Asking one student to correct another student in front of the class.

Providing group feedback only.

Providing general corrections only.

Correcting weaker students only.

The teacher asks a student to meet him after class to discuss a skill problem.

Providing negative feedback.

Ignoring a student.

Part B. Discuss your observational skills through these questions, specifying a particular dance form and a particular group of students.

How do you know which part of the skill needs correction?

How do you know which part of the skill is well learned?

Can you tell which students need corrections?

Can you tell which students prefer a certain type of feedback?

How can you tell when students understood the corrections?

How can you tell when they did not understand the corrections?

How can you tell when students are ready to learn a new skill?

How can you tell when they are beginning to detect their own errors?

How can you tell when they lose their concentration?

How can you tell when they are frustrated? Tired? Bored?

Summary

Knowledge of performance, or information about the form of a skill, is the type of feedback most appropriate in dance. In order to learn, novices require extrinsic feedback from the instructor, especially during the correct stage. With practice and experience, students will develop the ability to detect and correct their own movement errors, thus relying more on intrinsic feedback.

References

1. Magill RA: *Motor Learning: Concepts and Applications*, (6th ed). New York: McGraw Hill, 2001.
2. Rose DJ: *A Multilevel Approach to the Study of Motor Control and Learning*. Boston: Allyn and Bacon, 1997.
3. Schmidt RA, Wrisberg CA: *Motor Learning and Performance. A Problem-Based Learning Approach*, (2nd ed). Champaign, IL: Human Kinetics Publishers, Inc., 2000.
4. Hammond SN: *Ballet Basics*, (4th ed). Mountain View, CA: Mayfield, 2000.
5. Kassing G, Jay DM: *Teaching Beginning Ballet Technique*. Champaign, IL: Human Kinetics Publishers, Inc., 1998.
6. Schlaich J, DuPont B: *The Art of Teaching Dance Technique*. Reston, VA: National Dance Association, 1993.
7. Knudson DV, Morrison CS: *Qualitative Analysis of Human Movement*. Champaign, IL: Human Kinetics Publishers, Inc., 1997.
8. Overby LY: Principles of motor learning applied to the teaching of dance technique. Kinesiology and Medicine for Dance 14(1):113-118, 1991/92.
9. Smoll FL, Smith RE: The coach as a focus of research and intervention in youth sports. *In:* Smoll FL, Smith RE (eds): *Children and Youth in Sport: A Biopsychosocial Perspective*. Madison, WI: Brown and Benchmark Publishers, 1996, pp. 125-141.
10. Côté-Laurence P: The role of rhythm in ballet training. Research in Dance Education 1(2):173-191, 2000.
11. Stinson SW: Realities, myths, and priorities: Teacher competencies in dance. Journal of Physical Education, Recreation and Dance 64(9):45-48, 1993.
12. Hanna JL: *Partnering Dance and Education: Intelligent Moves for Changing Times*. Champaign, IL: Human Kinetics Publishers, Inc., 1999.
13. Consortium of National Art Education Associations: *National Standards for Arts Education: Dance, Music, Theatre, Visual Arts - What Every Young American Should Know and Be Able to Do in the Arts*. Reston, VA: Music Educators National Conference, 1994.
14. Knudson D, Morrison C: An integrated qualitative analysis of overarm throw. Journal of Physical Education, Recreation, and Dance 67(6):31, 1996.

Gabrielle Laurence

Where We Are Now – The Movement Sciences and Dance

Revisiting the Knowledge Base in Dance

Where Do We Go From Here—Looking Into the Future

   Research on the Learning Process Across Dance Forms

   Research on Children's Capabilities as Learners of Dance

   Research on Effective Teaching in Dance

   Recommendations

Chapter 12

Looking Into the Future

O ver a decade ago dance scholars and educators emphasized the need to broaden the core knowledge base of dance. They urged the dance community to study dance from a variety of educational and scholarly contexts, and to unite, rather than isolate, the arts with the humanities and the sciences.[1,2] The discussion in this book has aimed to integrate these components, and broaden the knowledge base in dance by uniting the movement sciences with dance. It is hoped that this approach will enable instructors to find answers about dance teaching and learning.

The knowledge base in dance must include foundation knowledge and application knowledge. Foundation knowledge represents the core knowledge, or what a dance teacher must know: the dance material, the nature of the learning process, and the learners' capabilities. Foundation knowledge is synonymous with declarative knowledge, or "knowing that" (see Chapter 7). Foundation knowledge alone does not guarantee good teaching. An individual's knowledge about a subject area is not always indicative of her ability to effectively disseminate that content to students. Effective teaching requires another type of knowledge.

Application knowledge is concerned with the transformation of the foundation knowledge into effective instructional content and methods. It is through this type of knowledge that the teacher uses her foundation knowledge in the dance class. Application knowledge includes selecting dance material and instructional methods that are appropriate for specific categories of learners. In a way, application knowledge is similar to procedural knowledge, or "knowing how to."

We know that what differentiates expert musicians and athletes from novices is their high level of procedural knowledge.[3] Therefore, the material in these pages argues that only when foundation knowledge includes the dance material, the learning process, and the learners' capabilities can it lead to successful application knowledge. Only then can researchers and educators claim that the dance knowledge base will lead to competent dance teaching.

Where We Are Now – The Movement Sciences and Dance

As a field of study and a discipline, dance has expanded exponentially in the last two decades. Several sub-disciplines have emerged as areas of research in dance, as evidenced by the diversity of publications that have appeared over the last two decades. The term "dance science" has also evolved to encompass more disciplines than anatomy and physiology. The original focus of dance science may have been primarily on preventing dance injuries. However, it is now recognized that motor learning may provide answers to the teaching process and learning capabilities involved in dance technique,[4] which, in turn, may lead to the end goal of enhanced performance.

Formal links between disciplines are frequently preceded by years of informal attempts, suggestions, probing, and exploratory studies. Modest links between motor learning and dance have been seen in recent publications by scholars and educators. For example, the need to examine motor learning research and applications to the technique class have been stressed in the 1980s.[5] This trend has continued to expand since the 1990s, as more aspects of motor learning applied to dance have been investigated.[6] The use of imagery in dance teaching, expert-novice differences in motor recall, observational learning, and developmental issues are but a few of the topics studied. However, many questions remain unanswered. Little is known, for example, about information processing in dance.

Another significant change is that more books on motor learning now include dance in the range of motor skills, and provide examples of practical applications in dance.[7,8] Why? Because dance scholars have produced good research, and the publications that their research appears in are being acknowledged by scholars in motor learning and control. There is recognition that dance is part of the repertoire of human motion, and as such, must be included in the search for answers. Clearly, dance has come a long way. Collaborative work between scholars in the fields of dance, motor learning, and motor development promises further understanding and enhancements.

The contribution of disciplines in the movement sciences to the study of dance, although still in its infancy, has immense potential. These disciplines have long investigated learning and teaching. Theories have been developed, and relationships between instructional practices and optimal learning and performance have been confirmed.[7,8] Despite these inroads, there continues to be a lack of information about how dance skills are learned. More than ever, it is now time to investigate the pertinence of movement science theories and findings to dance learning and teaching. As well, it is time to revisit the knowledge base required for teachers to plan for and effect optimal learning and teaching in dance.

Revisiting the Knowledge Base in Dance

A special 1990 issue of the *Journal of Physical Education, Recreation and Dance* addressed future trends in dance, with an emphasis what directions and changes in the discipline of dance must be seriously considered by dance scholars and educators. One particular message arrived loud and clear: dance knowledge had to expand and be more inclusive.[1,2] There has been a concern that teachers often lack knowledge of how skills are learned and what skills need to be learned. Too often and for too long, dance teaching has remained loyal to tradition. It is time to break away from tradition and demand greater understanding of how skills are learned and what teaching techniques produce the best results. More emphasis must be placed on learning and on the most effective ways to teach dance skills.

Dance teachers should know more than the dance material they teach. As part of their foundation knowledge, teachers must know about cognition, perception, and learning. They must know how dance skills are learned. They must know which factors inhibit learning and which factors enhance it. They must know about individuals' capabilities to learn and perform dance. They must know about cognitive differences between younger and older learners, and between beginners and advanced dancers. As part of their application knowledge, teachers must also know about effective ways to instruct students, demonstrate skills, and correct performance.

> Teachers must know about cognition, perception, and learning.

In order to comprehend what the dance knowledge base must be, let us see, at this point, how pieces of the dance education puzzle fit together. There is no doubt that the National Dance Standards[9] have had a tremendous impact on the dance education community at large. Consider, for example, three of the nine achievement standards attached to the first content standard for high school students. In order for students to meet the requirements of achievement standard c. "demonstrate rhythmic acuity," students must be taught perceptual skills specific to rhythm. Achievement standard f. "demonstrate the ability to remember extended movement sequences," requires that students have learned strategies to encode, memorize, and recall these long sequences. Finally, achievement standard i. "refine technique through self-evaluation and correction" requires that students have developed error detection and correction mechanisms. These mechanisms are based on a refined kinesthetic sense and reliance on intrinsic feedback.

Students must be taught strategies that will allow them to meet all these achievement standards. Evidence suggests that perceptual skills such as those required for rhythm acuity simply do not occur as a result of regular dance training.[10] These skills must be formally taught. Student must be taught explicitly through class exercises or implicitly through the way in which they have been taught. This kind of teaching, however, requires a specific foundational knowledge base. This text has illustrated that knowledge base in order to assist teachers in making correct decisions about planning their dance material, its delivery to students, and the promotion of optimal learning and performance in dance.

A revised knowledge base for dance teaching must be examined, scrutinized, and developed in teacher training programs. Training programs must include courses that provide this knowledge. Courses on motor learning theory applied to dance, motor development theory applied to dance, and on rhythm perception and production applied to dance, are but a few examples of courses that are critical in the training of dance teachers. It is critical that dance educators and scholars address teacher competencies that will meet the educational challenges of the new century. Teaching effectiveness is becoming increasingly critical. It is determined by the foundation and application knowledge proposed in this text. It is imperative that this new knowledge base must be imparted to future dance teachers.

Where Do We Go From Here? Looking Into the Future

Dance educators and scholars must continue to aim for new frontiers yet to be explored. The knowledge base in dance must continue to be periodically redefined and expanded. Practitioners and researchers, two key players in the dance community, must establish and maintain a dialogue. Each has expertise that, when combined, can achieve significant progress in understanding the nature of dance expertise.[11] Collaborative and multidisciplinary research endeavors must become the norm.[6] Links between dance and disciplines in the movement sciences must be solidified in order to test and apply motor learning and development theories to dance teaching. It is strongly recommended that collaborative teams of educators and researchers be formed, as they are the key to expanding the limit of knowledge further. What better way than putting different levels of expertise together to reach a common goal.

Consider research teams which include expert teachers in various dance forms, scholars specializing in observational learning, visual perception, skill kinematics, feedback, rhythm, learning stages, information processing, children's cognition, expert performance, or other related areas. The days of suggesting that one is an expert at everything are over. Significant contributions to the field of dance are most likely to result from collaborative work.

Collaborative and multidisciplinary projects must be encouraged in undergraduate and graduate dance programs. Extensive research initiatives must be undertaken in order to fully understand the learning process across dance forms, children's capabilities as learners of dance, and effective teaching in dance. Within each area, there are several potential research questions for investigation.

Research on the Learning Process Across Dance Forms

First, the proposed learning model must be tested. Systematic observations must be made on each stage of the model, and data must be collected as to what exactly happens when students learn skills in a particular dance form. Any viable learning model must be able to sustain challenges and modifications. Second, learning similarities and differences between dance forms must be examined.

Although dance teachers are generally familiar with a large repertoire of dance skills in a particular dance form, they must be encouraged to take a closer look at the level of complexity of dance skills, as they appear to the students. This is particularly necessary for the highly skilled dancer who embarks on a teaching career. Teacher preparation programs can no longer assume that graduates will teach only one dance form, or only adults and not children.

Future dance teachers must follow a comprehensive preparation that makes them cognizant of common learning problems across dance forms, as well as specifics attached to certain dance forms. For example, a dance form where beginners learn skills in a static balance position, gesturing with arms and legs for a long period of time provides challenges that are different than a dance form made up of sharp and angular body postures performed with explosions of energy. There are certain body types that appear to be more suited to one dance form than another, and also certain learning styles that may be more useful in certain dance forms.

Research on Children's Capabilities as Learners of Dance

Most of what is known about how children learn skills comes from studies with fundamental motor skills and sport skills and studies with discrete laboratory hand tasks. Little is known about how children learn specialized skills such as dance skills. It is crucial to know about the effectiveness of learning strategies and teaching techniques for children's dance learning. For example, the concept of readiness for advanced skills must be investigated. Questions raised in youth sports have prompted discussion on the influence of early exposure on later performance.[12] There is a great need for longitudinal studies on the effect of early dance training on performance.

How does one speculate on the most appropriate age to begin training? This line of thought leads to another question: what do we know about child experts? There are gifted young children in many sports, including gymnastics and dance. Questions relative to young experts' perceptual, attention, and memory skills must be studied in order to identify instructional methods most and least advantageous for these children.

Research on Effective Teaching in Dance

What actually goes on in the dance class? Research on teacher effectiveness offers guidelines that can certainly be useful in dance.[13,14] Nonetheless, it is imperative that dance educators and scholars continue to document what actually occurs in the dance class. Characteristics of effective teacher behavior common to, and specific to, dance forms must be carried to a higher level. Knowledge of these characteristics can lead to increased competency in dance teaching.

Recommendations

More research questions can be identified around the three areas of concern proposed above. Dance educators and researchers must continue to share their ideas and visions, and act upon them. In conclusion, we propose the following recommendations:

1. The dance knowledge base must include no less than two types of knowledge: foundation knowledge and application knowledge. Foundation knowledge must consist of knowledge about the dance material, the learning process, and the learners' capabilities. Application knowledge must include knowledge about selecting dance material and instructional methods. A comprehensive knowledge base will increase the probability that teachers will develop competent and independent learners.

2. The proposed knowledge base must become the foundation for teacher competencies. Teacher training programs must include courses that bring learning and developmental theory to the teaching of dance. The time has arrived to break away from tradition and establish new foundations for learning and teaching.

3. More research attention must be placed on the proposed knowledge base so that we understand dance teaching at a deeper level. In order to ensure significant advances in the discipline of dance, research must be encouraged in undergraduate and graduate programs, and the findings must be valued and more widely disseminated throughout the dance community.

4. Finally, dance practitioners and academics must unite across dance forms and work together in collaborative and multidisciplinary endeavors to shed more light into the complexity of dance skill learning and teaching. Although an inclusive approach to research is the new trend, cross-disciplinary dialogue and networking must be put in place before tangible results are seen.

The discussion presented in this book is an attempt in this direction. More efforts are needed to better understand what goes on in the dance class. We would like to make an ardent appeal to dance educators throughout the world to participate in this process of multidisciplinary research and the sharing of dance experiences.

References

1. Gray JA: Dance education in the future: Trends and predictions. Journal of Physical Education, Recreation and Dance 61(5):50-53, 1990.
2. Hanstein P: Educating for the future: A post-modern paradigm for dance education. Journal of Physical Education, Recreation and Dance 61(5):56-58, 1990.

3. Annett J: On knowing how to do things: A theory of motor imagery. Cognitive Brain Research 3:65-69, 1996.
4. Krasnow DH, Chatfield SJ: Dance science and the dance technique class. Impulse 4:162-172, 1996.
5. Clarkson PM, Skrinar M: *Sciences of Dance Training*. Champaign, IL: Human Kinetics Publishers, Inc., 1988.
6. Minton S: Research in dance: Educational and scientific perspectives. Dance Research Journal 32(1):110-116, 2000.
7. Magill RA: *Motor Learning: Concepts and Applications*, (6th ed). Boston: McGraw-Hill, 2001.
8. Rose DJ: *A Multilevel Approach to the Study of Motor Control and Learning.* Boston: Allyn and Bacon, 1997.
9. National Arts Education Associations: *National Standards for Arts Education: Dance, Music, Theatre, Visual Arts: What Every Young American Should Know and Be Able To Do in the Arts.* Reston, VA: Music Educators National Conference, 1994, p. 55.
10. Côté-Laurence P: The role of rhythm in ballet training. Research in Dance Education 1(2)173-191, 2000.
11. Côté-Laurence P: Reflections on dance in higher education. Canadian Association for Health, Physical Education and Recreation Journal 58(4):29-31, 1992.
12. Magill RA, Anderson DI: Critical periods as optimal readiness for learning sport skills. *In:* Smoll FL, Smith RE (eds): *Children and Youth in Sport: A Biopsychosocial Perspective.* Madison, WI: Brown and Benchmark Publishers, 1996, pp. 57-72.
13. Rink JE: *Teaching Physical Education for Learning.* St. Louis: Times Mirror/Mosby College Publishing, 1985.
14. Siedentop D: *Developing Teaching Skills in Physical Education*, (3rd ed). Mountain View, CA: Mayfield Publishers, 1991.

Glossary

Associated movement: Extraneous, unintended movements accompanying voluntary actions.

Attention capacity: The ability to consciously attend to one event. Attention capacity is said to be limited, serial, and selective.

Bilateral transfer: The ability to perform a skill learned on one side of the body on the other side.

Body schema: Conceptual body map; thought to be innate but needs to be completed through motor experiences.

Chunking: The tendency to group sounds or event. A strategy used to memorize more information.

Cognitive skills: Activities that take place in the learner's mind when learning a skill, e.g., detect, identify, recognize a stimulus, select a response.

Coincidence timing: Anticipation of the motion of an external object in order to intercept its path in space and time.

Dance skills: Complex versions of fundamental motor skills; consist of body actions performed in space and time, with a particular use of force.

Dance techniques: The collection of dance skills associated with a particular dance form such as ballet or modern dance technique; also refers to that part of a lesson that focuses on physical skill development.

Declarative knowledge: Consciously knowing about "what to do," and being able to verbalize it.

Deliberate practice: A theory that proposes that expertise is determined by structured and intensive practice.

Directionality: Awareness of dimensions in space, such as right, left, forward, backward; ability to identify pathways of movement of oneself or objects in space.

Egocentric: Used in a Piagetian sense, the child can only see the world from his own perspective; the opposite of allocentric, being able to take the perspective of others.

Extrinsic feedback: Information about an action provided by a source external to the body, e.g., the instructor.

Feedback: Information about the performance of a skill that allows a learner to improve the skill.

Fundamental motor skills: Locomotor, manipulation, and stability or body management skills such as running, throwing, balancing on one foot; show developmental progression in form through stages as child matures between two and seven years.

Information processing model: A model based on the premise that the learner, like a computer, is a processor of information. The model includes three stages: stimulus identification, response selection, and response initiation.

Intrinsic feedback: Information about an action provided by the sensory receptors within the body.

Kinesthetic sense: The conscious sensation of the position and movement of the body and body parts in space.

Knowledge of performance: Information about the form and quality of the movement.

Laterality: Conscious awareness that the body has a right and left side; the ability to correctly label and use the right and left limbs on command.

Learning process: The process that leads to the acquisition of a skill.

Long-term memory: A memory system in which learned information is stored permanently.

Mental rotation: The ability to mentally rearrange spatial patterns that have been visualized; for example, the ability to recognize an identical but reversed or upside down shape or pattern.

Metacognition: A mental process of awareness of one's own thinking; permits self-regulation and self-monitoring of one's behavior.

Modeling: Synonymous with demonstration.

Motor development theory: Descriptions and explanations of change in motor behavior over time due to maturation and experience.

Motor learning: A set of internal processes associated with practice that lead to relatively permanent changes in the capability for movement.

Motor learning theory: Term used to represent the current knowledge about learning and factors that influence learning. It includes empirical evidence that led to this knowledge.

Movement sciences: A grouping of the disciplines that study human movement; these include functional anatomy, exercise physiology, motor development, motor learning, biomechanics and sport psychology.

Perceptual integration: The coordination of many sensory inputs; initially involves the thalamus which channels input to the different sensory areas within the cortex; actual integration occurs in the association areas of the brain.

Perceptual skills: Ability to organize and interpret information received from our body and the environment through our senses

Procedural knowledge: Unconsciously knowing "how to do something"; something that an individual can do well, but cannot easily explain verbally.

Proprioceptive information: Information coming from the body sensory receptors.

Short-term memory: A "working memory" system with a limited capacity of about seven items. If not rehearsed, the information will be deleted. If rehearsed and used extensively, the information will be transferred to long-term memory where it is stored for later recall.

Specialized motor skills: Combinations of, or adaptations of, fundamental motor skills in new and more difficult contexts (e.g., a tennis serve, high jump, or pirouette).

Transfer of learning: The positive or negative effect of having practiced a skill on the learning of a new skill.

Index

Application knowledge, 5
Attention capacity, 55, 78, 120-121
    see also Memory capacity
Awareness, 72
Balance, 73
Bilateral transfer, 122, 182
Body actions, 17
    choices for teaching, 36
Body awareness, 72, 102
Body schema, 72, 103
Child
    body proportions, 92
    flexibility, 93
    fundamental skills competency, 94
    growth spurt, 91
    kinesthetic skills, 101-102
    learning abilities, 97
    learning strategies, 99
    perceptual skills, 100
    selecting material for, 164
    skill progression, 96
    stages of development, 90
Chunking strategy, 81-82, 99
Closed skills, 203
Cognitive capabilities, 6
Cognitive development theory, Piaget's, 109
Cognitive skills, 109
    metacognition, 110

    task comprehension, 110
Coincidence timing, 108
Complexity model, 24, 26, 161
Concrete operational stage, 109
Creative dance, 62
Culminating activity, 44
    evaluation, 153
Dance analysis, 16
Dance science, 210
Dance skill, 15, 20, 156
    accompaniment, 46
    acquisition, 24
    analysis, 13
    attempt stage, 53-54
        characteristics, 56
    biomechanical challenges, 17
    body actions, 17-18
    components, 20
    context, 23, 27
    correct stage, 53, 57
        characteristics, 58
    evaluating, 152
    movement quality
    perfect stage, 53, 59
        characteristics, 60
Dance technique, 16
Dancer
    body structure, 127
Demonstration (input), 52, 177

modeling, 176
Directional awareness, 72
Directionality, 105-106
Error detection and correction, 57, 71, 82, 122, 123
Feedback, 57, 189, 190
    augmented, 191
    categories, 199
    extrinsic, 58, 191
    frequency of, 20, 201-202
    intrinsic, 191, 199
    mirror, use of, 196-197
    negative, 193
    physical guidance, 194
    proprioceptive, 58
    role of, 190
    specificity of, 192
    tactile, 58, 194-195
    timing, 200
    verbal, 58, 191
    video, 198
Foundation knowledge, 5
Growth spurt, 91
Imagery, 173-174
Independent learner, 3
Information processing, 6
    attention
        capacity, 78, 120
        overload, 78
    beginners, 78
    beginners versus experienced learners, 70-71
    experience dancer, 128
    perceptual ability, 119
Information processing, 98
Input (demonstration), 52, 77
Instructional methods
    assessing effectiveness, 184
    evaluating, 205
    selecting, 169
    verbal, 170
Internal processes (mental activities), 52
Kinesthetic
    abilities, 73
    acuity, 102, 194, 199
    awareness, 73
    information, 83
    memory, 102
    sense, 83

skills, children, 102
Knowledge
    application, 5, 209
    declarative, 125, 209
    foundation, 5, 209
    procedural, 125, 209
    transfer, 69
Laterality, 103
Learner
    adaptability, 116
    adult beginners, 67, 81, 159
    beginners, 67, 71
    characteristics, 158
    child, 160
    evaluating needs of, 154
    experienced, 67, 115, 122, 161
        characteristics, 124
    independent, 3
    perception accuracy, 72
Learning
    stages, progressing through, 62
    stages of development, 90
    transfer of, 122
Learning abilities, 157
    adult difficulties, 88
    beginners versus experienced learners, 70
    child, 97
    child and adult beginners, 88
    child, chronological age, 89
Learning Model, 53
    attempt stage, 53
        verbal cues, 172-173
    correct stage, 53
    perfect stage, 53
    progressing through, 62
Learning strategies, 71, 183
Locomotor skills, 68
    dance skills, 47
    fundamental skills, 47
    variations of, 47
Long-term memory, 61, 81, 122
Manipulative skills, 68
Memory, 55-56
    capacity, 79, 82
    chunking, 81
    recall and recognition memory, 80
    see also long-term and short-term memory
Memory capacity, 79

long-term memory, 79-80
short-term memory, 79-80
Mental activities (internal processes), 52
Mental image, 55
Mental rotation, 106
Metacognition, 110
Mirroring, 45
Modeling, 176
Motor development, 72, 77
Motor learning theory, 5, 51-52, 78
    attempt stage, 53-54
        characteristics, 56
    correct stage, 53, 57
        characteristics, 58
    observational learning, 176
    perfect stage, 53, 59
        characteristics, 60
    physical capabilities, 67
    schema theory, 80
Motor performance, 72
Motor plan, 54
    assess, 58
    planning and control, 108
Motor proficiency, 117
Motor response (output), 52
Motor rhythmic ability, 74-75
Motor skill, 14
    fundamental, 15, 69, 156
    inter-limb coordination, 104
    related body actions, 69
Movement, 14
Multiple Intelligences Theory, 126
National Dance Standards, 211
Non-locomotor skills, 68
Novice adult, 68
    challenges, 68
Observation, role of, 202
Observational learning, 176
Observational skills, 202-203
Organizing dance material
    body actions, 36
    components, 39
    context, 41
    different dance forms, 34
Output (motor response), 52, 77
Perceptual abilities, development of, 72
Perceptual integration, 107
    coincidence timing, 108

Perceptual motor development, 101
Perceptual rhythmic ability, 75
Physical capabilities, 67, 117, 155
    health components, 67
    performance components, 67
Physical guidance, 194
Physical growth
    mature, 68
Practice, role of, 117, 130
Pre-operational thinking, 109
Proprioceptor, 73
Rhythm awareness (*see* temporal awareness)
Rhythmic abilities, 74
    motor, 74-75
    perceptual, 74
Selective attention, 99
Sensory information, 72
Short-term memory, 79, 81, 122
Skill analysis, 13
Spatial
    awareness, 72
    mapping, 105
    skills, 104
Teacher
    role and behavior, 67
    training programs, 212
Teaching methods
    see also Feedback
    assessing effectiveness, 184, 205, 213
    clarity of instructions, 170-170
    cues, 171
    demonstration, 176
    imagery, use of, 173-174
    ineffective, 4
    observational skills, 203
    organizing dance material, 33
Temporal anticipation, 76
Temporal awareness, 72, 74
    synchronization (of movement to music), 76
Temporal skills, 106
Timing, 74
Verbal
    cue, 55
    instructions, 169, 170, 172, 185
Vestibular apparatus, 73